CW00972298

SUBMARINE WARFARE
MONSTERS & MIDGETS

SUBMARINE WARFARE
MONSTERS & MIDGETS

RICHARD COMPTON-HALL

BLANDFORD PRESS
Poole · Dorset

First published in the UK 1985 by Blandford Press,
Link House, West Street, Poole, Dorset, BH15 1LL

Distributed in the United States by
Sterling Publishing Co., Inc.,
2 Park Avenue, New York, N.Y. 10016

British Library Cataloguing in Publication Data

Compton-Hall, Richard
  Monsters and Midgets.
  1. Submarine boats—History
  I. Title
  623.8'257'09   V857

ISBN 07137 1389 5

Typeset by Asco Trade Typesetting Limited
Hong Kong
Printed in Great Britain by BAS Printers and
bound by R. J. Acford.

*Whatever, keeping its proportion and form,
is designed upon a scale much greater or
much less than that of our general experience
produces upon the mind an effect of fantasy
. . .*

HILAIRE BELLOC

*If ever David and Goliath come up against
each other again, my money will still be on
David.*

AUTHOR

By the Same Author:
The Underwater War, 1939–45

To Eve, as always

Contents

Frontispiece. The monsters *en masse*: K-Class and
two M-Class in 1918.

Acknowledgements

I have so many people to thank for help of one kind or another that the following list is bound to be incomplete, and I sincerely apologise if any of the invaluable photographs, advice and fragments of first-hand information given, sometimes without a formal record, are omitted. Where, exceptionally, more than one print of the same photograph has been provided I have acknowledged what I believe to be the original source.

First and foremost, I am truly grateful to my wife Eve for expert, patient assistance and constant encouragement throughout the lengthy preparation of the text; and especially, for this particular book, for allowing me to use the private diaries and accounts of her late husband, Commander Donald Cameron VC.

Secondly, I thank my helpers and staff at the Royal Navy Submarine Museum, especially Gus Britton for his unfailing knowledge about past submarines and about the vast photographic library which he has helped to collect and annotate on the Museum's behalf; and also Lindsay Pirie, Micky Budd and Mrs Rosemary Corcoran for always knowing where to find the right answer in the archives.

For specific photographs, documents, letters and advice my thanks go to: The Trustees of the Royal Navy Submarine Museum, Gosport; Lieutenant Commander Mike Wilson of the Naval Historical Branch; David Hill (not only for his excellent drawings but also for his generous permission to reproduce his account of the Japanese *I-400* submarines); Ray W de Yarmin, Curator of the USN Pacific Submarine Museum; M J Malcolm; F W Collins; Lieutenant Commander C P Addis (Admiral Poland's albums) Lieutenant Commander M R Todd; Mr Kipling; Lieutenant Commander R S C Robinson (lately HMS *Vernon* historian); Lieutenant Commander R Baseden; C Debacker, J Devienne; R H Coltart; M Foley; Lieutenant Commander M Burbeck; the late Sydney Glazebrook; Jak Mallmann Showell; A Kevan; E Goddard; K Richardson; L W Benson; Commander H P Westmacott; Lieutenant Commander George Honour; J Bower; J Albrecht; G Kimbell; L Stannard; Mrs V Michell (daughter of the late Commander Kellett); Captain R W Garson; Captain J E Moore (editor of *Jane's Fighting Ships*); Commander R H S Thompson; Lieutenant Commander J M Maber; Dr Melville Balfour; Captain G E Hunt; Captain J S Stevens; G Clough; Lieutenant Maxie Shean; Lieutenant Commander T K Hornby-Priestnall; D Webb; Ruari McLean; Lieutenant Commander J M Maber; Dr Thomas O Paine, Chairman of Thomas Paine Associates (ex-executive officer of *I-400* prize crew and later Administrator of NASA); the Photographic team, HMS *Dolphin*, led by Len Cobbett; Captain Sergio Fontanesi; J Lambert; members of the Submarine Old Comrades Association; Scicon Consultancy International; Admiral Joe Vasey USN; Captain M R G Wingfield; Captain G B K Griffiths RM; General Dynamics, Electric Boat Division; Commander A S Hutchinson; J Bowers; Richard J Boyle; Professor Richard K Morris; US Naval Historical Center; B Ernst; K Wahnig; Commander E Grenfell; S Weatherall; M J Whitley; A Pohl; G Fagence and R N Commando Association; the Director, Royal Marines Museum.

PART 1
Monsters

HMS *K-3*, the first Fleet Submarine, looking the part.

1: Great Expectations

Captain Paul Koenig in 1916, the first mercantile submarine Captain. British submariners in both world wars came to envy the excellent clothing issued to U-boat men, and the crew of *Deutschland* were even better kitted up than most.

Alfred Lohmann who inspired the *Deutschland* project.

When HMS *D-1* emerged in 1908 with a diesel engine, its new propulsion machinery signalled the first significant increase in size for submarines and an enormous increase in their capabilities. Petrol engines had been dangerous and unreliable: early gasoline boats could be used as little more than an extension of coastal and harbour defences. Now, diesel fuel enabled submarines to go farther and faster. They could operate independently in supposedly enemy controlled waters and this effected a revolution in submarine warfare which, for some 40 years to come, was as far reaching both strategically and tactically as the nuclear revolution that succeeded it. Diesel-driven U-boats without the benefit of schnorchels, propelled by electric motors when submerged, nearly brought Great Britain to her knees in both world wars.

The most effective submarines during the 1914–18 war, armed with torpedoes and guns, were typically around the 800 ton mark. But it was soon realised in Germany that diesel power, with long range and the ability to remain hidden when necessary, conferred on a submarine potential advantages other than its well-proven ability to attack: if U-boats could impose a blockade on sea-borne trade they could also be employed as blockade-runners. True, they could not, whatever their size, carry so much merchandise as a merchant ship but a few essential items on the Kaiser's wartime shopping list, especially nickel and rubber, were comparatively small and the State Secretary of the Treasury suggested that U-boats might be able to import raw materials of this kind.

By the beginning of 1915, the British blockade was beginning to hamper Germany's war effort very seriously and merchant shipping was almost halted. International law forbade ships of war, which obviously included U-boats, from embarking commercial goods in neutral ports. It might, however, be possible to transfer merchandise, particularly rubber which would float, from neutral merchant ships far out at sea to German U-boats who would then run the blockade, diving when necessary to escape the vigilant watch kept by Allied cruisers, destroyers and submarines patrolling the German Ocean—or the North Sea as the British preferred to call it—and the Cruiser Squadron keeping guard off the East Coast of America. This way of doing things was rejected by the navy out of hand. Such transfers could only be accomplished in exceptionally calm conditions, which were rare and unpredictable in those areas where there was relatively little danger of the operation being surprised by anti-submarine forces; moreover, loading materials through the normal small hatches of a submarine would be a lengthy business, thereby increasing the risk of being caught by weather or the enemy.

The only possible answer, legally and practically, was to build totally unarmed underwater cargo vessels which would have to be considered as merchant ships in every sense with a merchant navy crew. Who first came to this conclusion is not clear, but the spring of 1915 found the head of a well known Bremen wholesale firm, Herr Alfred Lohmann, discussing possibilities with the German Treasury. The talks, which were initially kept strictly confidential for both commercial and military reasons, centred around the finance required for building one cargo-carrying submarine, with the State and Commerce sharing, for once, a common interest.

Agreement was soon reached. The notable shipping line North German Lloyd and the German Bank were brought together to form a limited liability Company with a capital of 2 million marks. The State undertook to indemnify the new company, Deutsche Ozean-Reederei GmbH, established on 8 November 1915, for the substantial capital investment and, moreover, to pay 5 per cent interest on it to the company. However, the State was to appropriate any profits which resulted from the venture. Lohmann's original company would not expect fees for negotiating cargoes, although it is hard to think that Lohmann & Company would not contrive to make something more than their share of the 5 per cent interest during the commercial transactions that were bound to follow: but, more importantly, Lohmann had the vision to see that the German economy might well collapse, and his firm with it, unless the venture prospered.

Meanwhile, the great armaments firm of Krupp seems to have arrived at a similar plan for recovering vast stocks of nickel belonging to the company in the United States. So anxious was Krupp to bring the desperately needed material to Germany that the firm declared itself willing to pay for a suitable cargo-carrying boat and to present it to the nation—provided that it brought home the nickel.

By now the project was by no means a close-kept secret; there was no real reason why it should have been. There was a great deal of German sympathy in America where, anyway, commerce was very reasonably considered more important than the political situation in Europe. Nor were Allied anti-submarine methods and communications sufficiently effective to deny Germany her proposed underwater trade route across the Atlantic—or so it appeared in the winter of 1915, when Germaniawerft, Kiel contracted to build two cargo-carrying U-boats at a cost of 2.75 million marks each, one to be paid for by Krupp and the other by the State-associated company. The latter was, in effect, to exercise operational and commercial control of both boats.

With a surface displacement of 1440 tons (1820 tons submerged) and a length of 65 metres (213 feet), the first U-freighter, *Deutschland*, although a monster for the time, was by no means the largest U-boat to be constructed during World War One. Some of the U-cruisers were considerably bigger, although few of these large ocean raiders actually took part in the war, and one giant steam-electric boat (Project 50) was designed with a surface displacement of 3800 tons and a surface speed of 25 knots, but it never left the drawing board.

Deutschland was a great idea rather than a remarkably great submarine in the literal sense, and the idea was even more attractive by reason of its comparatively low cost. The *U-139* type of U-cruiser, which was one-third larger, cost more than three times as much as *Deutschland* due mainly, of course, to the U-freighter not being equipped with any armament and also to having an inexpensive propulsion system: her two diesel-generators had originally been intended for supplying electric current in battleships and the electric motors were the standard U-boat pattern.

It would be interesting to see today how far purely commercial considerations, omitting military hardware, would cut the costs and building time of a submarine. In *Deut-*

schland's case, everything was cut, including bureaucratic red tape. No time was wasted while legal formalities were being resolved: complete plans were ready and the contract was signed in October 1915. *Deutschland* was launched on 20 March 1916, only five months later, and was entirely ready for sea trials six weeks after that. The sister submersible freighter *Bremen* followed and construction was started on another four cargo boats but, in the event, these were to be armed and taken into naval service as *U-151* to *U-154* when they were launched in 1917.

Materially, therefore, the first cargo submarine presented no difficulties and was produced with the usual German efficiency which the Allies had come, ruefully, to expect. The problem now was how to man her, bearing in mind the overriding need for *Deutschland* to be a merchant vessel acceptable as such to the neutral United States, whatever Britain and France might have to say about it.

Herr Lohmann considered the matter deeply. With Germany's shipping virtually swept from the seas (to quote the British newspapers), there were plenty of merchant navy captains looking for a berth and they included the ex-captain of the North German Lloyd's *Schleswig*, Paul Koenig, whom Lohmann had got to know personally in Sydney, where his firm was agent for the line. Lohmann knew that Koenig happened to be in Berlin and, in September 1915, he asked him to call upon him, urgently, at the Hotel Adlon.

Koenig was puzzled. He could not conceive of any possible job that Lohmann, despite his world-wide connections, could offer but, nonetheless, he hurried along to the luxurious hotel where the prices were beyond the reach of any merchant captain, even on full pay.

Lohmann did not bother about polite preliminaries. Was Koenig not bored sitting around Chesapeake Bay, where he had navi-off on a long cruise? The latter seemed a futile question and Koenig merely shrugged. Then Lohmann came to the point. Would Koenig be prepared to take command of the first of two merchant U-boats he planned to run between Germany and America? The first trip would be to Newport News, probably, and Lohmann knew that Koenig was well acquainted with the waters in and around Chesapeake Bay, where he had navigated in the Baltimore service of North German Lloyd. He had a pilot's knowledge of the soundings and much was made of this, which suggests that the available charts might not have been wholly adequate for submerged

navigation in the area. When dived at a depth sufficient to avoid small coastal vessels passing overhead, the captain of *Deutschland* was going to be navigating a vessel with an effective draft of some 20 or 25 metres, much greater than any surface ships of the day. It was something to which all submariners had to become accustomed, of course, but it was as well to make the point at the outset to a merchant skipper who would also find himself deprived of the Rules of the Road which he had followed so faithfully during a long career at sea. Then, too, there would be dangers and discomforts of a kind unknown even in the roughest tramps and steamers; and there would be no weapons for defence.

Koenig, as he himself admitted, was not fond of long deliberations. At the age of 45, he had despaired of taking an active part in support of the Fatherland's struggle and had not dreamed that such an opportunity would come his way. His answer was immediate, positive and enthusiastic.

A few weeks later, in early November, just at the time when the new company was being formally established, Koenig was summoned again to have his appointment confirmed; and for the next four months he devoted his energy to learning, in middle age, an entirely new trade. In this, he was helped unstintingly by the Chief Constructor at the Germania Works, Rudolf Erbach; but for the most part he had to find his own way through the bewildering, complex and totally unfamiliar submarine systems, a veritable jungle of wheels, vents, screws, cocks, pipes and levers, all of which had to be understood thoroughly if he and his crew were to survive, let alone succeed.

In the meantime, a hand-picked crew of 26 men had been recruited, led by First Officer Krapohl and Chief Engineer Klees. They, too, had much to learn, but the majority, at least, seem already to have had U-boat experience even though they were now—most strictly—merchant seamen.

Trials and training exercises in protected and shallow waters off the Baltic coast were thorough and extensive, and, very wisely, neither the company nor the naval authorities (who acted in an advisory capacity) sought to hasten them unduly, but, by the second week in June, the *Deutschland* and her company were ready. For the past six months the agents for Ozean Reederei had been buying up stocks of rubber in the United States and assembling them at Baltimore, where they now amounted to 1800 tons—nearly three full submarine loads if nothing else was carried. However, tin

and nickel had high priority and several hundred tons of these precious commodities also awaited shipment so that, even in the short term, there was a call for four or even five voyages.

Trade demanded that *Deutschland* should not make the trans-Atlantic run in ballast, so a cargo of concentrated dyes, dried stuffs, mail and precious stones—about 700 tons in all—was loaded through cargo hatches on either side of the hull down into the capacious stowage compartments forward and, amidships, between the control room and the engine room. Ample provisions followed, together with a generous quantity of luxuries, including cigars and gramaphone records: Koenig had no intention of being miserable during what was bound to be a long and tedious voyage, even at the maximum speed of nine and a half knots. The officers and ratings had already been issued with the superb leather coats and warm suits which made life in U-boats so much more tolerable than in their British and French counterparts as well as with pre-war merchant marine uniforms.

On 23 June 1916, the *Deutschland* sailed from Kiel carrying a cargo worth nearly 1.5 million dollars. The crew were in excellent spirits. The port of destination was, as far as Koenig knew, still Newport News but, in fact, it was Baltimore. Perhaps Lohmann was unwilling to worry the Captain before sailing with the thought that he had the whole length of Chesapeake Bay ahead of him—some 120 miles of pilotage in American territorial waters—and nobody could be quite sure what political reaction in the United States might be. Relationships with Germany might change dramatically and *Deutschland* could find herself forced, suddenly, to take the only evasive action open to her, diving.

Four patrol boats escorted *Deutschland* out into the North Sea, and then, with the German coastline fading to the south-east, they turned back, leaving Koenig and his men to forge their way alone across the mine-strewn 'Barrage', known to U-boat men as the 'Rose Garden', around the heavily patrolled coast of Scotland and out into the Atlantic. Prudently, Koenig dived at once to catch a trim. It was just as well, because the Chief Engineer had to take in 17 tons of water more than had been needed in the fresher Baltic. It took a long time to

Deutschland at anchor.

Opposite top
Control Room looking forward—steering wheel amidships, hydroplane wheels on port side.

Opposite left
Conning tower: the usual German kiosk arrangement.

Opposite centre right
Motor room looking aft. The ladder leads up to a store and thence to the steering compartment.

Opposite bottom right
Steering compartment.

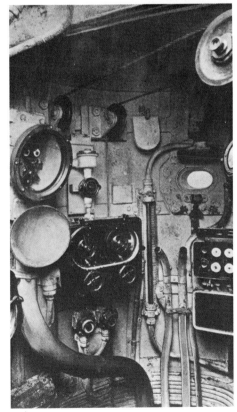

Coming up Chesapeake Bay.

Coming alongside at Baltimore on 10 July 1916.

The manifold dangers of being seen were obvious and Koenig impressed them on his crew. The crew, stolid and experienced seamen, were unworried: '*Ach!* They won't get *us*' said the gigantic Bos'n Humke.'[1]

Humke was a simple soul. The Captain asked him what he thought of voyaging to America in the very midst of war. What was his opinion about the purpose of the enterprise? The reply came with a grin: 'Why, to make money, of course!'

Koenig tried to explain that if the voyage was successful it would mean the resumption of trade relations with America in the face of the British blockade with all that this implied, but the Bos'n did not want to know about such matters. When some men came up from below to stretch their legs on the bridge Koenig, according to his own account,[2] gave the longest speech which he ever made in his life: it was still commendably short considering the political indoctrination to which he had clearly been subjected.

Koenig's theme was that the goods they were carrying would prevent envious English traders not only from damaging German imports and exports but also from injuring American manufacturers and American trade. Without carrying guns or torpedoes the *Deutschland* would revolutionise transoceanic commerce and international law. Even armed U-boats were only employed to protect Germany against the barbaric methods of starvation adopted by the English contrary to all international law. Yet the English armed their merchant ships and bombarded every U-boat which approached them for the legal purpose of sinking contraband. That, said Koenig contemptuously, is what the English call defence. Although Germany was compelled to sink English merchant ships without warning, that was only so that U-boats might not be sunk by ramming or gunfire.

Now, continued Koenig, the English had begun to whine for help, and, with existing international law, they had managed to win the Americans over to their point of view. Germany only desired peace with the great American people, so the government did not argue. But the *Deutschland* was both a U-boat and a merchant vessel; and defenceless merchant vessels could not be sunk without warning. It followed that a merchant submarine had to be examined before being sunk—and that would be very difficult to do so long as it was capable of diving.

So, if the *Deutschland* was not to be searched before being attacked *all* merchant ships could be sunk without warning—

submerge. When finally satisfied that the boat was in trim and could dive quickly, he surfaced again and started to run the long British gauntlet.

At this stage, a present-day Trident or Polaris SSBN captain setting off on a nuclear deterrent patrol through inshore waters would recognise and sympathise with Koenig's problem. It was imperative to avoid discovery by any other ship or submarine: even a neutral could, and probably would, tell tales; and, quite apart from the danger of attack with no means of retaliation, *Deutschland*'s mercantile identity could not be revealed until she arrived in America.

Triumphant return at the mouth of the Weser on
24 August 1916, with American flag flying aft.

Above right
Deutschland armed and taken into naval service as *U-
155*. On wide-ranging cruises off the Azores from May to
August 1917 and February to May 1918, she was extremely successful, using mainly her two large 15 cm
(5.9 inch) guns. In all, under Kptlt Meusel and KK Eckel-
mann, she sent 42 ships to the bottom, totalling 118, 373
tons. The money invested in *Deutschland* first as a
cargo-carrier and then as a U-cruiser could scarcely
have shown a better return!

including British vessels. Thus, the *Deutschland* would bring about the collapse of what
was a one-sided interpretation of the former
law and the laws of warfare would once
more be justly balanced by means of a
peaceful unarmed merchant-submarine.

Such was Koenig's logic. There is no record of the crew being particularly interested
in it and it sounds far from convincing.

Koenig had no intention whatever of putting his theories about search before sinking
to the test; but he was nearly caught in the
North Sea by what seemed to be a neutral
steamer which he unwisely allowed to come
in sight of him. The steamer's subsequent actions suggest that it might well have been a
Q-ship but, fortunately for *Deutschland*,
Koenig did not delay his dive too long and
the submarine slipped away unharmed.

During hours of total darkness where
destroyers were expected, Koenig at first
decided that the boat should remain submerged because he thought, wrongly, that
the sighting advantage would otherwise lie
with surface ships: a submarine is, in fact,
extremely difficult to see at night on the surface. However, he could not afford to run

long on the electric motors because the battery had only a few hours endurance even at
a modest and fairly economical speed of four
knots so, in the event, he proceeded almost
entirely on the surface. When bad weather
blew up he knew from experience in Baltic
storms that diving would be, to say the least,
tricky if he could not choose the most
advantageous course beam to sea: and
then, rolling during that critical period of
half-submergence could be dangerous. The
length to breadth ratio of *Deutschland* was
almost ideal for fully submerged control at
7:1, but diving from the surface into a head
sea of the kind that they were now ex-
periencing would be difficult for any submarine. A dive could either be held up inter-
minably while the bows were continually
being lifted or alternatively they might very
suddenly be forced steeply downwards to the
point where control was lost. And that,
when Koenig was forced to dive for a destroyer that appeared over the horizon, was
exactly what happened.

At first the boat refused to go under, even
when the motors were put to full ahead at
seven and a half knots. Then, with a sicken-
ing suddenness that many submariners know
only too well, Koenig felt the deck tip
violently beneath him as the manometer
(depth gauge) needle started to move with
alarming rapidity.

The angle grew still steeper and the crew
lost their footing, clinging to whatever they
could and unable to right the situation.
Klees in the engine room had evidently met
this kind of situation before and, being a
very small man, found a corner to crouch in

so that when, with an angle of 36 degrees
bow down, there was a heavy thump, signifying that they had hit the bottom, he was
able to reach for the telegraphs and wind
them to stop. The switchboard operator
somehow managed to haul himself up and
break the switches and a disciplined silence
fell throughout the boat.

The manometer, registering amidships,
showed 15 metres and some quick mental arithmetic, together with the rapidly
fluctuating propeller revolutions before the
motor was stopped, made it clear that the
stern was sticking out above the surface
while the bows were buried in the seabed at
the charted depth of 31 metres. The destroyer, which was probably fully occupied in
trying to avoid pooping with the sea astern,
did not observe *Deutschland*'s predicament
and went on its way while the submarine
sorted itself out and regained a level trim.
The whole incident lasted no more than a
minute or so, although it must have seemed
much longer; and during that time Koenig, a
true merchant skipper, thought only of his
cargo. Had it been securely stowed? Or had
it shifted? He was much relieved to find that
it had remained in place.

Other ships were seen and successfully
avoided, but bad weather and constant vigi-
lance had exhausted the crew and Koenig,
with many years of battling with the sea behind him, knew that enough was enough for
the time being. They were not in a hurry;
there was no glory to be gained nor any med-
als won by fighting the elements; and tired
men were not, in his experience, depend-
able. While still in fairly shallow water, be-

It was decided on 16 December 1916 that four cargo U-boats being built by Reiherstag and Flensburger should be modified and equipped by Kaiserliche Werft as U-cruisers, designated *U-151* to *U-154*. Three of these monsters, with two bow tubes (eighteen torpedoes) and two 15 cm (5.9 inch) guns, can be seen here soon after the war at Harwich with *U-152* in the foreground, *U-151* and *U-153* outboard. They scored heavily: *U-151*, 37,210 tons; *U-153*, 12,742 tons. *U-154* was herself destroyed by the British submarine *E-35* on 11 May 1918 after sinking three ships (7,958 tons).

fore breaking out into the Atlantic, he elected to bottom the boat deliberately so that his men could rest and recuperate.

For the first time since leaving Kiel, everybody was able to wash and relax without listening constantly for whistles and orders from the speaking tubes. The cook set to work in the galley; the gramophone records were brought out; the wardroom steward, Stucke (a 'dear soul' the Captain called him) laid the table with clean linen and bright silver as though he was still in the saloon of the *Kronprinzessin Cecilie*; and French champagne, a gift before sailing, filled the officers glasses.

It was a pleasant night and it did wonders for morale. The following day found *Deutschland* well under way and clear of British patrols. The weather was unseasonably bad for the month of June but *Deutschland* had been well built and, apart from a good deal of water coming down the conning tower, which made life below thoroughly unpleasant, no damage was done. When the weather cleared, all hands brought up damp mattresses, blankets and boots for airing. Underwear was fastened to the jumping wire, which served as a clothes line, and the men sunned themselves on deck like lizards.

The two gramophones were constantly being wound up, for Koenig, ahead of his time, reckoned that life on board a submarine would be unthinkable without canned music.

Far out into the Atlantic, it was most unlikely that any ships would prove hostile but, as a precautionary measure and to avoid diving unnecessarily, a framework was rigged to simulate the outline of a small steamer. The camouflage came complete with a dummy canvas funnel fastened to the periscope. When a tramp eventually loomed up cotton waste was lit inside the 'funnel' but it only produced a thin wisp of smoke; so Bos'n Humke climbed to the bridge with a packet of tar and this did all that was required of it—and more. The passing ship, perfectly convinced by the disguise, assumed that the *Deutschland* was on fire and in need of assistance. Dutifully, it turned straight towards her in order to assist. This was not the result that the disguise was intended to produce and Koenig ordered everything to be dismantled at top speed. However, it was not necessary to dive: the merchantman, recognising at last that he was very close to an undeniable U-boat, veered off and departed, billowing clouds of smoke which Koenig and Humke could not but envy.

Despite this misadventure, the camouflage was re-assumed with rather more care and better regulated smoke and Koenig thought he had succeeded in avoiding the suspicions of passing traffic until, about 100 miles from the American coast, he decided that he could no longer take the smallest risk of being identified. From

now on, he invariably dived as soon as smoke was sighted on the horizon; but *Deutschland* had already, in fact, been sighted—and identified, furthermore, as a very large submarine.

Not knowing this, Koenig nevertheless assumed that British intelligence sources knew something of his movements. And indeed they did. Vice Admiral Sir George Patey, Commander-in-Chief North American and West Indies Station, told the Admiralty on 1 July 1916:

The Ambassador in Washington informs me that the expected German submarine would fly the German merchant flag. I cannot conceive that any enemy's submarine can have any status except that of a belligerent enemy and I shall treat her accordingly if met. The fact of flying a merchant flag, or any other flag, would be no guarantee.

So much for Koenig's argument.

In the summer of 1915, American submarines had caused a certain amount of worry by exercising (quite properly) near British patrols off the US East Coast. The same concern was evident in 1916 and Admiral Patey was worried about the possibility of a dangerous incident, the more so when he received a report from the Admiralty on 30 June that the Dutch merchant ship *Westerdyk* had sighted a large submarine (estimated 400–500 feet!) steering west at 0545 on 24 June in position 50,58N 29,18W. He warned the cruiser on the New York patrol to take every precaution but also instructed that, 'should favourable opportunity offer', the submarine was to be attacked.

On 11 July, the British Ambassador was informed that US submarines would keep away from the vicinity. But Koenig was ahead of the schedule predicted by intelligence services. He had come within sight of the American coast some three days earlier and had appreciated that the final approach to Hampton Roads and the Chesapeake might well be hazardous until within the three-mile territorial limit.

It was the ten-mile band to seaward of this limit which common-sense suggested was most dangerous and the outer edge of this band was reached early in the evening of 8 July. It was a question of whether to wait for dawn and cross the danger zone in daylight, depending on sighting and evading any enemy vessels before they could endanger *Deutschland*, or simply going ahead under cover of darkness in the hope of not being sighted at all. As it happened, British units were not in the right place. At the time that Koenig was wondering what to do next, the armed merchant cruisers *Caronia* and *Calgarian* and the light cruiser *Isis* were either en route or relieving each other on the established New York patrol; and Patey signalled the Admiralty that he did not propose to send any cruiser to the Norfolk (Virginia) and Baltimore area. His proposal was approved on 10 July.

Although submariners of any navy might be reluctant to admit it, they quite often take decisions which are based more upon considerations of personal comfort backed up by wishful thinking than upon reasoned logic; and those decisions are almost always right. So it was on this occasion.

A stiff south-westerly breeze had sprung up which brought with it a short and choppy sea. It was, as the Captain remarked, extremely disagreeable[3] and the crew had all had enough of seasickness. So Koenig went straight ahead, almost blinded by the lights of passing steamers, and crossed the three-mile limit into American national waters half an hour before midnight. Switching on navigation lights, he made the customary signal for a pilot boat and caused something of a sensation when one appeared. Although the name had to be repeated twice, the pilot clearly expected *Deutschland's* arrival (justifying Koenig's earlier fears). His first words were: 'I'll be damned, here she is!'

Koenig's fulsome account of the extraordinarily warm welcome that then ensued is probably correct and Captain Hinsch of North German Lloyd, whose liner the SS *Neckar* had been lying in Baltimore since the outbreak of war, was in the tug *Timmins* to greet the awaited U-freighter. Hinsch told

Koenig that the destination was now Baltimore and assured him that everything was arranged: there would be no trouble—quite the contrary. The German Ensign was hoisted in *Deutschland* and, at first light, the huge U-boat, escorted by *Timmins*, started the passage up Chesapeake Bay, a passage made more pleasant by a block of ice passed over from the tug to cool another couple of bottles of champagne.

At 2300 on 9 July 1916, while the British warships were still taking up other positions, the first mercantile submarine in the world anchored off the Quarantine Station at Baltimore. The Press and 'movie men' were there in force. A hastily gathered German-American band rendered suitable Teutonic airs when the boat finally came alongside and a crowd of enthusiastic girls on the quayside rained flowers on the deck. Captain Koenig's first ride in an automobile to the North German Lloyd Agency in Baltimore City was like a triumphal procession. Such was the warmth displayed by the good citizens of Baltimore that the automobile with Koenig embarked was wearily recognised by the City Police as an inevitable traffic obstruction whenever it appeared during the next few days. When any of the crew appeared in public, they were greeted with the *'Wacht am Rhein'* sung loudly (and apparently with the right words) in German. The German Club and others with decidedly anti-British sentiments had prepared the ground well.

The dangers of overt publicity must have been apparent in Germany, where the threat of Admiral Patey's Cruiser Force was well known; but there is reason to think that the risks, correctly interpreted as minimal, were accepted because the whole affair was intended to foster German-American goodwill as much as, if not more than, to promote some advantageous trading. This point is supported by the extraordinary speed with which Captain Koenig's subsequent book *The Voyage of the Deutschland* was written, translated and published by Hearst's International Library Company at New York in the same year, only a very short time after *Deutschland's* safe arrival back in Bremen on 24 August.

The book is extraordinarily well written and, without denying Koenig the ability to write interestingly and amusingly, it bears all the marks of Public Relations expertise although PR was not a recognised craft at the time. Yet, if this suspicion is founded, the book aligns with the facts recorded elsewhere: it is only the sheer brilliance with which the political theme is underlaid that

tends to raise a questioning eyebrow.

Meanwhile, the frustrated Admiral Patey reported on 14 July that he was, after all, sending at least one cruiser to the Chesapeake. His appreciation of the situation and directive read as follows:[4]

WATCH OFF CHESAPEAKE ON GERMAN SUBMARINE

No M/9 MEMORANDUM.

It is most probable that the submarine will come out at night, in which case it will probably be impossible to see her, whether on the surface or submerged.

But if no Allied Man-of-War is in sight off the Chesapeake the submarine would come out in daylight and submerge at her leisure. Under these circumstances I propose to station one or two ships off Chesapeake.

If there are two, one should keep fairly close in by day, retiring further to seaward at night, and returning again at daylight.

The second ship should patrol about 100 miles SE of Cape Henry, as I am of the opinion that the submarine would proceed in that direction before shaping course for Europe.

If there is only one ship she should proceed as in the first case, but should not START *her return to the coast until daylight.*

It is reported that the submarine is unarmed, but she should be attacked at once if sighted clear of neutral waters, as the Germans cannot be trusted, and would submerge at once to escape or to attack.

NB. *The possibility of another submarine arriving from seaward must not be overlooked.*

(Sgd)GEORGE E PATEY
Vice Admiral
COMMANDER-IN-CHIEF

It was unfortunate and not due to any intelligence gambit that Captain Guy Gaunt, the British Naval Attaché in the United States, had only recently and very publicly announced from New York that it was impossible for the Germans to send a submarine to America. The confident Attaché went on to explain that a U-boat left a trail of oil on the surface which would be followed and that it was a dead certainty that it would be captured. Gaunt had seven years seniority as a Post Captain but anti-submarine warfare was not his strong point.

When British patrols off the Chesapeake were instituted, late in the day and initially by the *Isis* on 15 July from the New York area, it was inevitable that there should have been reports in the American press of the British violating American waters. On 28 July, Associated Press, and others, told how a British cruiser of the 'Berwick' class passed between Cape Henry and Cape Charles on the night 24/25 July and then steamed up the Chesapeake. When challenged, the ship was reputed to have replied 'British Cruiser', and then to have extinguished all lights. The two ships on patrol at this time were *Carnarvon* (Senior Officer) and *Berwick* herself (inshore station) but both obeyed the orders in the C-in-C's directive and it is certain that neither violated American territorial waters. *Berwick* was relieved in the area on 1 August by *Cumberland* and sailed for Halifax.

Deutschland remained at Baltimore until 2 August, by which time Koenig must have been exhausted by hospitality, although he permitted himself (or was permitted) only one reference to 'somewhat wearily' accepting another invitation.

For the return journey, the submarine was fully laden. Some of the external ballast tanks were stowed with 275 tons of rubber (27 tons more than the constructors had thought possible) and another 91 tons were carried in the cargo holds. Nickel, tin, copper and silver amounting to about 525 tons filled the remaining stowage spaces. The rubber alone was said to be worth 17.5 million dollars (which seems unlikely, despite inflated wartime prices) and the total value of the cargo could have been in the region of 30 to 40 million dollars—many times the capital and running costs of the submarine itself if the figures were not unduly exaggerated.

The British, naturally enough, were not prepared to tolerate these goings on. *The Morning Post* of 18 July announced that 'the *Deutschland* in consequence of its character

as a submarine is to be regarded as a war vessel and is to be treated as such. The warships of the Allies will, therefore, seek every opportunity to waylay the vessel beyond the American 3 mile limit and will sink it without warning.' Koenig protested that English brutality had never been more clearly displayed: the greatest of the neutral powers had expressly recognised *Deutschland* as a merchant vessel and yet the English now intended to sink her without warning. The arguments on both sides were nicely balanced and had all the ingredients for making one of those endless wrangles from which only the legal profession emerges as a winner. On the whole, history would probably agree with the British point of view.

Koenig was warned that the English had assembled a Squadron, vastly overestimated at eight ships, outside the threemile limit off the entrance to Chesapeake Bay. They reportedly carried nets with explosive devices attached and they used boats in laying them. If he was going to meet trouble immediately after leaving American territorial waters, Koenig knew that he must get the boat back into trim as soon as possible after sailing on 2 August. He therefore made a trim dive while on the way down Chesapeake Bay, with the faithful *Timmins* standing by.

It was nearly a disaster. The trim itself was perfect in spite of having embarked a lot more cargo than the specifications allowed for. But, when the Captain ordered the boat to bottom in a supposed 30 metres of water, the chart, just as Lohmann had originally feared, proved wrong. The boat, deliber-

ately trimmed a little heavy to settle at the expected depth, continued to go down and down until it thudded onto the bottom at 50 metres and burrowed itself into the mud. The manometer inlets were blocked, the needles fluctuated wildly and the compass went mad. Pumping and blowing eventually succeeded in freeing the submarine and, as a result of the incident, the crew were a good deal more alert they had been a couple of hours earlier. Hangovers evaporated quickly.

Deutschland emerged from the Bay well after sunset to find powerful searchlights playing on the water ahead and occasionally illuminating the conning tower. An American cruiser was patrolling the territorial limit to ensure fair play but the lights of fishing vessels, which could be acting as netlayers, were also visible in several directions and it had to be assumed that these were backed up by warships just outside the limit waiting to pounce if the U-boat became tangled in the netting. There was, however, no reason to think that the opposition had any kind of underwater listening apparatus and, if *Deutschland* remained submerged, there was nothing other than the nets that could stop her; but Patey reported on 3 August:

There are detailed accounts, all of course inaccurate, in the United States papers of the disposition of Allied vessels on watch off the United States' coast—fast patrol boats, laying of submarine nets, etc. I do not contradict these reports as I consider they have a good effect.

Poor Patey. He was struggling with elderly, unsuitable forces to block a new kind of political, economic, semi-covert submersible operation with disputed legalities surrounding it. The British efforts, supported later in August by the French cruiser *Marseillaise*, cost a good deal more than the German mercantile submarine that provoked them; and it was the U-boat that won—easily and profitably. However, the British were, perhaps, the winners in the end because ten British submarines (*H-11* to *H-20*) built in America but held under neutrality laws in Boston, were released during the diplomatic skirmishing occasioned by the voyage of the *Deutschland*. Six of the H-boats went to

Deutschland's torpedo tube space. After the war, *Deutschland* (*U-155*) was taken over by a British crew, brought back to England and put on show. She was a very popular attraction and proceeds from the sale of souvenirs went to King George's Fund for Sailors. The project was sponsored by the proprietors of *John Bull*.

Allied and Axis submarines were frequently used as blockade runners during World War Two, a quarter of a century after *Deutschland* had shown the way. This is HMS *Rorqual* carrying stores, mail and personnel to Malta under siege in the summer of 1941.

Above right
Several large submarines laid the 'magic carpet' to Malta in 1941–42: here, Yeomen of Signals 'Ginger' Facer is hoisting the Porpoise Carrier Service flag under the Jolly Roger on the bridge of HMS *Porpoise*.

Chile in exchange for Chilean ships taken over in British yards. It is an ill wind that blows nobody any good.

Koenig, the centre of all this turmoil, was unaffected by strategy, diplomacy and debate. Single-minded, he had a job to do and he pressed on with it. Maintaining periscope depth through and past territorial waters, he slowly made his way eastwards while steering clear of the many ships, all well lit but not necessarily harmless, that lay between him and the open ocean.

By midnight, the U-boat had covered some 25 miles submerged and the surface ships were no longer visible. Thankfully, Koenig surfaced, recharged the batteries and made for the Fatherland at the painfully slow best speed of nine and a half knots. He was sighted on 12 August by the British

steamer *Sachem* and had to dive when she turned towards but, otherwise, the passage passed without incident.

The welcome home at Bremen on 24 August was rapturous. Even the Chief Stoker of the battleship *Posen*, who had recently seen action at the Battle of Jutland, was moved to write a congratulatory poem of nine rather tedious verses; and in the evening there was a State Banquet at the Rathaus. The formal celebrations included the singing of the hymn of thanksgiving, 'To the God of Justice we Offer our Prayers', and the festivities were brought to a close by the President of the Senate proclaiming: 'Deutschland, Deutschland uber alles! Long live Kaiser and Empire!'

It had indeed been a remarkable voyage. *Deutschland* had covered 8450 miles, of which 190 critical miles were submerged.

A second cargo trip was made between October and December, this time to New London and, again, the British failed to intercept the *Deutschland*. But her sister U-freighter *Bremen* was lost en route to Norfolk, Virginia. She had been sighted 300 miles south of Iceland and the big armed merchant cruisers of the Tenth Squadron were spread to intercept her. Both the flagship HMS *Alsatian* and HMS *Mantua* reported ramming a heavy submerged ob-

ject and this was almost certainly the unfortunate blockade-runner. Curiously enough, neither ship claimed that the ramming was deliberate in order to take credit.

At the turn of the year it was decided to convert *Deutschland* to a fighting U-boat and equip her with torpedoes and guns. The navy adopted her as *U-155* on 18 February 1917.

What had been accomplished? The commercial value of the enterprise is obvious and the merchandise brought back from America was perhaps as valuable as supposed. But the propaganda value for Germany at home and in the United States was beyond price. *Deutschland*'s exploits reversed American public opinion, which had been incensed by *U-20* sinking the *Lusitania* on 7 May 1915: for a while, at least one German U-boat seemed to be sinned against rather than sinning. This temporary change of attitude could not and did not persist and America entered the war against Germany on 6 April 1917. But the whole business, from every point of view, was handled faultlessly by Lohmann, the State, and Koenig alike.

The *Deutschland* in her mercantile role deserves to be remembered with more respect than she has so far been accorded in the history books.

2: Great Disasters

The extraordinary thing about submarine construction over the years is that, almost invariably, the vehicle has taken precedence over the weapon systems. The first consideration has usually been speed, linked with endurance; then, propulsion machinery has been formulated to generate the necessary power; then, a hull has been designed to accommodate the machinery and fuel in a shape suited to the speed; and, lastly, weapons have been chosen to fit the hull.

This is hardly a logical process: it is as if submarine designers have been determined not to be accused of putting the cart before the horse. But, surely, it would make better sense to load up the cart before deciding what kind of horse will have to pull it. The first question ought to be: what weapon system do we want for such and such a task? And the second: what is the best vehicle to carry it?

The consequences of reversed thinking are curious and far-reaching. For example, weapon engineers have nearly always been constrained by constructors to fitting new weapons into existing torpedo tubes which may or may not be of the right size or in the best position for discharging a new kind of torpedo or missile. Furthermore, far more money and effort has been spent on developing submarines than on developing the weapons which, ultimately, it is their principle purpose to carry.

Thus, when the Submarine Committee of the Admiralty sat in February 1912, they recommended a new *high speed* Overseas Type Submarine and weapons were almost an afterthought. The term 'Overseas' simply meant ocean-going as opposed to coastal defence and the requirements for a large vessel to out-class continental designs were, in the customary order of priority: twenty knots surface speed; high submerged speed for a short distance; large surface and submerged

endurance at economical speed; diving time, three minutes; good accommodation for officers and men; and two bow, two beam and two stern torpedo tubes.

The aim was to build a submarine which had sufficient speed to accompany the Fleet with good sea-keeping qualities in all conditions. How and when the boat would be expected to fight was not stated and, at the design stage, there is good reason for thinking that this was scarcely considered—certainly not by submariners themselves.

In 1914, just before war broke out, disquieting news arrived about new German U-

Commander E W Leir, DSO, 'the Arch Thief', with the Ship's Company of *K-3* in late 1916. In 1915, *The Maidstone Magazine* listed him as first in the Light Finger Stakes with the German Crown Prince as 'also ran'. He was reputed to have disposed of 300 tons of lead ballast, profitably, following the trials of *E-4* at Barrow. It was Leir in *Ithuriel* who loyally but tragically turned back with three K-boats to assist *K-14* and *K-22* and inadvertently contributed thereby to the disastrous 'Battle of May Island' in January 1918.

K-4 aground off Barrow during trials in January 1917: this was a minor mishap compared with her tragic loss after colliding with *K-6* on 31 January 1918.

boats with a surface speed of 22 knots. The report was unfounded but, by 1915, the speed requirement for a new British boat had been raised to 24 knots and it was from this high speed requirement alone that the steam-driven K-class evolved. En route, the diesel *Nautilus* and the steam *Swordfish*, intended as intermediate steps between the 670-ton E-boats and the much larger new class, were ordered in April and August 1913 respectively; but, although much was learned during the construction of these boats, they are not significant in this story of the monsters.

K-boats were prompted by the Grand Fleet. They were not the product of the Submarine Branch nor were they a submariner's idea of what a submarine should be.[1] They were to be the first Fleet Submarines and one of the early Vickers drawings was labelled 'H.M. Flotilla Leaders'. It is impossible to say what was meant by that; but clearly the K-boats were to be prestigious, and that intention may well have overridden other, more practical, considerations.

Steam was the only possible method of achieving high speed (just as it is today with nuclear propulsion), and the size of the power plant demanded a surface displacement of 1980 tons. A high reserve of buoyancy (32.5 per cent) was obviously necessary and the displacement submerged was 2566 tons. It was found that such a large boat could accommodate four 18-inch internal tubes forward and four beam tubes amidships together with two (initially three) guns. Two additional bow tubes were included on building, but they were subsequently re-moved because they drastically decreased stability.

The K-boats were probably the most hazardous and undoubtedly the most notorious submarines ever built. Eighteen of the class (including the greatly modified *K-26*) were completed and no less than eight of them suffered disasters of one kind or another. There were sixteen major accidents altogether and an uncounted number of lesser mishaps. Most of the monstrosities were in service for some eighteen months during the latter part of the 1914–18 war but they accomplished nothing against the enemy and were responsible for the loss of many British lives.

So far as submariners were concerned, the K-class and its *raison d'être* made little sense. When the first keel was laid at Vickers by His Majesty King George V on 21 May 1915—for *K-3* as it happened—British submarines and German U-boats had already proved their effectiveness as lone wolves. The dislike, suspicion and contempt with which surface sailors greeted the emergence of the Navy's new Submarine arm fourteen years earlier in 1901 had largely been dissipated by the exploits of British submarines in the North Sea, Baltic and the Dardanelles: indeed, the Submarine Service had achieved, in the first few months of war, more than the big ships that looked down upon them with such disdain. And, on the German side, *U-9* under Kapitänleutnant Otto Weddigen had demonstrated all too clearly what a single submerged U-boat could do by sinking, only a few weeks after war was declared, the three British cruisers *Aboukir*, *Cressy* and *Hogue* with a loss of life—1459 officers and men—greater than that suffered by the whole of Nelson's fleet at the Battle of Trafalgar. It must have been obvious that submarines were most gainfully employed independently and underwater; but now it seemed that the Admiralty wanted to bring them up to the surface again.

It is going too far to suggest that Their Lordships favoured the idea of Fleet Submarines on account of their greater respectability as predominantly surface vessels, but this could well have been a factor in the minds of older Admirals and politicans. It was, of course, the Hun in his U-boats who skulked beneath the waves, hit below the belt and did not play the game (presumably cricket): British submarines were quite different (so long as they succeeded), even if their sailors did look like 'unwashed chauffeurs'; but there must have been those who thought it would be a very good thing if some at least could rejoin the Navy proper as a part of the Grand Fleet. How they should be employed was another matter.

The fact was that the Submarine Branch was not properly represented at high level in the Admiralty. It was really the fault of the submariners themselves that the Admirals knew so little about them. Spurned in the beginning as being in a service that was 'no occupation for a gentleman', British submariners withdrew from naval society, with all its pomp and circumstance, gunnery and gaiters, into a tightly knit clan. The consequence was that submarine design and submarine operations were inhibited for decades and misemployment was common. If, halfway through World War One, submariners felt that the K-boats had been foisted on them, they were right, but they lacked the ability to plead their case, so when the K-boats, almost at the beginning of their short careers, became objects of extreme dislike and K-boat men were known collectively as the 'suicide club', there was only grumbling beneath the surface and little or no positive arguing one way or the other. Serving submarine officers, who seldom had Staff training, were in any event no match for the highly professional Staff Officers sitting in Whitehall.

As seamen and submariners, however, the quality of the officers appointed to K-boats was exceptionally high: just as in the nuclear giants half a century later, the cream was skimmed off to man the monsters. Size more than purpose dictated rank, and K-boat captains were usually full Commanders with four other officers and 64 ratings. K-boat command was prestigious in 1917, but it was to become a cachet allied to catastrophe before the year was out.

Despite their vast seniority, compared with the abundant juniority of captains in far more effective D and E class submarines, the K-boat captains retained the individuality that formerly had made them famous— or occasionally notorious—in earlier commands. There was Kellett, who had made a German trawler tow him back to Harwich when his engines in *S-1* packed up in the North Sea in 1916; Laurence of *J-1*, who was the only man ever to hit two battleships— the *Grosser Kurfurst* and the *Kronprinz Wilhelm*—with a single salvo (of four fish from the bow tubes), as well as having earlier torpedoed the battleship *Moltke* in *E-1*; Herbert, who had a price on his head for sinking *U-27* and then shooting the crew in what the Germans claimed to be cold blood; Leir, known as the 'Arch Thief',[2] who plundered His Majesty's Navy of anything portable, and of whom it was said that only his DSC was earned honestly; Harbottle, who had disguised *E-21* as a U-boat in a spy-catching operation off Crete; Dobson, who had been towed submerged by a trawler in *C-27* to trap U-boats attacking British fishermen in the North Sea and sunk *U-23* thereby; Bower, who was a well-paid and humorous writer under the pen-name of Klaxon; Calvert, who, according to confidential reports by his Flotilla Captain in September 1917, was 'one of the best all round officers I know'[3] but who, by June 1918, was 'suffering the stress of K-boat life'; and Shove, who was, perhaps, the most curious character of all.

Shove, at a time when officers (outside their submarines) took pains with their appearance, stood out from the remainder with 'matted dishevelled hair' and a 'high-water mark above his collar'. On one occasion he was heard to remark to one of his officers: 'Sub, I must wash. I can smell myself.'[4] He had a pet rodent called Ratto which he kept up one sleeve of his monkey jacket: the creature had a habit of obeying quite frequent calls of nature without leaving this warm nest whereupon his owner would shake the droplets out of his sleeve with apparent unconcern. It may have been this practice which defeated the Bishop of Stepney, whom Shove chose, on board HMS *Maidstone*, to engage in a profound theological argument which, it was said, reduced the Bishop to gibbering impotence.[5]

Such were the personalities who found themselves appointed to K-boats and who foresaw, after a life of action, a boring existence ahead, mostly in some remote fastness with the Grand Fleet, towards the end of the war. They could not know that all too much

excitement was to come and that none of it would be welcome, for it would not arise in battle with the enemy.

An ordinary submariner's reaction on seeing the strange and exceptionally long outline of a K-boat for the first time was a mixture of wonder and disbelief. It was commonly believed that an illicit union had been consummated between a destroyer and a submarine when nobody was looking. Signalman George Kimbell, being ferried to his new chimneyfied home, *K-17*, in the Gareloch, and seeing smoke coming out of two small funnels, was moved to remark to the boatman, 'that's never a submarine surely?'

The surface navy voiced no such doubts. The K-boats looked magnificent and appeared fully capable of supporting the Fleet. They were indeed handsome vessels. But handsome is as handsome does; they were

Top
Steam and Sail: *K-6* on builder's trials in Plymouth Sound early in 1917. On her first dive in a non-tidal basin in North Yard, Devonport, *K-6* obstinately refused to surface for two anxious hours and many of the dockyard workmen refused to dive in her a second time.

Above
K-6 with the fleet at Invergordon *circa* 1920, with the aircraft-carrier *Argus* and an M-class submarine in the background. Lord Louis Mountbatten was, for a short time, appointed to the boat as a midshipman. In later life, he wore the Submarine Badge as a result: he was not entitled to do so but nobody grudged it to him.

frighteningly difficult to handle submerged, and that was not their only fault. However, looked at from above so to speak, they were all that had been asked of the constructors.

The maximum speed of 23½ knots came within half a knot of the revised speed requirement and the endurance at full power was normally 800 miles or about 1200 miles if emergency oil fuel was embarked; alternatively, the cruising range at 10 knots was an astonishing 12,500 miles.

The armament, too, was impressive at first sight. The four bow tubes, with four re-loads could presumably deal with any ship from submerged and the beam tubes (two to port and two to starboard with re-loads) would, in theory, simplify maneouvring on the surface during a close night action, where pointing a target might be difficult. However, 18-inch torpedoes were not nearly so effective as 21-inch weapons, which had twice the punch. The smaller tubes were excused by saying that larger ones would involve an entirely new design, implying delay; but this argument was weak, and typical of the low priority given to weapon systems, because *Swordfish* and the G-class had already tested 21-inch tubes successfully.

W/T communications with the Fleet were ensured by telescopic masts, and 40 square feet were allocated to the Wireless Office, which compares favorably with the space available in many boats today. There were no hydrophones for tracking U-boats or anti-submarine vessels although Fessenden underwater signalling apparatus was sometimes installed; but, true to their vaguely conceived surface role, a number of boats carried a loaded depth-charge thrower aft for anti-submarine work—a nasty thought when going deep or when under attack.

So far as the vulnerability of a submarine on the surface was concerned, some misleading gunnery trials had been conducted on 17 October 1912 against the primitive *Holland*

IV, with the boat, unmanned, fifteen feet below the surface. A wildly over-optimistic conclusion was reached despite the boat being sunk by the second shot bursting directly over the submarine and fracturing one of the glass scuttles in the conning tower: it was believed that 'if the hull is twelve to fifteen feet below the surface a 6-inch Lyddite shell cannot do any damage beyond causing the conning tower lights to leak.' A K-boat with its partial double hull and most of the pressure hull underwater was consequently held to be a satisfactory platform which, if not immune from enemy gunfire, was relatively no more vulnerable than a surface ship. A substantial gun armament was therefore included because there was plenty

of room for it. Although the original outfit was reduced and repositioned, one four-inch and one three-inch gun were carried, the former on top of the superstructure between the funnels and the latter at bridge-deck level between the bridge and the forward funnel. With weapons coming last on the list, it is not surprising that the disappearing

K-22 with the funnels half lowered preparatory to diving. She once left them up by mistake.

Bottom
In the words of the 'Song of the BKBS' (The Brighter K-Boat Society):
Early in the morning the Inconstant *hoists a signal*
See the little K-boats all in a row
Man in the control-room pulls a lot of levers
Swoosh—Swish—Down we go.

K-2 gunnery practice.

K-2 recovering a practice torpedo.

type of gun-mounting tried in *Swordfish* was not pursued on the grounds that the water resistance of a gun when dived was not as great as first thought; the 'complicated mechanism' was not reckoned to be necessary or worthwhile but, in fact, quite simple air or hydraulic mechanisms for turning a gun upside down or simply lowering it into the casing were long known, tested and available in at least three navies. (Incidentally, something on these lines might well have proved invaluable half a century later when submariners were once more asking for guns in the 1960s, while being, by then, much concerned about the effects on speed and, more importantly, on noise; but, repeating history, the constructors did not seriously consider the possibilities).

With all their apparent attributes, K-boats seemed, on the surface, to be valuable and flexible additions to the surface fleet. From below, the picture was rather different.

With a length to breadth ratio of 12.8:1, the submarines were bound to be unhandy when they dived—and so they proved. There is a well known story of one Captain telephoning his First Lieutenant in the distant fore-ends: 'I say, No. 1, my end is diving—what the Hell is your end doing?' [6] It illustrates the point. Once a bow-down or bow-up angle developed, it tended to increase see-saw fashion—a horrible feeling—because the broad flat casing itself started to act like a gigantic hydroplane, making it difficult, if not impossible, to level the boat

without recourse to flooding and blowing tanks and, in desperation but against instructions at the time, using full power astern. (A similar but manageable effect—give or take a few heartbeats at first—was to be felt 40 years later in Polaris submarines.) To make matters worse, the hydroplanes themselves had an unpleasant habit of jamming at the most awkward moments. As Able Seaman Crouch in *K-14* resignedly remarked, 'you never knew what was going to happen next.'

With a length of 339 feet and a designed diving depth of only 200 feet, the danger in deep water was clear enough: a steep angle could take the bows to crushing depth in seconds. Senior officers were of the opinion that no submarine should deliberately be taken below 150 feet. In shallow water most K-boats hit the bottom at one time or another: *K-2* did it with the Prince of Wales, later King George VI, on board. It was claimed, not altogether laughingly, that visitors to the Firth of Forth when the Flotilla was at Rosyth would, as a daily occurrence, see parts of a K-boat projecting above the water: sometimes there would simply be two propellers idly whizzing round and sometimes a large, sinister-looking bow looking like a basking whale.

The diving arrangements were immensely complicated with no less than twenty external and eight internal main ballast tanks. With 40 vent valves involved, even with the new centralised telemotor (hydraulic) controls, a very careful drill was needed to flood

the tanks evenly and to avoid a list or a longitudinal angle. The fastest diving time ever recorded from full buoyancy was three minutes 25 seconds, and five minutes was more usual: this contrasted with a small H-boat of the same period which could, in ideal conditions, submerge fully in about half a minute. However, when already trimmed down after an initial dive, and provided the Engineer Officer did not fiddle with the feed water for the boilers, it is evident from torpedo-practise firing records that K-boats were able to do a little better on occasion.

The telemotor control, which also operated major hull-valves as well as the periscopes and raisable W/T mast, was provided by a Westinghouse hydro-pneumatic system, previously untested save in a floating dock, but it was a prudent precaution to man each and every valve at diving stations in order to revert to hand operation if necessary. Reliable remote indicators were not available: the numerous orders and reports concerned with diving, added to those resulting from shutting down the boilers and checking twelve hatches shut, as well as various other openings in the hull—'too many damned holes', as contemporary submariners complained—made diving a noisy and bewildering evolution.

The largest holes, and by far the most dangerous, were the four air intakes in the boiler room, each three feet in diameter. These were covered by domes operated by telemotor rams which raised them ten inches from their seatings in the open position. Each cover weighed about eight hundred-weight, and the weight helped the shutting operation, which was quick and effective, with hand gear for use if the telemotor supply failed. When *K-13* was lost in the Gareloch during trials on 29 January 1917, it was because the air intakes were left open on diving when verbally reported shut.

The funnels were lowered electrically, while a telemotor operated 'top door' hull-valve and a secondary 'lower door' sealed off the uptake. The time specified to shut down the boiler room and secure was nominally 30 seconds but, with all the time in the world available while the submarine struggled to submerge, it would have been a very unwise Engineer Officer who endeavoured to hasten the drill for the sake of smartness. Meanwhile, it was not unknown for the Captain to climb down from the bridge, after having pressed the hooter (klaxon), in order to see for himself that the funnel doors were properly shut.

The control gear for operating the funnels and the air intakes was in the turbine-room; and the boiler-room amidships was completely isolated when preparing to dive. The heat in the boiler-room was bad enough when the induction fans were forcing air into the furnaces; but when the diving hooter sounded and the fans were stopped, the temperature rose to almost unbearable limits while frantic stokers shut off all the valves and machinery before thankfully vacating the inferno through the twin doors of an airlock which led into the turbine-room.

At the business end forward there was continual trouble with the torpedo-tube bow-shutters—the fairings necessary for speed—which were not strong enough to withstand heavy bow seas. A K-boat's tubes could not be relied upon after a period operating with the Fleet. The guns could not be brought into action quickly and a sustained rate of fire was not possible because the 175 rounds of 4-inch and 100 rounds of 3-inch ammunition were stowed in magazines right forward and right aft; the ammunition route was long and tortuous through several watertight bulkheads. Gunnery control was rudimentary and it was difficult to pass orders from the bridge to the guns.

The seagoing capabilities, too, were disappointing. Although, in September 1918,

two K-class submarines overtook the Grand Fleet hove-to in a heavy gale in the North Sea and thereby demonstrated a degree of sea-worthiness in extreme conditions, the class was unable to keep up with the fleet in moderate weather at reasonably high speeds and the superstructure worked alarmingly in a seaway. E and L-class submarines, by comparison, were superior seaboats, much steadier in heavy weather, and their crews were notably less prone to sea-sickness.

All things considered, it is no wonder that K-boat men described their boats as untrustworthy, and that was one of the milder expressions to be heard. They were not even comfortable despite their size, although the officers were looked after well enough. The whole wardroom area was about 30 feet long and officers had their own heads and washplace, but ratings lived as best they could in awkwardly shaped messes and odd corners; each man had a twenty-fifth share of a lavatory seat and usually had to wash himself and his clothes, with rationed water, in a bucket.

Only the cockroaches and rats which infested the cluttered accommodation spaces were thoroughly happy: they thrived and prospered in great numbers and nothing would get rid of them. After Commander Benning ran *K-1* aground in the Orkneys, he pleaded at his court-martial that rats had eaten the relevant portion of the chart—and the court believed him. It has to be said, however, that some K-boats were more efficient than others and their crews were

more content and less worried than the rest. As always, efficiency, and hence a reasonable feeling of confidence, depended on the command. A rigorous surface-ship type of discipline of the sort that Commander Geoffrey Layton imposed in *K-6* seems to have made the ship's company a good deal happier than the more casual type of authority which submariners were used to and which resulted in perfect efficiency in other, smaller classes—but probably not in K-boats.[7]

There were no trained chefs or stewards and any seaman or stoker could be told off as cook for the day. It was convenient to detail the morning-watch quartermaster for the task since he would, anyway, be up and around at daybreak and could conveniently prepare breakfast for the ship's company while at the same time looking after the safety of the submarine. This practice led to what may well be the only K-boat accident ever regarded as a joke. As such it deserves to be recorded.

Able Seaman Sidney Glazebrook was cook-cum-quartermaster one morning when *K-12* sailed early out of harbour, bound for independent surface manoeuvres and gunnery exercises. There was no intention of diving and the ship's company were so informed. Glazebrook settled himself comfortably in the cramped but comfortable confines of the external surface galley in the after part of the bridge superstructure, far removed from the bridge, where he was invisible to his superiors. The range glowed red and warm in front of him. The fire was

Taking the supporting role to the limit, K-boats were occasionally invited to lay a smoke screen for the surface fleet—perhaps the most inappropriate employment ever devised for submarines.

fed with coal from its own bunker and Glazebrook reflected on a recent argument ashore when a destroyer man accused the K-boats of having coal-fired boilers—an insult which was repudiated with vigour. Now, a frying pan full of sausages was sizzling merrily on the coals as the submarine passed the outer buoy and the acting chef devoted himself to a detailed study of the unclothed French female figure in an interesting imported journal. It was an unusually advanced publication for the period.

The water lapped at his boots as the submarine's speed increased but Glazebrook was high, dry and happy. The sausages smelt delicious and his mates below would undoubtedly appreciate his efforts. Suddenly, the sea on his starboard seaboot began to lap less lightly. Then the seaboot started to fill. Absorbed as he was in abundant and pneumatic femininity, he eventually had to turn his attention to an unwelcome intrusion of salt water into the galley. There was no doubt about it: *K-12* was submerging steadily, albeit slowly and sedately as was her wont. The Captain had changed his mind and had decided to dive, but nobody had thought to tell Glazebrook, despite the Charlie Noble aft which was smoking lightly as evidence of an unseen presence outside the pressure hull.

The ship's company below were counted and told off in the normal way; Glazebrook was not amongst them. The Coxswain counted again but he was still one short.

It took a long time for *K-12* to dive—four minutes or more—but it also took a long while to surface. Glazebrook was even-

tually picked up by a passing destroyer, annoyed and wet but otherwise not much the worse for wear. The tragedy was that the girlie magazine, something not easy to come by and much coveted in those days, was lost forever.

Apart from this small incident there was not much to laugh about. Throughout 1917, rumours of operational problems and mechanical failures filtered through the Flotillas. They were entirely believable in the light of *K-13*'s sinking during her acceptance trials in January and a host of lesser but alarming incidents that followed. Morale fell steadily and inactivity at Scapa Flow, where Layton started a garden ashore to provide some diversion for the crew, did nothing to help. *K-2* came close to mutiny following the loss of a stoker overboard while keeping anchor-watch: the men refused one Sunday to go ashore to church, which was compulsory, but this was the only order to be disobeyed, for the Captain, Laurence of *J-1* fame, was a first-class leader and won the crew round before matters came to a head. Scapa was a bleak, dismal place and there were some unpleasant occurrences in the fleet.

It is not surprising that there was some exceptionally heavy drinking in K-boat wardrooms even when judged by the lavish standards of the day. Whisky was the antidote for officers and could easily be afforded at duty-free prices. There were less attractive beverages in the ratings messes where, legally, only the standard ration of one eighth of a pint of rum per day was allowed. Boot-polish strained through bread provided al-

K-22 dwarfing the much more practical 265-ton German *UB-28* minelayer soon after the Armistice. For all their size, the K-boats achieved nothing while small U-boats like the UBs played a large share in nearly bringing Britain to her knees.

cohol of a sort and magnetic compasses, floated in spirit, mysteriously tended to run dry in harbour.

It has to be remembered that appointing the best and most experienced men to K-boats meant that many of them had a long hard war behind them and were worn out by danger, discomfort and sheer fatigue. Senior officers did not, apparently, recognise the tensions that started to build up in these new Fleet Submarines almost as soon as they commissioned, although individual confidential reports show clearly enough that all the pointers were there. There were too many incidents like the illicit party for Petty Officers invited by the Boatswain to the Wardroom of *K-8* in March 1917 and for which he was dismissed to General service;[8] and perceptive observers, like Lieutenant Commander Samuel Gravener coming to *K-7*, were disturbed at the spirit, or lack of it, which they found among the crews. *K-7* under her former Captain, Kellett, was the only K-boat to fire a salvo of torpedoes in anger: one of these was thought to have hit *U-95*, but it failed to explode. When *K-7* first went to sea with Gravener in command, he asserted that the Coxswain's knees were trembling when he was sitting at the hydroplane controls. A number of officers and men were formally reported as having neurasthenia (which, synonymous with bad morale, was the popular diagnosis by doc-

Boiler being lowered into a K-boat while building.

Two views (*below*) of *K-6* undergoing full-power trials.

tors and captains alike), but very few were transferred or given adequate medical examinations.

Comprehensive medical reports about these problems were not written until some time after the war ended and, when they did emerge, they tended to gloss over the danger signals that must have been apparent. In those days of public-school muscular Christianity and stiff English upper lips, no sympathy was wasted on men with 'cold feet' who today would quickly be recognised as a potential menace to themselves as well as their messmates and be given proper treatment.

Reactions must, in some cases, have been slow and probably contributed to the disasters which overtook the class. Furthermore, it was not possible for the Captain, in one of these huge compartmented boats, to keep a constant eye on every member of the crew in the same way that he could in other British submarines. British officers disliked the German practice of positioning the Captain in a kiosk above the control room during an attack beacuse he was isolated there and they appreciated that a good commanding officer needed to employ his ship's company as an extension of his own senses: lacking an adequate internal communication system, this meant that he had to keep the crew in

Bow 18-inch torpedo tubes in *K-2*. There was no bulk-head between the tubes and the stowage compartment (as in later classes) to prevent flooding after a collision forward.

sight as well as in mind. That was impossible in a K-boat: it was very hard for a Captain to know exactly what was going on or how the crew were reacting in any given situation.

However, there was an interesting and important innovation resulting from a K-boat Captain being distanced from many of the crew. Exceptionally heavy reliance was placed on the Engineer Officer who not only had much greater engineering responsibility than usual but also had to exercise considerable power of command within his large and extensive department under operational conditions. This occasionally led to Engineer Officers being encouraged to assume duties of seamen officers; and at least one, Lieutenant (E) Owen W Phillips, progressed from keeping watch at sea as a regular officer-of-the-watch in *K-4* (Commander D de Stocks) in 1917 to commanding *F-2* and *H-22* in 1918–19.[9] This, for the Royal Navy, was a revolutionary departure and it is good to know that Phillips eventually became a Rear Admiral, not retiring until 1944.

Whatever submariners might be thinking about joining the surface fleet in 1917, Admiral Sir David Beatty, commanding the Battle Cruiser Flotilla and flying his flag in HMS *Lion*, was determined to make his new flock as welcome as possible; and Lady Beatty concentrated her formidable abilities on ensuring that baths, recreation facilities and a reading room ashore were provided for submarine officers and men who still lived in the supposedly self-sufficient K-boats when

the Admiral transferred the K-boat Flotillas from Scapa Flow to Rosyth in December in the hope that they would operate more advantageously from the Firth of Forth. It was a welcome move for the K-boat men but they could not foresee the tragedy that came to be known as the Battle of May Island.

By now it was being rumoured, almost unbelievably, that ratings being drafted to K-boats were trying all kinds of ways to escape joining one. Moreover, even at a submarine Signalman's level, there were considerable doubts about operating with the Fleet. In particular, a qualified Signalman like George Kimbell in *K-17* felt uneasy about formation orders which laid down that the Twelfth and Thirteenth Submarine Flotillas, consisting of four and five K-boats respectively and each led by a light-cruiser leader, were to follow astern of the battle cruisers when leaving harbour in daylight but were to precede them in line ahead during hours of darkness.[10] His unease was well founded.

No account was taken of the difficulties of station-keeping and keeping a good lookout from the bridge of a K-boat at sea and it seems that the submarines were credited, quite wrongly, with the same capabilities in this respect as a destroyer. In theory, the fleet formation on leaving harbour was sound, remembering that the submarines were intended to surprise an enemy which evaded the guns of the surface fleet. In the open sea, the idea was for the K-boat flotillas to submerge and lie in wait, generally in

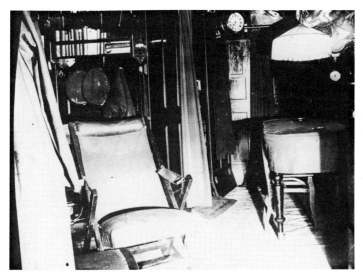

Above, top right and right
The wardroom in *K-2*, luxurious compared with the crew's scattered accommodation spaces.

Centre right
The beam torpedo tubes. These were unclipped to fold open so that reload torpedoes could be lowered into them from a gantry running along the fore-and-aft beam overhead.

Below right
HP and LP ahead and astern turbine throttles.

Left and below
K-2 control room looking forward with hydroplane handwheels on the Port side. The helmsman was, unusually, abaft the planesmen.

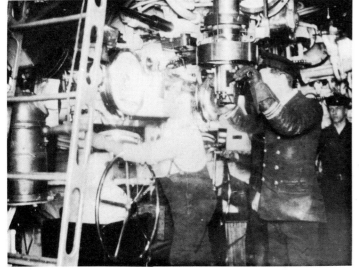

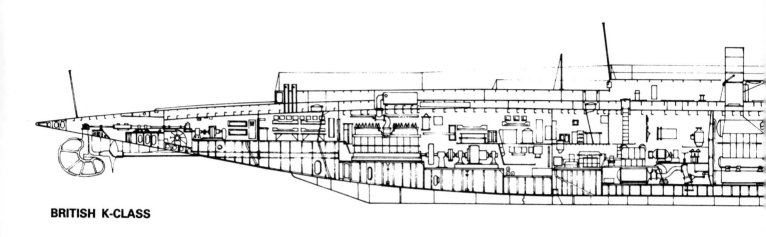

BRITISH K-CLASS

pairs, either spread across the enemy's expected line of advance or on one bow of
approaching German heavy units, ready to
fire torpedoes while the British battle fleet
engaged the enemy with big guns on the
other bow. So it was logical in daylight, on
leaving harbour, which in this case entailed a
long passage down the Firth of Forth, to
bring up the rear and remain, hopefully, unseen by an enemy whose attention was
focused on the surface units; by night, it
was thought, presumably, that the enemy
would not be alerted prematurely if the sub-

marines, which were very difficult to spot in
the dark, went first into the attack and led
the fleet out of the estuary. Unfortunately,
though, it was just as difficult for friendly
vessels as for the enemy to see a long, low
K-boat at night.

High-speed fleet manoeuvres in close
formation can be tricky at the best of times
for novices: exercises for surface ships were,
and still are, graduated gently from basic
manoeuvres in daylight to complex evolu-
tions at night. But no such exercises were
planned for the inexperienced and ill-
equipped submarines which now joined the
well-practised Fleet. It was just the sort of
omission that, in retrospect, might be expected in view of the wide-spread ignorance
about submarine capabilities and the un-
willingness of submarine officers to make
plain their limitations.

On Thursday, 31 January 1918, the ships
in the Firth of Forth were ordered to sail at
dusk and rendezvous in the North Sea with
the remainder of the Grand Fleet from
Scapa Flow for a full-scale exercise designated 'ECI'. Vice Admiral Sir Hugh Evan-
Thomas, wearing his flag in the battle cruiser
Courageous, devised the departure plan and
placed himself at the head of the line.
Courageous was followed at five-mile intervals by the leading ships of battle squadrons
and submarine-flotilla leaders. The light
cruiser *Ithuriel* (Commander[S] XIII) led
five K-boats and *Fearless* (Captain[S] XII)
led four. The flotillas were sandwiched,
respectively, in line ahead between
Courageous in the van and the 2nd Battle

The bows of the light cruiser HMS *Fearless* after colliding with *K-17* during the Battle of May Island, 31 January
1918.

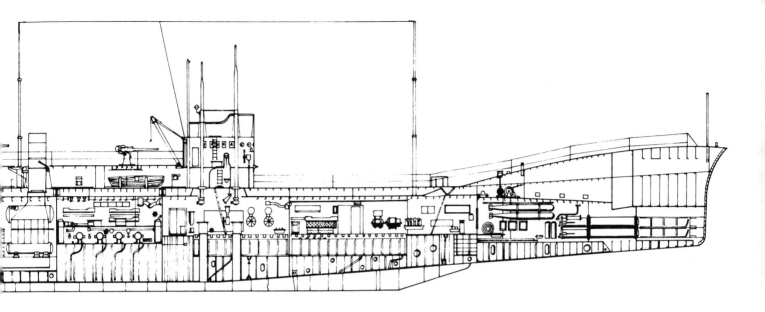

Cruiser Squadron's flagship *Australia*, and between the 2nd Squadron's rear ship and the 5th Battle Squadron bringing up the rear. With escorting destroyers, there were more than 40 vessels in the long procession strung out over some twenty miles and all proceeding at the ordered speed of 16 knots.

Courageous was to increase speed to 20 knots (later amended to 21 knots) on reaching a position north of May Island (which marked the mouth of the estuary) and alter course eastwards for the rendezvous. The ships and submarines in her wake were to conform.

A U-boat was reported off May Island; the night was pitch black with patches of mist; the fleet was darkened with only dimmed blue stern-lights showing; radio silence was enforced; the swept channel was narrow; the K-boats were but poorly equipped for station-keeping; and a group of armed trawlers, engaged in mine-sweeping from their base on May Island, were not informed of the fleet's movements.

All the ingredients on that January night added up to a recipe for disaster; and disaster duly struck.

Courageous increased speed and altered course as planned on passing May Island and, although *Ithuriel* had lost sight of the flagship in the mist, she followed suit at about 1930, but, unknown to Commander (S), only three of her flotilla followed. The captain of *K-14* had put the wheel hard over a few minutes earlier to avoid two of the unwarned minesweepers and, typically, the helm jammed—for a long, long six

minutes. From then on, with submarines altering course in all directions to avoid each other and clear the line of battle cruisers and destroyers coming up fast from astern, confusion reigned. *K-22* sliced into *K-14* at 19 knots and *Inflexible* (last in the 2nd Squadron line) rammed *K-22* in turn.

Although severely damaged, both submarines eventually returned in safety to Rosyth, but others were not so lucky. Commander Leir, in *Ithuriel*, by now well to the east of May Island, received garbled and inaccurate news of the collisions, late and in two successive coded signals when radio silence was eventually broken. Impulsively, unwisely but very understandably, he decided to turn back with his three remaining K-boats and do what he could to help. Leir may have been an arch-thief but he could never be accused of not doing his utmost for men under his command.

Reversing course to the west back towards May Island, with *K-11*, *K-17* and *K-12* following in line astern, was, all the same, a tragic mistake, although he switched on navigation lights to minimise the risk. He assumed that the huge company of ships maintaining their easterly course would all be following identical tracks, but he was wrong. Finding *Australia* dead ahead on the opposite course, he jinked the flotilla to port—by ill chance right across the path of *Fearless* (Captain[S] XII) and her four K-boats which were offset a mile to the south of the main fleet.

At 2032 *Fearless* collided with *K-17*, which sank eight minutes later. *K-4*, directly astern

of *Fearless*, veered away to port and stopped; *K-6*, third in line, also went hard-a-port, stopped engines and went full astern but, with way still on, hit *K-4* a little forward of amidships. It was a mortal blow. Layton in *K-6*, with his bows buried deep in the sister submarine, had difficulty in pulling clear as *K-4* settled in the icy water, threatening to take *K-6* with her. *K-7*, last in line, bumped hideously over the sinking wreck as Gravener drew slowly up, without any clear picture of what had happened, to pick up such survivors as there were. He rescued eight of the crew, including one of the engineer officers, and, while doing so, he was very nearly run down by the escorting destroyers which passed on, still at high speed, straight over the spot where *K-17* had gone down, washing away or cutting down the men who had swum clear. Apart from the handful rescued by *K-7*, there were no survivors from the two submarines sunk at the Battle of May Island: 103 officers and men lost their lives.

The First Lord of the Admiralty, Sir Eric Geddes (notorious after the war for the 'Geddes Axe') blamed the officers—'it looks as though there was something wrong with the standard of efficiency.'[11] Submariners took another view. One is quoted as saying, succinctly and correctly, that the K-boats came to grief because they had the speed of a destroyer, but the turning circle of a battle cruiser and the bridge-control facilities of a picket-boat.'[12]

Their Lordships at the Admiralty were not deterred either by the disaster off May Island or by numerous other accidents which

K-boats looking handsome at Algiers in 1924. *K-26* (right) was the last and considerably improved submarine in the K-boat line, but she was not immune from disaster: two men were scalded to death when faulty valves in the boiler-room failed when raising steam for trials.

had befallen the K-class. In June 1918, a redesigned boat, *K-26*, was laid down at Vickers and launched in August 1919. She was not completed—at Chatham Dockyard—until June 1923, but when she finally went to sea she was able to display some notable improvements. She was expected to be the first of a new class; but a much more powerful bow salvo, afforded by six 21-inch tubes forward, a rather better diving time made possible by transferring more main ballast to internal tanks, and marginally improved

habitability failed to disguise that she was still one of the calamitous K's. Nobody in the submarine service showed any signs of real regret when she was struck from the list in April 1931 after only seven years service. The class was not continued.

It is not easy to find a fitting epitaph for the K-boats, save that they were a monstrous example of the surface fleet forcing on submariners a concept which they did not want and which they, the submariners, failed to oppose.

3: Great Guns

At the beginning of the twentieth century, Admiral Sir John Arbuthnot Fisher—'Jacky' Fisher to his friends and far more numerous enemies—was almost the sole supporter, with any real power, of submarines in the Royal Navy. His vision was astonishing but his objectivity was even more remarkable: in 1904, just when this greatest gunnery enthusiast of all time had at last won the battle to build *Dreadnought* battleships and revolutionise naval gunnery, Jacky was importuning King Edward VII and writing impassioned letters to officials at the highest level about the battleship's greatest potential enemy and 'the vast impending revolution in naval warfare and naval strategy which the submarine will accomplish!'[1]

The Admiral was well aware that the two revolutions would war against each other; and it was not long before his stalking horse, Admiral Sir Percy Scott, was openly saying that 'as the motor has driven the horse from the road, so has a submarine driven the battleship from the sea.'[2] By an ironic twist of fate, however, HMS *Dreadnought* herself was to ram and send the German *U-29* to the bottom on 13 March 1915, only a few months after these portentious words were written: the U-boat took down with her the brilliant Otto Weddigen, the 'polite pirate' who in *U-9* had sunk the three British cruisers *Aboukir*, *Cressy* and *Hogue* at the beginning of the war, and, a little later, *Hawke*.

Fisher, despite being notorious for personal favouritism and unfairness within the Navy (and, it was said, for certain infidelities in private life) was too great a man to allow professional partisan feelings to blur the picture. The pity was that his idiosyncracies and pride were eventually to cloud his judgement but, while he was still respected and in power, if the underwater fleet threatened his long years of work perfecting big ship gunnery, so be it. It was the Service as a whole that mattered; and in truly believing this he was rare amongst admirals.

From the start, with HM Submarine Torpedo Boat *No. 1* (*Holland I*) launched in 1901, British submarines carried reasonably effective, albeit short-range, torpedoes but gunnery armament was another thing altogether. The little *Holland* boats and their immediate petrol-engined successors could not bear any additional top weight and it was not until 1911 that one of the first diesel boats, HMS *D-4*, was fitted with a serviceable 12-pounder; and that was not gunnery as Jacky Fisher knew it. However, if a submarine could be equipped with a really big gun as well as with torpedoes, it would embody, in one vessel, everything that Jacky had fought and connived for over the years.

Fisher resigned the post of First Sea Lord in May 1915, at the age of 74, in circumstances that made him the subject of much criticism; but he was appointed as Chairman of the Board of Invention and Research in July and, from Victory House in Cockspur Street, he applied his formidable talent for getting his own way to achieving ends previously denied him when in office. The BIR soon became known as the Board of Intrigue and Revenge and did not by itself achieve much (although it did promote the development of ASDIC) but, on 5 August 1915, Fisher put forward a plan to Arthur Balfour, First Lord of the Admiralty, for a 'submarine *Dreadnought*' with a 12-inch gun mounted forward of the conning tower in addition to normal torpedo armament. He had already remarked, unfairly but privately, that 'our torpedoes won't hit and, when they do hit, produce no more effect than sawdust.' The Admiral's protégé. Sidney S Hall, now serving a second term as Head of the Submarine Service, was easily persuaded to back the argument for arming submarines with a large gun: 'No case', said Hall, 'is known of a ship-of-war being torpedoed when underway at a range outside 1000 yards. The result is that opportunities of inflicting damage on the enemy have often been missed, even though the submarine has been brought unobserved within a mile of them...'

The Admiralty dockets circulated in the normal elephantine way for six months before it was decided in February 1916 to proceed using the keel of *K-18*, which had already been laid down at Vickers, and as much framework as possible. A second boat, based on *K-19*, was ordered from Vickers in May 1916 and two more, *ex-K-20* and *ex-K-21*, from Armstrong Whitworth in August 1916. The new class fortuitously followed the L-boats, so the next letter M was able to stand, legitimately, for Monitor.

The 12-inch breech-loading Mark IX guns for the M-class were similar to those in *King Edward VII* battleships, although when replacements became necessary, these were

M-1 in war paint!

Mk VIIIs taken from the obsolete 1895 *Majestic*-class. The Mk IXs were selected not only because of their immediate availability but for their considerable girder strength. The weight of each gun and mounting was 122 tons and its 40 rounds of ammunition weighed 29 tons. A smaller 3-inch high-angle disappearing gun was to be fitted aft in recognition of an increasing threat from the air but it was the monstrous 12-inch weapon which dictated the shape and line of the submarine, so it would be fair to say that the M-class was exceptional in that the vehicle was, for once, built around the primary weapon system.

The gun itself demands description before looking at the intended tactics. It was, by any standards, a huge piece of artillery and the submarine's total complement of six officers and 59 ratings included eleven specialist gunnery ratings as well as sixteen others for the ammunition party. The anti-aircraft gun required yet another four gunnery ratings and a loading party of two on deck, so the intake from HMS *Excellent*, the Gunnery School at Whale Island, together with an armourer, was impressive. Happily, this high proportion of gunnery specialists did not bring with it the parade-ground atmosphere of boots and gaiters which submariners associated with 'The Island' or 'The House That Jack Built'; this was another of Fisher's original creations, where it was asserted that all gunners were deafened by their own excesses.

The gun barrel, once appropriated from its battleship, was sawn off and shortened. It could be elevated to twenty degrees or depressed to a standing ten degrees which gave it a dispiritingly droopy appearance in harbour. Training was restricted to within ten degrees either side of the fore-and-aft line. The gun and its loading chamber and director tower were forward of, and incorporated in, the bridge structure and there was a common access compartment to the tower and the bridge. The 12-inch magazine with passageways each side, the 12-inch shell room (it was, of course, 'separate' ammunition) and the hydraulic machinery compartment occupied about 30 feet along the length of the pressure hull, directly below the gun.

The mounting was protected by a non-watertight fairwater carried on a turntable, but to the rear of the mounting there was a watertight tower which carried the machinery for loading the gun with its heavy projectile and propellant. The gun itself was therefore wet and subject to pressure when submerged. This meant that it could only be loaded when on the surface, so the gun-

The M-boats had a reputation for being seaworthy but the Bay of Biscay was no respecter of reputations.

house decking was confined to steel girders with a minimum of plating to ensure that the water drained away rapidly. Reloading took about 75 seconds.

The concept of firing with only six feet or so of the barrel and a periscope protruding above the surface has long been popularised, but, in fact, it was impractical. It would have meant elevating the gun nearly to the highest angle, implying near-maximum range, while the short aiming-periscope's range from the director tower, with a low height of eye, would be limited to far less. Even when on the surface, the chance of hitting anything, including shore targets, at ranges approaching the extreme 32,700 yards was negligible.

However, there was no need to surface fully for short-range engagements. Under an experienced captain like Max Horton, the first commanding officer of *M-1*, the submarine could be brought up on the hydroplanes at speed on the main motors, with perhaps a puff of air in the ballast tanks for safety, without blowing tanks completely. The practise was to 'dipchick' up and down again from periscope depth—20 feet, measured not from the keel as nowadays, but from control room level at the surface waterline. From the order to break surface and fire, it took between 30 and 40 seconds for the first round to get away and another 50 to 55 seconds to regain periscope depth.

Even from full buoyancy on the surface, the diving time was very much better than the K-class; it averaged 80–90 seconds. The weight of the gun itself assisted downward movement when the tanks began to flood and, conversely, the barrel (which was sealed) gave a degree of buoyancy high up when submerged, helping the make the submarine handy and stable. *M-1* and her sisters were very different from the K-boats on whose keels they rested; they were deservedly popular with the crews.

Fortunately, there was no room to contemplate installing steam machinery, so the M-class was equipped with the same diesel engines, motors and batteries that were being fitted in the successful L-class still building. They gave a maximum speed of 15 knots on the surface and eight knots submerged for one hour or two knots for 40 hours.

The watertight director tower, with a combined raisable telescopic and periscopic director sight, was directly astern of the loading tower and forward of the bridge proper. The gun was laid and fired from here, but the training and elevating hand wheels were operated from below in the wardroom area, following pointers. Fixed-angle loading was necessary and, with an unusually long recoil to minimise the forces coming on the vessel's structure, loading was arranged to be carried out with the gun in the run-in and depressed position. The gun was kept dry by a hydraulically operated

A Mutton-boat (*M-3*) lying alongside a trot of K-boats with the ships' companies waiting for divisions in the depot ship inboard.

M-1 and *M-2*, like two prehistoric monsters, basking on the surface.

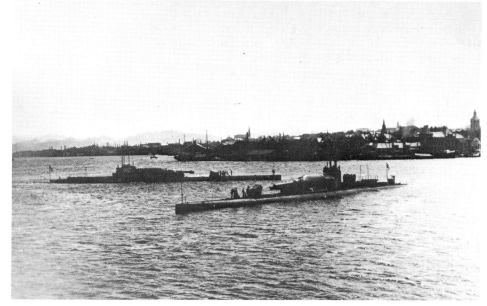

muzzle-sealing device or tampion when submerged.

The 863 pound shell was transported from the shell room at the bottom of the submarine by hydraulic lifting and traversing gear to a working chamber at main-deck level and then rolled into the upper shelf of a two-tier cage. Meanwhile, the cordite charges, two for each round, were conveyed from the magazine on an open trolley and worked by a hand-winch through the shell room to the handling room where the bags were placed on the lower shelf of the cage. The trolley wheels, however, had a habit of slipping sideways and partially flattening the copper telemotor leads which ran alongside the track and led to submarine services: it is possible that a reduced volume of hydraulic fluid and consequent loss of control contributed to the disaster which was tragically to end the career of *M-1* seven years after she commissioned.

The cage, now carrying a complete round, was raised by an independent hydraulically-operated lift, not unlike the sort of apparatus found in an old-fashioned butler's pantry. From this, the projectile and the cordite were rolled out on to waiting trays behind the breech when the lift reached the right level. There was a watertight hatch where the hoist passed through the pressure hull: this had to be opened, hydraulically or by hand, before the cage went up and it had to be shut after the cage descended.

Only when the gun was locked fore-and-aft with a two degree depression could the watertight door at the forward end of the loading tower be opened. The loading tray could then be run out towards the breech for the shell and full charge to be rammed into the gun by a chain-rammer. The system was worked hydraulically but the gunnery tele-motor system was entirely separate from the controls supplied by the leads in the passage-

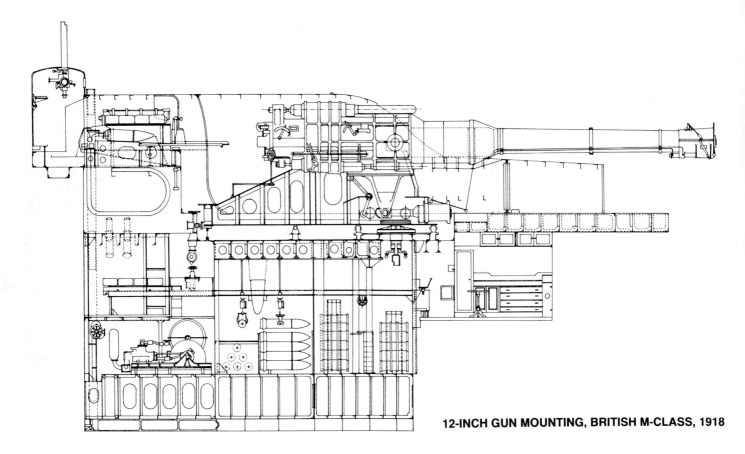

12-INCH GUN MOUNTING, BRITISH M-CLASS, 1918

The business end of a 12-inch gun.

way, upon which the submarine depended for dived control.

Turning to tactics, Rear Admiral Hall's reasoning was that if a submerged submarine observed an enemy ship, came to surface and then fired quickly, there would be no time to elude the shell. Moreover, a submarine was able to carry only a small number of torpedoes, whereas a much larger number of shells could be embarked. A single shell would be sufficient to sink a merchant ship or a U-boat.

On sighting a target it was planned that a submarine should close to within half-a-mile of its projected track because a virtually flat trajectory was necessary to make sure of hitting with a single shot. Training and elevating restrictions as well as range meant that the boat had to be pointed and manoeuvred in much the same way as for a torpedo attack; this in itself was a severe limitation on gunnery tactics if the target was zigzagging.

The Captain provided the Gunnery Officer and director tower with the necessary information concerning course, speed and range of the target so that deflection and elevation could be calculated and continually applied to the gun. The gun would already be loaded, but the tampion, hydraulically

operated, had to be opened before firing. The idea was to wait for the appropriate moment and plane up to the awash condition. The tampion was then opened; the Captain gave the permissive order 'Shoot'; and, when the sights were on, the Gunnery Officer gave the executive order 'Fire' to the director layer, who pressed the trigger.

The general instructions listed in CB1475 (1919) relating to the 12-inch Mark IX open mounting and drill are a splendid and well-preserved example of the sort of orders that were issued for many years by the Royal Navy's School of Gunnery. For example:

DISCIPLINE *at a gun is at all times to be rigidly observed. There are to be no departures from the drill at any time. There is to be no leaning about or slackness during drill.*

WASHING THE MUSHROOM HEAD. *One member of the gun's crew is to wipe all over the mushroom head with a wet cloth and is to see that there is no residue left burning on any part of the mushroom head or obturating pad (special care being exercised when using SFG primers).*

DUMMY PROJECTILES. *When using wood projectiles, care is to be taken that splinters do not get in the breech threads or the mechanism where they are liable to cause damage.*

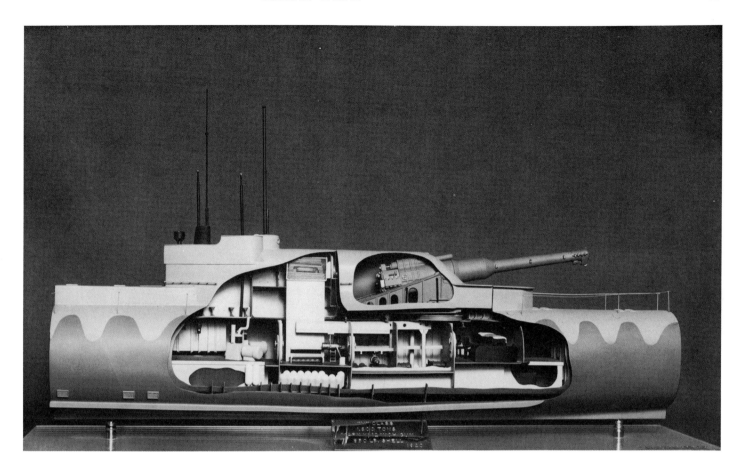

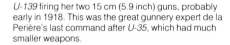

DUTIES OF GUN'S CREWS AT CLEANING QUAR-
TERS. *The first thing to do is to clean and oil
all working (i.e. moving) parts thoroughly;
any spare time then remaining may be spent
in polishing brasswork etc.*

CLEANING GEAR. *There are only two places
for cleaning rags: in use, or in the rag bag.*

OIL. *Men should know the difference between mineral oil, olive oil and mineral jelly.*

The detailed drill has a heavy-booted
stamp upon it that will evoke nostalgia from
officers of the big-ship gunnery era:

*At the order "Test safety and loading gear"
No. 1 opens the loading door and orders
"Out tray".
No. 2 should find this impossible and reports
accordingly.
No. 1 closes the loading door and orders
"Open the breech".
No. 2 opens the breech.
No. 1 orders "Out tray".
No. 2 should find this impossible and reports
accordingly.*

And so on. Everything wrong should be
impossible in gunnery language. Gun-action
in a submarine equipped with a nineteenth
century battleship's 12-inch gun must have
been wonderful to watch—from a distance.

The tactical possibilities were undoubtedly attractive, but the M-boats never saw action in war. Nevertheless, they had some exciting times during trials and exercises. The
barrel of the guns in different submarines
burst four times without, incredibly, hurting
anybody or damaging anything other than
the gun itself. Twice, a barrel burst because
water got into it through the breech-end before firing. Great efforts had been made to
make the tampion watertight but, for some
reason, nobody had thought to take similar
pains with the breech-end, where it was
found, too late, that the aperture for the
electrically-operated firing tube leaked. And
once, in *M-3*, the tampion was opened

Model by Paradigm Models of *M-1* gunnery system, in
the Submarine Museum, Gosport

U-139 firing her two 15 cm (5.9 inch) guns, probably
early in 1918. This was the great gunnery expert de la
Perière's last command after *U-35*, which had much
smaller weapons.

A distinguished group of visitors inspecting *M-1*'s monstrous weapon at Piraeus in 1919. The gunnery team could see when the tampion was open because the indicator spike (top of picture) was automatically raised. It was the failure to check the tampion open before firing that caused at least one barrel to burst.

before surfacing, fully flooding the bore and resulting in eight feet of the barrel being blown off.

The other occasion, in *M-1* exercising off Portland, was even more dramatic. The director-layer, his mind fully occupied with erotic fancies about a young lady he was planning to seduce at a Ship's Company dance that night in Weymouth, failed to check the tampion open before firing; the firing-switch interlock also failed to do its job.

The gun was wire-bound, meaning that it had an inner rifle-tube strengthened by massive wire binding, the whole being encased by the visible barrel; and the sleeve of the tampion was connected to the wire-binding. When the layer pressed the trigger, the tampion opened alright—and flew off, closely pursued by a 12-inch shell; but after the tampion went the wire, fathom after fathom.

The tampion was heavy and so was the wire; in a moment, the submarine found itself securely and humiliatingly anchored by its own gun. Nothing could be done. There was no tool on board which could cut the wire quickly and it was many hours before *M-1* was free.

The able seaman director-layer was totally unrepentant. Nobody was particularly concerned about the enormous and expensive damage caused to the ship's main armament by his mistake. So far as he was concerned the only disaster was that the submarine did not get back to harbour in time for the dance, and the ship's company, as well as his girl friend, rightly laid the blame on him.

As well as attacking shipping, shore-bombardment was much in the Admiralty's mind for monitor submarines, but whether they could continually surface and reload safely close to the well-patrolled coast of Heligoland was doubtful. A maximum range of 21,000 yards was quoted for bombardment but it is inconceivable that single shots unspotted would have been effective at that distance. However, exercises later—in 1923—with aircraft and submarines spotting the fall of the shot, were very satisfactory and Max Horton (by then Captain of the K and M Squadron) reported that:

The ability of such a squadron to approach unseen until a few seconds before opening fire is an important factor, especially where the standard of efficiency of the enemy is of a lower level than that of the Germans in the late war.[3]

M-1 showing herself off at Venice in 1919.

Top left
The wardroom of *M-1* with Max Horton's trophy, a silver chanticleer, on the table. The officers were accommodated in comparative luxury: how the arm-chair was brought down the hatch is not known!

Top right
Although spartan by comparison with the wardroom, the mess-decks for ratings, like this in *M-1*, were regarded as exceptionally comfortable; but some sailors still had to 'sling' as shown by the lashed-up hammock at the right of picture.

Above
M-3 in Stokes Bay with the crew saluting a senior ship.

The crew standing by while completing *M-3* in early 1920.

The crew of *M-3*, alongside the giant liner *Aquitania*, waiting to go ashore after engine trials, probably October 1920.

The 'disappearing' 3-inch gun on *M-1*.

Commander Max Horton, captain of *M-1*, with the 3-inch gun.

Above
M-1 breaking surface for a 'dip-chick' practice firing with the gun trained 10 degrees (maximum) to starboard. The guard rails would not, of course, be rigged on a war patrol.

Above right
Gun being laid and trained.

Below
Tampion open (as shown by raised indicator).

Right
Tampion shut, submarine diving again.

Gun barrel of *M-1* bursting on firing as photographed by the Bo'sun of HMS *Conquest* with Captain(S) on board. The cause, on this occasion, was water in the barrel with the resulting cloud of steam and splashes from the disintegrated forward part of the gun, which can be seen. Nobody was hurt!

HMS *M-1* about to return to Gibraltar minus the forward few feet of her 12-inch gun after it burst.

M-1 at Gibraltar showing the damage. The wire-binding of the gun (which on another occasion anchored the submarine by the tampion) is hanging loose.

Horton scribbled a note beside this paragraph on his own office copy of the report: 'Aircraft carried in submarines—another use for?'

After the completion of *M-1* in April 1918, the Admiralty reconsidered her employment. It seemed by now that there was little chance of gunnery targets appearing for her to engage and Their Lordships were, anyway, anxious not to give the declining Germany's capability for swift and effec- still relentlessly waging war against British shipping and, even when the Kaiser's surface fleet was demoralised and on the point of mutiny, the U-boat crews remained staunch. Germany's capabilities for swift and effective improvisation was well known and if *M-1* had demonstrated her gun in action, especially in the shore bombardment role, one or more U-boats might have followed suit. Some of the larger U-boats already carried one or two 5.9 inch (15 cm) guns; and Arnauld de la Perière in the comparatively small *U-35* had sunk nearly *half a million* tons of shipping mainly with a single 4.1 inch (10.4 cm) weapon. The fear of retaliation had, in fact, delayed the completion of *M-1* earlier, 'as it was recognised that if the enemy employed similar submarines he could do more damage to us than we could

to him.' *M-1* therefore joined the Eleventh Submarine Flotilla for ordinary patrol duties 'until any special operations for her arose' and ended the war in the Mediterranean.

It was suggested that *M-2*, *M-3*, and *M-4* should be completed as overseas patrol vessels without the 12-inch guns, but the First Sea Lord turned this down and ordered the M-class—becoming popularly known as

HMS *M-1* at Ancona, Italy during her Mediterranean tour in 1919, still in the horse-and-cart era. She attracted a great deal of interest everywhere she went but the Italian, Greek and Turkish navies could find no use for monitor submarines.

HMS *M-1* with Commander C G Brodie in command at Fort Blockhouse (HMS *Dolphin*) in 1921. Brodie, later Rear Admiral, wrote *Forlorn Hope 1915* about the Dardanelles campaign and became a respected and popular writer for several journals under the pen-name of Seagee.

THE BRITISH NAVY MOURNS THE HEROES OF THE M.1.

FUNERAL SERVICE FOR "SUBMARINE M.1" OFF START POINT.

A token of remembrance of the men
who lost their lives in

SUBMARINE M. 1

Thursday, 12th November, 1925.

The Sea hath claimed them for her own,
And keeps them, one and all,
Beyond the reach of bugles blown,
Or fluttering flags' recall.

Famed ships, brave men of days of old
Live in historic scenes;
But Valour writes your names in gold,
Men of the Submarines!

—LOFTUS DALE.

Memorial card for HMS *M-1*.

Mutton-Boats because of the leg-of-lamb appearance topsides—to be completed as originally designed. *M-2* and *M-3* went to sea complete with their big guns in 1919 and 1920 but work on *M-4* was halted in October 1919 and the large hull was ignominiously used as a fender at High Walker Yard on the Tyne before being broken up in 1921.

Not unnaturally some people who saw such a monstrous gun mounted on a submarine wondered whether it was just some kind of bluff. After all, dummies of various kinds had been known in Germany during the war.

One evening in June 1923, when the Flotilla which included M-boats in its number was on a visit to Norway, the submarines anchored off Odda at the head of the Hardanger Fjord. With rather noticeable stealth a small rowing boat pulled out from the shore towards *M-2*. When almost alongside the submarine, the solitary rower lay down

his oars, picked up an air rifle and proceed to fire pellets at the gun barrel. He was quite sure it was wood but eventually, as the pellets fell flattened to the deck, he became convinced that the gun was real and sadly sculled his way back. The submariners did not trouble to pursue him.

M-2 and *M-3* are better known after conversion to an aircraft-carrier and a mine-layer respectively: their stories as such are told later. But *M-1* retained her gun and continued in service after the war, albeit without any clearly stated purpose, until on Thursday, 12 November 1925, she was struck while submerged by the Swedish SS *Vidar* 15 miles south of Start Point. *M-1* was screening a simulated troop convoy (with three other submarines, including *M-3*) at the time, in the face of four minesweepers representing a cruiser squadron. The track normally followed by merchant shipping ran through the middle of the exercise area.

The merchant vessel scarcely noticed the shock and the captain only realised later, when reports were transmitted around the world, that he had unwittingly been responsible for the loss of a British submarine. It was apparent from *Vidar*'s log that the collision occurred at 0745 in good visibility.

No conclusions were reached about the cause of the tragedy, but it may be that Lieutenant Commander Alec Carrie in *M-1*, perhaps while coming up to periscope depth, found himself at the depth most dreaded by all submariners—neither shallow enough to see through the periscope nor deep enough to avoid an oncoming ship. If, as seems probable from some reports, the telemotor system was barely adequate at the best of times for all the services simultaneously and if, further, trolley-loads of heavy shells had continued to flatten the telemotor pipes running along the deck from the magazine area, it is conceivable that the hydroplanes and periscopes were robbed of hydraulic power at the critical moment. It was—and still is— not unknown for services to behave sluggishly while hydraulic pumps and accumulators struggle to restore full pressure in certain circumstances. And this always happens at the worst possible time, because that is when the services are being used most energetically.

Then again, it may have been no more than an error of judgement that caused the disaster—inaccurate ranges at the periscope or a wrongly estimated angle-on-the-bow. Whatever went wrong, it was an unmitigated tragedy: there were no survivors.

The disaster was all the more poignant because the M-boats were happy and efficient. In sharp contrast to the K-boats, morale was always excellent and *M-1* in particular never lost the faultless stride set by Max Horton on commissioning—until that fatal day off Start Point.

The confident attitude of a Mutton-Boat's ship's company was nicely summed up by (then) Commander C.G. Brodie, who took command of *M-1* in 1921. At Fort Blockhouse, where the submarine lay alongside, there was a small shed on the jetty housing a 'convenience'. This had a partition and officer-users on one side could see the men's boots under it and hear their voices over the top.

'Brodie?', the new captain heard, 'oh, he's alright. He don't know nothing about it, but we'll see him through.'

The phrasing was not wholly flattering but Brodie had never heard praise that pleased him more. He knew that he had been accepted by a fine team, exceptional even by the high standards of the submarine service.

4: Great Cruisers

In the spring of 1915, while being pressured to produce submarines to accompany the Grand Fleet, the Submarine Committee had ideas of their own. *Nautilus* and the steam-driven *Swordfish* were building and eight three-engined J-class had been ordered in January. Now the Committee, chaired by Rear Admiral (S), turned its attention to the possibilities of a Cruiser Submarine. Such a boat was thought to be feasible and submariners were anxious to have a vessel that could roam the seas around the far-flung Empire independently, like a surface cruiser, but with the great advantage of surprise that a submersible conferred. A heavy cruiser-style gun armament as well as torpedoes would be required, so none of the current designs would serve.

Such a boat would obviously need to be fast, although it would not necessarily have to reach the Fleet speed of 24 knots, and it would need exceptionally long range. Hence it had to be large. There was so much else going on in the submarine world during the critical war years that the idea was not taken up seriously until some three years later, after the Armistice, by which time the design and capabilities of the 1512/1875 ton

German U-cruisers *U-151* to *U-157* had been thoroughly examined, together with the other large and advanced U-boats produced towards the end of the war.

By 1921, the plans for a cruiser submarine, designated *X-1*, were well advanced: the project was included in the Naval Estimates for 1921/1922. It was not a propitious period for new developments. The Washington Conference, attended by the five largest naval powers, was in progress. It had the intention of avoiding an arms race and the members were bent on negotiating a treaty of limitation for submarines. The British, who had so recently been very nearly defeated by the U-boat, strongly advocated the abolition of submarines altogether and maintained—or pretended to maintain—that the submarine was effective only as a commerce raider and then only if it disregarded international law.[1] They went on to say that the submarine was of no use as a purely military weapon, but this was so patently absurd that the British argument thereafter carried no weight. When the resulting Washington Treaty was finally signed, four of the five countries concerned were constrained to developing the sub-

HMS *X-1 circa* 1926. Despite her two huge 5.25-inch twin turrets she had fine lines and handled well.

BRITISH XI

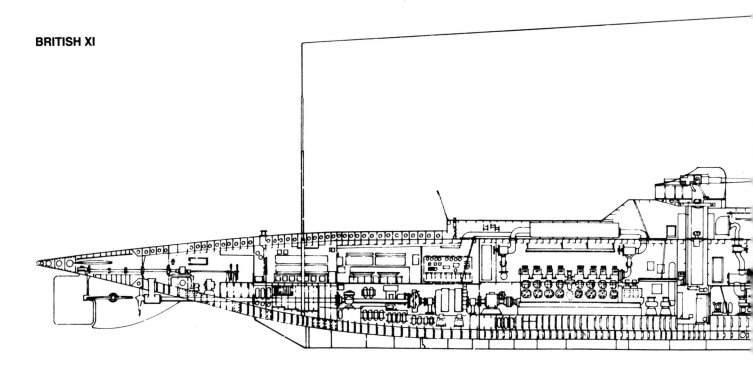

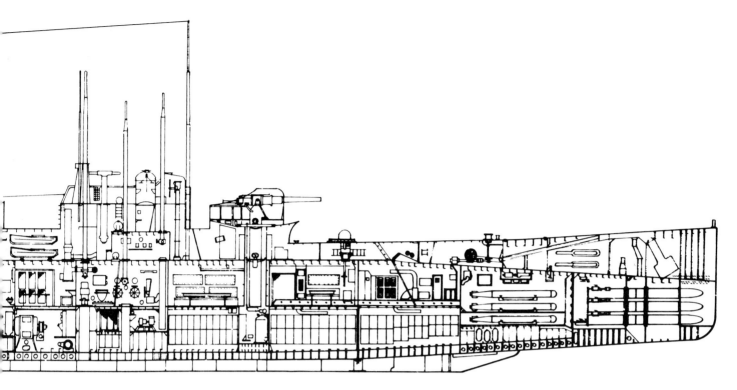

marine only as a purely military weapon. The intention was that there should be no more wholesale war on trade of the kind so successfully waged by Germany's U-boats (and Germany herself was already precluded from building U-boats altogether), but the wording was imprecise and it must have been obvious, even at the time, that the Treaty would be ineffectual in the long term. France refused to ratify that part of the agreement dealing with attacks on merchant shipping and was therefore free to build submersible commerce raiders if she wished.

There was certainly no intention of employing *X-1* for commerce raiding (although she would be admirably suited to the task) and plans went ahead despite a major cutback in the British Fleet amidst severe economic restraints in all quarters. It is surprising that the project was progressed: its protagonists seem to have succeeded more because it was time to investigate totally new submarine technical designs (which might be used by a future enemy) than because a specific new submarine was wanted. The one-off building cost was high: £1,044,000 which compared with a contemporary *Kent*-class cruiser (1926) at £1,970,000.

At any rate, *X-1* was laid down at Chatham on 2 November 1921—the first new boat to be put in hand since the war had ended in November 1918. She was com-

pleted on 23 September 1925, commissioned in December of the same year and finally accepted in April 1926, when she became the largest submarine in the world at sea. After a passage to Gibraltar and back, the first signs of persistent main engine trouble became evident and she spent the rest of the year in Dockyard hands. After a successful full power trial in January 1927, *X-1* joined the Mediterranean Fleet but, only a year later, further major engine troubles occurred. These were made good at Malta but the engines failed again in April 1928. Over the same period, the auxiliary engines and HP air compressors also gave trouble. Thereafter, *X-1* spent much of her short life in Dockyard hands. Continual mechanical problems were frustrating to say the least, but the huge submarine handled well both on the surface and submerged when she was able to show her paces. She twice went out of control when diving, achieving 26 degrees bow down on the second occasion, but the captain's private diary[2] strongly suggests that these alarming mishaps were due to the Chief Stoker putting the trim on wrongly or dipping the tanks incorrectly. It can also be inferred that whatever went wrong in *X-1* it was always the fault of the engineering staff—in the opinion of the executive officers!

It says much for the new-found arguing power of senior submariners that what was really no more than a gigantic mechanical, gunnery and tactical test-vehicle should have

been built in such difficult times. But, true to form, the admirals were much more interested in propulsion and the hull than in the primary weapon systems. On 11 March 1921, while the design was still open to discussion, Rear Admiral (S) wrote a strongly worded minute to the effect that it was the submarine itself (i.e. the vehicle) that was important and that 'the gunnery arrangements throughout are of secondary importance.' Meanwhile, the torpedo tubes were given scant attention by the operational staff, who found to their dismay (too late) that although the hull was safe to 350 feet, with a safety factor of 70 per cent beyond that (giving an estimated collapse depth of 595 feet), the tube rear doors could only withstand 200 feet.

The principle design objectives, as seen by the Admiralty, were to evaluate a diesel engine of considerably greater power per cylinder; to ascertain the diving and control capabilities of a large submarine 363 feet 6 inches long, displacing 2780 tons on the surface and 3600 tons submerged; and to determine the practicability of installing and operating a relatively heavy gun armament—two twin 5.2 inch turrets—capable of engaging a destroyer if necessary.

The form was more of a complete double-hull type than any previous British design and the pressure hull was almost completely surrounded by external tanks, comprising main ballast, oil fuel and oil-fuel compensating tanks.

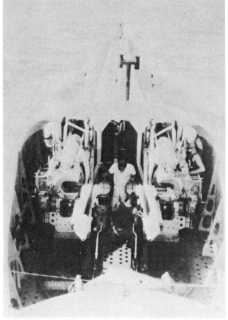

Above
X-1's forward turret looking very like a surface ship's armament but with the Charlie Noble (galley funnel) blocking the line of sight! The cook was presumably hard at work in the surface galley beneath the casing.

Above right
X-1 diving: despite deliberately underrating her performance to mislead the Japanese, *X-1* could probably submerge fully in about one minute.

One of the eight-cylinder 'Chathams': the Port main engine.

With a view to damage-control in the event of being hit during a surface action, there were nine watertight bulkheads, each with a circular door 2 feet 9 inches across, subdividing the pressure hull into watertight compartments. The double hull would also have afforded some defence against shell-fire—a principle adopted 60 years later by the Soviet *Typhoon*-class for protection against torpedoes and other impact weapons.

An exceptionally large bridge was devoted primarily to gunnery control and it included an upper control room, a range-finder room and a director tower. The normal submarine conning tower was positioned abaft these gunnery spaces. A high superstructure at bridge deck level carried one 5.2 inch twin-mounting just forward of the bridge and a second about 50 feet abaft the bridge. Three large buoyancy tanks forward were installed to keep the bows up in heavy seas, and there were adequate compensating tanks to allow for the useage of shells and the wide changes in seawater density to be expected when shifting areas over the almost world-wide range allowed by the submarine's endurance, 16,200 miles at an economical speed of ten knots—well over twice the range of the surface-cruisers. Even at a near maximum speed of 18 knots, *X-1* could go for 5300 miles without refuelling. However, the endurance submerged fell far below the predicted 50 miles at 4 knots: only 18 miles at 4 knots was actually achieved. Presumably, insufficient allowance was made for the massive external fittings which must have imposed a considerable drag when dived; or perhaps the 336 special battery cells, each weighing 1475 pounds (as against the normal 920 to 960 pounds), had a lower capacity than expected.

The propulsion system was unusually flexible. Besides the two four-stroke eight-cylinder main diesel engines, one on each shaft and known as 'the Chathams', there were two MAN auxiliary engines (taken from the German *U-126*) which drove two generators. They were put into action by the splendid order 'Start the Deutschlands' which led to a mistaken belief that they came from the German mercantile submarine of that name. The generators would drive the main electric motors in combination with the main engines to give full power on the surface, but they were normally employed to charge the battery which, of course, was the usual source of power for the main motors. Surprisingly, in the light of the usual excellence of German machinery, the auxiliary engines gave even more trouble than the main diesels.

The Engineer Officer was not a man to be envied. Perhaps his need of solitary meditation was foreseen because he was given a cabin to himself, something unknown in other submarines where only the Captain was accorded a modicum of privacy. The technical problems were certainly appreciated at high level from the start for,

Top left and right
No. 15 dock, Portsmouth, on 26 June 1931: *X-1*'s most embarrassing mishap. The lower deck story (probably correct) was that the lunch-time whistle sounded and the Portsmouth dockyard maties dropped everything and went to lunch before shoring up the submarine in the normal way. Unfortunately, nobody stopped the pump and the submarine heeled over to 55 degrees, doing extensive damage to the Port tanks.

Above
HMS *X-1* looking superb under the envious gaze of L-class crews at Gibraltar.

Gunnery exercise off Gibraltar during one of the relatively few periods when the main machinery was working properly.

even while *X-1* was being laid down, the Engineer-in-Chief was gloomily remarking that the design of the propelling machinery was 'already outside the limit of our experimental knowledge' without adding the complications of auxiliary drive.

Successive engineers, who seem to have been chosen for equable temperament as well as for their unusually high seniority, weathered the storm well, but one Engine Room Artificer had had enough after one month in the boat. With his wife 'in a very nervous condition' and himself 'of a nervous temperament', he was 'put under the observation of the Senior Medical Officer' at Fort Blockhouse for a period of three months and discharged to General Service. Fortunately, the rest of the engine-room staff were made of sterner stuff.

By contrast, the gunnery system was reported by the Captain, Commander C S T Allen, in August 1928 to be first class:

... the manner in which the whole control personnel, including layers and trainers, have merely to sit quietly in their seats, and not climb rapidly through hatches etc at the critical moment when breaking surface, and just before opening fire, is excellent. In fact the whole arrangement seems to have been designed almost ahead of its time. [3]

When the customary teething troubles had been overcome, the gunnery performance was impressive. The time of opening fire with both turrets laid and trained accurately was about 90 seconds from breaking surface.

The timing of salvoes thereafter was apt to be erratic, due partly to the crowded conditions in the magazine and around the hoist arrangements, but eight salvoes in two minutes was the normal rate, and it was maintained with accuracy out to about 10,000 yards using the 12-foot range finder. At a closing range between 9000 and 8000 yards on trials, the last five out of eight salvoes straddled the target.

Tactics against major warships, and aircraft carriers in particular, were not confined to gunnery. The idea was first to fire a full salvo of torpedoes from the six 21-inch bow tubes; the moment these crossed the target's track (whether they hit or not), it was intended that *X-1* should surface and engage the enemy with HE shell while turning away at full speed and breaking off the engagement by emitting CF smoke, diving after about two minutes on the surface.

Diving was a very carefully regulated operation with the range-finder to be housed and sixteen large holes in the pressure hull to be checked shut. Nevertheless, the advertised diving time of three minutes was almost certainly exaggerated: she could do better.

Reliable evidence, which has only recently come to light, shows that *X-1*'s operational deficiencies were made to look worse than they really were. She proved undeniably clumsy and ill-suited to attacking warships in fleet exercises and she was handicapped by self-noise which deafened her ASDIC listening apparatus while making her prone to detection by anti-submarine vessels; but attacking *heavily escorted* fleet units was not her intended role. Then again, it was never certain what her real role was.

The fact was that, roaming alone, the giant submarine was potentially a superb commerce-raider—and commerce raiding, so far as Britain was concerned, could not be contemplated. The Admiralty, however, was desperately anxious that a future enemy, seen clearly as Japan by the late 1920s, should not be inspired to build similar cruiser submarines. Hence, a most favourable report on *X-1*'s capabilities forwarded by her first Captain, Commander P E Phillips, was regarded in the Admiralty with much alarm.

So, according to Phillips, 'some feller' came down from London with the report and asked the Captain, Friedburger the Second Captain (First Lieutenant) and Roberts the Gunnery Officer to rewrite it 'and put in a number of nasty little statements which, if digested by the Japs ... could make them think that the British had tried out a real wrong-un'. [4] The report was duly rewritten and, with the exception of the engine failures which were all too genuine, it thoroughly condemned *X-1* as virtually useless to Britain or any foreign power.

This did not prevent successive ship's officers from enthusing about their boat: it was 'superb' and 'gorgeous'. Nor did it stop them from making proposals in 1928 for an even bigger and better cruiser submarine with either two triple or three twin 5.2 inch gun turrets. Taking into account the advantage of an 'X-2' engaging with gun action from submerged, she could, avowed the Gunnery Officer, engage any cruiser in single combat with even a chance of annihilating her. This was essential 'when the tactics of commerce destruction are considered [sic]

Action stations: full calibre shoot.

The bridge showing the director tower.

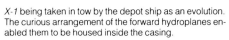

X-1 being taken in tow by the depot ship as an evolution.
The curious arrangement of the forward hydroplanes enabled them to be housed inside the casing.

as convoys are certain to be escorted by a cruiser or cruisers in future wars'.[5] It was an ambitious opinion, typical of the imaginative and radical writer, Lt Cdr Philip Ruck-Keene, who had a most distinguished service career but, even if commercial shipping was eventually to be attacked, Ruck-Keene, like most of his contemporaries, did not take into account the anti-submarine aircraft—carrier or shore-based—that were bound to accompany many convoys.

Excessive fear of what an enemy could do with a submarine like *X-1* and bursts of over-enthusiasm in the submarine itself, together, of course, with the unreliable engines, brought about *X-1*'s early demise. In May 1933, Their Lordships decided that her age and limited operational value no longer justified her retention as a fighting unit, but, since the London Treaty forbade her being replaced by equivalent new construction tonnage if she were scrapped, she was laid up in reserve in Fareham Creek. She was taken off the active list late in 1936 and scrapped in 1937, by which time the London Treaty was dead, having expired on 31 December 1936.

It is possible that the Admiralty's caution in denigrating *X-1*'s potential had the desired effect because Japan did not in the event build cruiser submarines for commerce raiding although, as will be seen later, they built giants for other purposes. If the Japanese had indeed adopted the idea, such boats could have wreaked havoc in the Indian Ocean during World War Two and might well have succeeded in cutting Allied communications between Australia and the Cape.

Surcouf

France, meanwhile, was in no better economic state than anybody else following the cessation of hostilities in 1918. But she had long realised, and much earlier than any other nation, that submarines as commerce raiders were the most economical and effective vessels for waging the *Guerre de Course* first advocated by the *Jeune École* led, in the underwater field, by Admiral Aube in the 1880s. *La Guerre de Course* meant the destruction, piecemeal, of merchant ships on the high seas. The greatest mercantile nation in the world was still Great Britain. France, without saying so *actuellement*, was still determined to rival the Royal Navy at sea and be ready again to engage her most consistent enemy, perfidious Albion, if necessary, while guarding her own quite substantial overseas interests and possessions—all at the least possible expense. Hence, with the German fleet out of the way, the French navy turned to the old policy of the young school.

Inspired by the *U-151* class of German U-cruisers, plans were made to build a sub-marine which could roam the oceans and destroy merchant shipping wherever it could be found; and, having declined to ratify the Washington Treaty with regard to submarine commerce-raiding, the French designers were able to include, in a massive building programme, a giant submersible which was to become the *Surcouf*.

The name was chosen to honour Robert Surcouf (1773–1827), a native of St Malo, who started his naval service at the age of thirteen in merchant ships which were mostly engaged in the slave trade between Africa and Ile de France (Mauritius). Given command of the merchant *Creole* in 1794, he defied the new revolutionary law against slave-trading and made a slaving voyage to Mozambique for which he narrowly escaped condemnation by the Colonial Committee of Public Safety.

He then turned privateer and, in command of the 180-ton *Emilie*, captured a number of British prizes, only to have them confiscated by the Governor of Ile de France because no Letter of Marque had been granted and his actions were again illegal. However, the Revolutionary Government at home were more sympathetic this time: Surcouf fought and won his case in the Courts when he returned to France. Encouraged by this, he operated between 1798 and 1800 in the Bay of Bengal in command of the privateers *Clarice* and *Confiance* and

The ship's company of *Surcouf* fallen in smartly at Toulon. Good radio communications were essential in the cruiser role, hence the exceptionally high masts.

captured numerous East Indiamen, including the 1200-ton *Kent*.

Surcouf was offered the rank of Post Captain in the French Navy by Napoleon when war with Britain was resumed in 1803 after the brief Peace of Amiens, but he refused to work other than on his own account—like the seventeenth century buccaneers who plundered the Spanish Main and used to say they were 'going on the account' because it sounded more respectable than 'turning pirate'. With ample funds resulting from earlier captures, he prepared a number of piratical vessels at St Malo and, in 1807, he built for his own command a large powerful ship whose lines so pleased him that he called her *Revenant*.[6] He enjoyed further successes in this ship before it was commandeered by the Governor of Mauritius, whereupon Surcouf returned to France. Back at home and created a Baron of the Empire, he busied himself for the remainder of the war in fitting out privateers for his old shipmates.

Robert Surcouf was, so to speak, self-employed: his motives and methods were hardly inspired by deep feelings of patriotism. But his exploits caught the French imagination in much the same way that John Paul Jones (who, by contrast, was formally commissioned) had sparked the spirit of the American Navy a few years earlier. One might wonder at France in the 1920s choosing the name of such an unorthodox character for the pride of her navy, but some arguably disreputable Elizabethans like Drake and Hawkins were equally honoured in England. Surcouf embodied the *élan* which the French Navy sought to recapture in its underwater fleet between the wars.

Succeeding X-1, *Surcouf* was, until the huge Japanese aircraft-carrying submarines were commissioned, the largest submarine in the world. Laid down in 1927 at Cherbourg, she took seven years to complete. With a length of 361 feet and displacing 3250 tons surfaced and 4304 tons submerged, she has been criticised as being unnecessarily large for the task assigned to her. Certainly she was complicated—and the French have always delighted in complexities—but the size was, as usual, primarily dictated by the requirements for speed, range and endurance. Intended for raiding far overseas, she could easily make 18 knots on the surface and was credited with 20 knots at full power. At a cruising speed of 10 knots, she had a

range of 10,000 miles and stores and provisions sufficient for a 90-day independent cruise could be embarked and stowed comfortably. High speed submerged was not particularly important for her primary role as a submersible raider and, like practically every other submarine, *Surcouf* was limited to little more than 8 knots for one hour when dived, with an endurance of 70 miles at 4.5 knots.

The submarine's vast bulk enabled her to carry what, to all appearances, was a truly formidable mix of weapon systems. Two 8-inch (204 mm) 50-calibre guns in a twin watertight turret provided the main surface armament with torpedo alternatives in two triple mountings, each comprising one 21.7-inch (550 mm) and two 15.75-inch (440 mm) tubes; placed externally on traversing platforms. There were four fixed 21.7-inch internal bow tubes for attacking submerged. Eight 21.7-inch reload torpedoes and four 15.75-inch reloads were carried—22 torpedoes in all, and none of them reliable. The smaller weapons intended for finishing off merchant targets at short range, were an almost total failure and the larger 'fish' could not be guaranteed to run straight except under ideal conditions.

The external tubes could be reloaded at sea, but only in very calm weather where there was no threat from the air. It would have been an optimistic Captain who depended on reloading at all in the open ocean; but in the true traditions of buccaneering, it was intended to slip into quiet bays or inlets for the purpose.

The reconnaissance so essential to privateering was afforded by a Besson MB Floatplane carried, with wings folded, in a watertight hangar abaft the conning tower. The aircraft could be fully assembled, prepared for flight and lowered into the water by its crane within 30 minutes of surfacing; recovery and stowage took about the same length of time. It was discarded early in the war and was never employed operationally.

A boarding launch with a speed of 16 knots might also be considered as a part of the armament, but it was not carried after war broke out in 1939, presumably because, by then, the submarine's projected operations did not include a use for it—or perhaps it was seen as too liable to disintegrate into revealing splinters under depth-charge attacks. In fact, it would have been very useful indeed during some of the political excursions which *Surcouf* took part in later.

Two single 37 mm semi-automatics with 1000 rounds of ammunition and two twin Hotchkiss anti-aircraft and general purpose

machine guns with 16,000 rounds were supplemented by two portable Colt machine guns in 1942. At least 600 8-inch shells could be embarked to support the rate of fire of three rounds per minute from each gun. The stereoscopic range-finder on its 4-metre base could range with reasonable accuracy out to 12,000 metres (about 6.5 nautical miles) but the maximum gun-range of about 15 miles was tactically unuseable except for shore bombardment.

In short, *Surcouf* had just about everything that could be crammed into a submarine of the period; but whether it would all have worked effectively is questionable. She has been described as clumsy, but that is hardly fair because she could dive in less than one minute if necessary. The established complement was 129 officers and men but secure, if not luxurious, accommodation was also provided for 40 prisoners of war from sunken (or conceivably captured) merchantmen.

Although *Surcouf* was commissioned into the 2nd Submarine Flotilla at Brest on 17 August 1935 and made two distant cruises to the Antilles and Africa in late 1935 and the Spring of 1938, the latter lasting for four months, it is most unlikely that she was ever properly worked up before war was declared. The cost and effort to do so would have been enormous and her role in any future war, with Germany rearming rapidly, must, anyway, have been in doubt by the latter half of the 1930s.

On 28 August 1939, *Surcouf* left Dakar for a secret destination, but the outbreak of war found her at Fort-de-France, Martinique whence she moved to Kingston in Jamaica in mid-September to help escort the second of two fast convoys headed for England. It was the first of several convoy-escort duties but, on this occasion, it was a situation of mutual advantage because the submarine herself urgently needed a refit and required some kind of support while crossing the Atlantic.

Detaching from the convoy in the Western Approaches, *Surcouf* reached Brest on 19 October, having covered 22,000 miles since leaving that port. Work was not complete when she was forced to sail on 18 June 1940 to avoid capture by the Germans. Under the command of Capitaine de Frégate Paul Martin, she sailed for Plymouth where she arrived in the early hours of 20 June and lay uneasily while her crew debated the confused political situation. The ratings, and particularly the engine-room staff, seem to have had left wing leanings, but the officers were predominantly right wing to the point of being fascist. The ship's company was, therefore, split in much the same way that France herself was divided.

Meanwhile, the new French Government at Vichy was negotiating an armistice with Germany and the British Cabinet was awaiting the outcome with considerable apprehension. If the French Navy was to be handed over to the enemy, the German invasion forces would be immeasurably strengthened—and it was expected that Germany would attempt to invade England very soon. The pressures on the French Navy mounted on both sides and, on 3 July, Hitler demanded that all French ships must return to France 'or the entire Armistice would be reconsidered'. The bulk of the French Fleet was at Oran and Mers el Kebir and the contrasting British demand, to the French Admiral at Oran, was to fight on or to neutralise his ships, or see them sunk within six hours. A fortnight earlier, the British had already made secret preparations to deal with French vessels lying in British ports in the event that force had to be used, and these vessels now included *Surcouf*.

Nobody on the British side relished the task, code-named Operation CATAPULT. During the night of 2/3 July, Churchill signalled Vice-Admiral Somerville in HMS *Hood*, the flagship of Force H waiting at Gibraltar:

You are charged with one of the most disagreeable and difficult tasks that a British Admiral has ever been faced with, but we have complete confidence in you and rely on you to carry it out relentlessly.

At 0300 on the morning of 3 July, at about the time this signal was being decoded in the Mediterranean, Commander Denis 'Lofty' Sprague, Captain of the large submarine HMS *Thames*, together with Lieutenant Patrick Griffiths from *Rorqual*, two engineer officers and a small escort, of ratings and Royal Marines, boarded *Surcouf* at Plymouth and confronted Commandant Martin who, with calm dignity, insisted that the boarding officers waited while he changed from pyjamas into uniform. The engineers passed aft to the engine-room where they were regaled with wine at this early hour, while the French officers were all brought into the wardroom. Here, Sprague read out to them a statement which said that they were under arrest and that they and the crew would be taken ashore. If they wished to be repatriated to French territory they would be allowed to go or they could stay in Britain and continue the fighting against Germany.

Martin asked Sprague if he might go and talk the matter over with his Admiral, de Villaine, in the battleship *Paris*, promising

that he would return immediately. Sprague accepted this request and also agreed not to remove any of the crew until Martin came back. Meanwhile, two British ratings were left to guard five French officers in the wardroom while Sprague escorted Martin up to the casing. One of the Frenchmen asked if he could go to *les poulaines* (heads) and here, evidently, a number of pistols were hidden, for moments later Sprague heard a shot. He drew his pistol and ran back down towards the wardroom where he received six bullets before the Gunnery Officer, Bouillaut, shot him fatally in the head. Griffiths, following Sprague, fired at Bouillaut and wounded him in the shoulder, tripping over Sprague's body as he turned to run for help. As he fell, he in turn was shot in the back by the submarine's doctor who then fired his pistol at one of the British ratings, who succeeded in bayonetting another member of the crew before he, too, died.

Sprague, Griffiths, one British Leading Seaman and one French sailor were killed in the scuffle (or died soon afterwards) and two men were wounded before the remainder of the boarding party gained control. It was a sad, secretive affair and even Churchill was not apprised of the deaths of the two officers: he wrote to Sprague's widow in 1949 apologising that his book *The Finest Hour* had failed to recognise their loss.[7]

Practically all the French records concerning *Surcouf* during the war were seemingly destroyed, and if any significant papers remain they are not being released from the archives at Vincennes. From now on it is difficult to be sure of what really happened during the remainder of *Surcouf*'s service under British orders. Even British records are incomplete and facts are mixed inextricably with fantasies. Mysteries, rumours, coincidences and accusations abound on all sides. The best that can be done is to hold securely to those facts that can be cross-checked and interpret the remainder with common sense and a knowledge of how submarines do and do not operate: a careful look at *Surcouf*'s real capabilities will at least dispose of some of the legends.

The tragic bloodshed at Plymouth resulted in only 40 (one source says fourteen) of the 129 men in the original crew being retained. The remainder were replaced—mainly by untrained men—under the command of Capitaine de Vaisseau Ortoli with Lieutenant de Vaisseau Blaison as First Lieutenant. As in all Allied submarines serving under British operational control, one officer, a Signalman and a Telegraphist from the Royal Navy were also drafted to the boat, not to tell the

French how to go about their business but simply to make sure that orders were understood and signals were correctly transmitted and received.

Morale throughout the scattered French Navy was understandably low and *Surcouf*, following the shooting incident, had special problems. Moreover, it was quite impossible to train the new crew of the giant submarine to the peak of efficiency which would have been necessary for her to make best use of her substantial armament. However, to the French, represented by Admiral Muselier, she still appeared to be a powerful force that could be employed in helping to protect French interests abroad, particularly in the West Indies and the Pacific. For the British, her value lay principally as a convoy escort —and a submarine was by no means ideal for that purpose although, reluctantly, British boats were increasingly to be sent on convoy duties to Russia. Much thought was given by the Admiralty to how else she might be brought to bear on the war at sea.

Surcouf recommissioned with her new ship's company on 15 September 1940 and went to sea for the first time on 20 December, making her first dive two days later before sailing for an inadequate one week's work-up in the Holy Loch from 7 to 14 February 1941. She sailed for Halifax on 19 February and remained there throughout March until joining Convoy HX 118 on 1 April. On 17 April, the submarine arrived back at Devonport, having been attacked by a German seaplane the previous day. During the following week, German bombs on Plymouth resulted in superficial damage. One man was killed and six wounded: morale did not improve.

It is worth recalling at this point a succinct report by Sub Lt Ruari McLean, Liaison officer in the Free French minelaying submarine *Rubis*:

RUBIS *is a French submarine not a Free French one ... Patriotism and loyalty is not to de Gaulle (who, however, they admire) but to France and is as strong as an Englishman's to England ... if they are captured by Germans they may not be shot but if they are captured by Vichy Frenchmen they certainly will be shot ... they are fighting Germany for France not for Britain....*

These remarks described the situation well in *Rubis* which was an efficient and successful boat whose ship's company felt that they had a definite aim in the war. It might be felt that they equally applied to the crew of *Surcouf*, but here the state of affairs was far less clearly defined. Ortoli, and Blaison

F F submarine *Surcouf* at anchor in Holy Loch in February 1941 during work-up.

Surcouf at Portsmouth, New Hampshire, USA on 9 November 1941 after trials and exercises under her new captain Louis Blaison who had assumed command on 7 October.

who succeeded him in command on 7 October 1941, had a ship's company with little sense of direction and no figurehead to follow. It says much for the leadership of the successive captains (particularly Blaison) that there was no open unrest but, equally, besides the training problem the determination and drive required to make the submarine run smoothly were clearly lacking.

One of the original 'alternative employment' suggestions while at Devonport had been to prepare *Surcouf* for carrying urgently needed stores to Malta as a part of the invaluable submarine 'magic carpet' which kept the besieged garrison supplied from June 1941 to October 1942. Admiral Muselier had strongly resisted an earlier proposal to convert the submarine to a store carrier but agreed in April when persuaded of the urgency. However, the Admiralty now

looked more closely at the giant submarine's characteristics and decided that 'she was unsuitable owing to her poor diving qualities [sic] for this purpose.[8] It was becoming more and more apparent that *Surcouf* was something of a white elephant. On 14 May 1941, she sailed for an uneventful Atlantic patrol en route to Bermuda from which base she made a three-week anti-surface raider patrol before moving to Portsmouth, New Hampshire, where the newly promoted Capitaine de Frégate George-Louis-Nicolas Blaison took command, for a three-month refit. The end of November found her still unemployed and once more in Bermuda. She sailed for Halifax on 7 December.

On 12 December, Admiral Muselier also arrived at Halifax with the three corvettes *Mimosa*, *Alysse* and *Aconit*. This small force, together with *Surcouf*, was secretly

assembled to annex the St Pierre and Miquelon Islands—a project which met with strong opposition from the United States Government because it would imperil the US State Department's agreement with Vichy. But, on 18 December, the Admiral received a formal order from General de Gaulle to proceed without informing any foreign nationals. It is not clear how much the British knew about *Surcouf*'s movements at this time, but it is possible that they promoted the annexation clandestinely because the radio stations on the islands, while controlled by Vichy, could well be reporting Allied convoy movements to the enemy. However, the Admiralty seems to have been largely kept in the dark.

Ten days earlier, on 8 December, when the submarine was nominally on passage to Halifax, the Norwegian tanker *Atlantic* re-

Surcouf in dock, Portsmouth, New Hampshire, in September 1941.

ported sighting a large submarine flying the French flag 546 miles south of Halifax, but the British Admiralty seems only to have surmised that this was *Surcouf*. The submarine's precise movements were probably unknown and it is not certain who had operational control of her. The tanker reported being 'chased all round the compass before the submarine made off in a NNE direction.[9] Presumably, *Surcouf*, having established the friendly nature of the *Atlantic*, simply went on her way for she had a speed advantage of some eight knots over the tanker and could have caught her if she had wished. This small incident has relevance because rumours were going around to the effect that *Surcouf* was carrying out some kind of Fifth Column activity and torpedoing Allied ships when the opportunity arose to do so while supposedly escorting them in convoy. One of the two British ratings on board later alleged that two torpedoes were mysteriously lost during each convoy operation.

It is as well to examine this allegation before going any further with the story. First, it has to be said that the British Liaison Officer and the two ratings were extremely unhappy on board; they distrusted the French submariners, who were gratuitously unpleasant to them, and their evidence, which is only hearsay anyway, must be treated in that light. Secondly, it is unthinkable that everybody on board would not have been fully aware when and if torpedoes were fired, even from the external tubes. Thirdly, there is plenty of evidence to show that *Surcouf*'s crew were not sufficiently worked-up to per-

mit torpedo attacks being made covertly and under difficult tactical circumstances with any chance of success. Furthermore, the French torpedoes differed in size from the British weapons and were not replaceable abroad so that the Captain would have been most reluctant to risk wasting them. Finally, the *Atlantic* would surely have been a prime and easy target, yet the submarine left her alone. Sheer common sense suggests, then, that the ugly tales of double-dealing which surrounded *Surcouf* (and persist to this day) are without foundation.

However, such suspicions were constantly refuelled by the secretiveness of the French.

In Halifax, Muselier put it about that he had brought the ships together only in order to inspect them. On 13 December, he duly inspected *Surcouf*, congratulating Blaison and his crew in glowing terms, well aware that they needed a shot in the arm: 'I have never seen the inside of a submarine so well kept— immaculate, well painted and brightly polished.'[10] The Admiral did not comment on the external appearance of the boat which was almost entirely sheeted in ice with icicles hanging from the giant guns.

It was not a healthy time of the year for any kind of landing operation, but, at noon on 23 December, *Surcouf* and the three corvettes sailed out of Halifax harbour in the general direction of Newfoundland, supposedly for independent exercises. The weather was appalling and *Surcouf* rolled heavily, spilling acid out of the battery cells and starting a fire which recalled similar incidents during the previous year in the same waters. The crews of the four vessels must have guessed that there was something more in the wind than horizontal sleet but Muselier was unwilling to commit any instructions to paper until clear of the land. Accordingly, secret orders were passed by line-throwing guns when well out to sea, and the little flotilla set course straight for Miquelon. There was no doubt now about who had operational control.

By the early hours of Christmas Eve the weather had moderated and the island's flashing light was clearly visible on the horizon. *Surcouf*'s draught was too great for her to enter the port of St Pierre herself and she

FRENCH SURCOUF

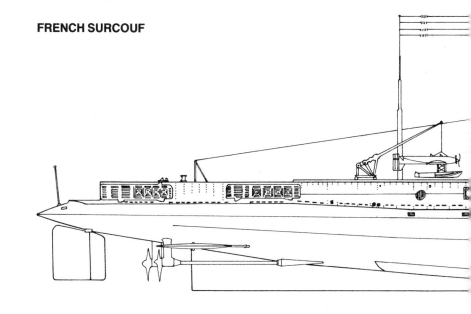

transferred her landing party to the corvettes which pressed on in to seize, without any resistance, the Customs House and the Gendarmerie. Militarily speaking, the operation was successful and it passed without incident. The Free French flag was hoisted and Muselier triumphantly informed the Admiralty on Christmas day. The Admiralty did not want to know: the British Government was disassociating itself from the whole affair for fear of upsetting the United States.

Meanwhile, *Surcouf* was left at sea exposed to the dangers of U-boat attack but with orders to torpedo any ship which, under cover of darkness, entered the islands' territorial waters. Armed intervention by the Americans or the Canadians was possible—even probable—and these orders put Blaison in the same uncomfortable situation in which other French Commanding officers had found themselves earlier in the year off North Africa. Muselier ordered *Surcouf* to return to Halifax, but the political situation created by the operation boiled up and the submarine was kept on patrol off St Pierre for a fortnight before matters calmed down sufficiently to allow her to berth again in Halifax on 14 January 1942. Here she remained, trying to put right her ever growing list of defects until once more she sailed for

Surcouf's main and secondary gun armament showing the director tower. The guns were never used in anger.

Bermuda, where she arrived at the end of the month, reverting to British control.

Despite French accounts[11] which describe movingly the farewells to Muselier, their Commander-in-Chief, at St Pierre, the officers and men drawn up on the casing 'as it for a naval review at Toulon' all was far from well. Even making due allowance for the British Liaison Officer's prejudices and for the mutual dislikes which had built up in a crowded wardroom, the reports which he rendered to the British Commander-in-Chief (America and West Indies) at Ber-

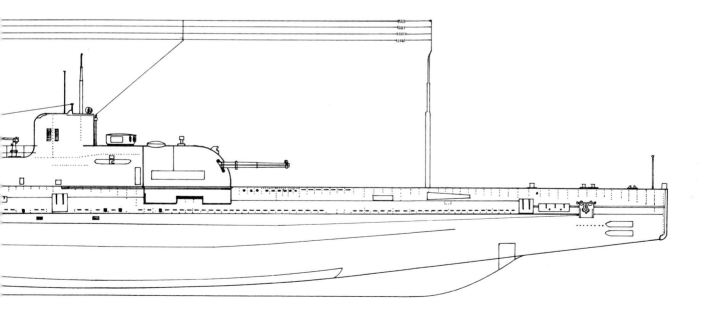

muda, summarised by the latter's signal of 6 February 1942 to Flag Officer Submarines, reproduced adjacent ring all too true.

The final tragedy in the giant submarine's unhappy and unfruitful career, ill-starred since that fateful day in Plymouth a year and a half earlier, now started to unfold with orders to proceed to Tahiti. The following Most Secret signals, shorn of inessentials, tell the remainder of the story:

> *6 February 1942*
> *From C-in-C America and West Indies*
> *To   Flag Officer Submarines.*

SURCOUF *now reports defective main motor armature ... propose ship proceed UK and pay off.*

> *6 February 1942*
> *From Flag Officer Submarines*
> *To   Admiralty*

I adhere to my previous opinion. The CO of SURCOUF *is a seaman who knows his job and his ship well. The First Lieutenant is a good officer and experienced in submarines. The Engineer and key ratings are well experienced. The crew have suffered inaction and anti-British propaganda in Canada. To get any results from these Free French they must be put in the front line and kept there. I am sure Commander Cabanier at Tahiti can make use of* SURCOUF *and in an active war area. In defence of their own soil I consider* SURCOUF *may be of considerable use.* SURCOUF *occupies a peculiar position in French Naval mentality and the Free French would hate to pay her off. In any case a large crew would be required for care and maintenance and she would be a nuisance in this country. I strongly recommend* SURCOUF *proceeding as already ordered.*

> *7 February 1942*
> *From Flag Officer Submarines*
> *To   Admiralty.*

... even if temporary repairs at Bermuda prove unsatisfactory on passage to Tahiti F.S. SURCOUF *can still dive using one shaft. At Tahiti her 8-inch guns would provide a valuable addition to defence of this or other islands. If it were found necessary to pay her off this should be done at Tahiti where her crew could add to strength of local defence force. A few of the better officers and key ratings being sent back to UK to act as spares for Free French submarines in this country...*

Surcouf sailed for Bermuda bound for the Panama Canal on 12 February. She probably had 130 men on board but, in view of her mission, the figure could have been higher although the Memorial at Cherbourg

shows only 129 names. Only one main motor was working. The Admiralty signalled calmly that 'though she will not be fully efficient submerged'—a considerable understatement—'she will be an asset in the defence of the Free French Pacific Islands. It is confidently anticipated that morale will improve as soon as she becomes operational.' It appears that Their Lordships were anxious to be rid of the monster, but they could not foresee the fate that awaited her. The first indication of this came in a cable from the British Consular Shipping Adviser at Colon, Panama:

French Cruiser-Sub SURCOUF *not repetition not arrived.*

'THOMPSON LYKES *USA Army Transport northbound convoy yesterday now returned after collision with unidentified vessel which apparently sank at once at 2230R 18th February in latitude 010 degs 40 North longitude*

MOST SECRET   MESSAGE   1221P/5th February   IN

From C.in C. America and West Indies.   Date 6.2.42.   Recd. 0459

Naval Cypher XD by Cable.

Addressed - F.O. Subs. Repeated Admiralty.

IMPORTANT.

898.   B.N.L.O. SURCOUF has given me copies of his reports dated 17th December 1st January and 16th January addressed to you.   After discussion with B.N.L.O and from my experience of SURCOUF I am convinced that this most unsatisfactory state of affairs is not in the least exaggerated.

2.   The two main troubles are lack of interest and incompetency (the E.R.Department is however moderately clean and efficient and the machinery is in fair order) discipline is bad and the Officers have little control. I have no suggestions to make which are likely to assist in eliminating these defects which I am afraid are inherent.

3.   SURCOUF is a large complicated and indifferently designed submarine and in my opinion could only be of operational value if manned by an exceptionally well trained crew.   Even then her size places severe limitations on her sphere of usefulness.   At present she is of no operational value and is little short of a menace.

4.   SURCOUF will leave Bermuda on 7th February for Tahiti via Panama Canal unless otherwise ordered. For Political reasons it may be considered desirable to keep her in commission, but my view is that she should proceed to U.K. and pay off.   Request very early decision on this question, and in any case before 13th February when SURCOUF will be due at Colon.

1221P/5

Advance copy D.C., D.O.D.(F)., D.D.I.C.

1st Lord.	D.A/S.W.
1st S.L.	Hd. of M.(6).
2nd S.L.	D.C.(2).
V.C.N.S.	D.D.I.C.(2).
A.C.N.S.(H).	D.N.I.(4).
A.C.N.S.(F).	D.D.O.D.(M).
Nav. Sec.	I.P.(2).
D.O.D.(H).	W.D.
D.D.O.D.(H).	
D.O.D.(F).	

The aircraft hangar, used only for stores during the war.

079 degs 30 West. She searched the vicinity until 0830 today 19th February but no survivors or wreckage. Only sign was oil. Considerable bow damage made to THOMPSON LYKES at fore foot.

Three days after the accident on 21 February, the Consular Shipping Adviser at Colon assembled the facts in a message to the British authorities concerned:

Following additional information obtained from perusing statements by Master, Officer of the Watch and two military gunners on board THOMPSON LYKES.

(a) United States Ship without lights course 356 degrees at full speed approximately 14 knots. Originally steering for Windward Passage but diverted for Cienfuegos, Cuba.

(b) Other vessel not observed until white light flash seen one point to starboard bow about half minute before collision. Wheel put hard to port but before ship answered helm light again seen this time right ahead so wheel reversed hard to starboard engine still full ahead.

(c) Heavy collision very shortly afterwards. On reaching bridge after collision Master stopped engine. While still close on port beam vessel seen sinking with great disturbance of water. Gunner states bow of other vessel thrown up clear of the water before sinking. Calls in English for help were heard by witnesses but their ship carried headway lost contact. Master delayed lowering lifeboats allegedly on account of sea running intending to do so later when party of survivors were located.

(d) Meanwhile shortly after vessel sank violent underwater explosion was felt in United States ship. Having carried her

way about half mile ship put back to where Master estimated other had sunk. Searchlight revealed no sign of survivors or wreckage but much oil. Weather described as rather heavy sea fresh wind; visibility not mentioned. United States Authorities informed by W/T. Search abandoned 0830, 10 hours later.

(e) Consider statement either taken badly through inexperience or considerably condensed and important evidence either not elicited or not recorded e.g. no statements produced from helmsman or seaman look-outs.

(f) From personal observation 15 yard distance, nature of damage to US ship points to other not being surface craft, as upper two third stem post and of pole plate not damaged.

(g) US Authorities now severely limit communication to ships and preserve close secrecy. Nothing has been told me officially but local Naval Intelligence persuaded by US Navy Port Captain at my request allowed me unofficially to read above statements. They know that I am reporting facts and inference to you but have probably not repetition not informed their superiors of my reading statements or reporting on them. Army officers also interrogated candidates witnesses later.

(h) Understand that although carrying Army personnel US ships manned solely by Merchant crew. Do not know if Master warned he might meet French cruiser S/M SURCOUF [SIC]. British and other Allied merchant ships leaving here show dim navigational lights in Caribbean Sea.

What the (probably American) Consular Shipping Advisor at Colon did not say was

that he, the responsible authority, had failed to warn either Surcouf or the convoy that the submarine was routed on a reciprocal track to the convoy that would take her straight into its grain.

Nothing more, of any significance, was immediately established about the ramming but fresh rumours were now circulated, and it is reasonable to suppose that they were prompted by German agencies. The most unpleasant and damaging of these stories gained widespread credence: it was to the effect that Surcouf was deliberately rammed and sunk in the belief that she would otherwise be handed over to the enemy.

Leaving aside circumstantial evidence, which is admittedly less complete than might be expected, there are two good reasons for rejecting this version of the events.

Premeditated ramming by a merchant ship, especially one carrying troops, could not possibly have been contemplated by responsible authorities; it could well have resulted in the ramming vessel herself being sunk, and the Thompson Lykes did indeed sustain heavy damage. Nor would a collision necessarily result in the submarine sinking. Repeated attempts to ram U-boats, throughout the war, were often unsuccessful: they required very nice judgement and a good deal of luck. Ramming was not the way to make sure that Surcouf went to the bottom.

Supposing, however, that the Americans and, presumably, the British had connived at Surcouf's destruction by some means, the top intelligence men on both sides would certainly have known about the plan. But a day or two after the collision (before the signals started flying), the very people who would have been privy to such a devious scheme were busily—and genuinely—looking into further uses for the submarine.

The collision was, beyond any reasonable doubt, either a pure accident—an accident to which submariners were particularly prone before the days of radar—or, just possibly (according to one officer present at the Board of Enquiry), it was the result of an instant reflex action by the Thompson Lykes which was certainly not planned. It does not really matter either way: it was still a dreadful tragedy.

Surcouf never accomplished anything for which she was designed and she had an unhappy knack of being at the centre of political trouble; but it is sad that, even in death, she should continue to attract suspicion and hostility towards herself and ill-informed speculation about the manner of her passing. She and her company should be allowed to rest in peace.

5: Great Aircraft Carriers

At about the time that *Surcouf* was being laid down, HMS *M-2* had her giant gun removed and a seaplane hangar installed in its place, with a derrick forward, in order to allow her to operate a small seaplane. A Carey compressed air catapult was added later.

The project originated in the progressive and imaginative mind of Captain Max K Horton during the summer of 1923 when Horton was Captain of the First Submarine Squadron. He had commanded HMS *M-1* during her first commission 1918–19. In a secret memorandum to RA(S) (Rear Admiral Submarines) Horton wrote:

... the more the probable conditions of a possible future war are studied, the more obvious it becomes that greatly increased reliance, in comparison with the late war, must be placed on submarines and aircraft for early information of enemy's movements.

The practical combination implied by a submarine carrying aircraft has vast possibilities. The submarine, with its inherent advantages of great endurance and power of acting unsupported far from its base, is perfected where its greatest defect lay, viz. in lack of vision.

... the ultimate addition of a Flotilla of such craft to the Main Fleet would do much to relieve the serious anxiety that is now experienced as a result of a close examination of the various sources from which enemy information can be expected in a war over wide seas.

... for this purpose, an M class submarine presents advantages which can only be described as peculiarly fortunate ...

RA(S) was not, by naval custom, permitted to approach the Admiralty directly with a new idea and had to forward it through the Commander-in-Chief, Atlantic Fleet who, on 27 July 1923 was immediately 'pleased to place before Their Lordships' the proposal in Horton's original words—always a good omen. From there on, with the idea safely tucked inside an Admiralty docket, matters moved less swiftly.

The Air Ministry as well as many naval departments had to be consulted and, on 1 October 1924, the Head of the Air Section of the Naval Staff felt compelled to write to RA(S):

I am afraid it all appears to be a very slow business, but I think it of no use pushing on and converting a submarine to carry one of these machines until we are sure that the Air Ministry can produce an aircraft that is suitable.

The Air Ministry promised to build a specially designed machine, which could be folded when housed in the proposed submarine's hangar, by March 1925, which was not bad going for a totally new aeroplane. Meanwhile, drawings were produced by the Director of Naval Construction and Their Lordships finally approved the conversion of *M-2* in September 1925. Chatham Dockyard was to do the work at a cost of £60,000.

HMS *M-2* recommissioned in her new guise towards the end of 1927 and started trials and work-up in April the following year. She retained her four 18-inch bow torpedo tubes and the 3-inch 'disappearing' high-angle gun but, of course, her most interesting feature was the Parnall Peto spotter aeroplane. Her new complement, under Lieutenant Commander JDA Musters, DSC, consisted of three other officers and 46 ratings with the addition of two officers and three ratings from the Fleet Air Arm and Royal Air Force.

M-2 was not the first aircraft-carrying submarine: HMS *E-22* had two Sopwith Schneider seaplanes in 1916, primarily to make bombing and reconnaissance raids over the German Zeppelin bases at Cuxhaven and Tondern. Indeed, designs for a submarine-based flying boat were submitted to

the Admiralty by a Mr Pemberton Billing, evidently a persistent gentleman, a year earlier than this with the idea of bombing Berlin and the Baltic, but they were turned down because the project, at that stage, was said to be inhuman. And, long afterwards, at the 1929 Olympia Show, a visitor came to the stand of the magazine *The Aeroplane* to see one of the Peto aeroplanes which was on display close by. The visitor happened to be deaf and dumb (which somewhat complicated the subsequent interview), but it was eventually gathered that, very forcibly as best he could, he was putting the question 'who has stolen my idea?' Scribbling on scraps of paper he claimed to have suggested to the Admiralty that a submarine could convey an aeroplane as far back as 1913. *The Aeroplane* was sure that 'the visitor was not Mr Pemberton Billing—who is certainly not dumb though he is sometimes deaf to argument'. Whoever he was, the claimant might equally have accused Germany, the United States and Italy, who also experimented at various times with aircraft on submersibles.

However that may be, *M-2* was the first submarine with a reasonably practicable aircraft-carrying system capable of submerging with the aeroplane on board. Quite why the aircraft, three of which were built, were called Petos is uncertain; but it must be more than coincidental that the much liked and respected officer, Lieutenant Commander H F Peto (later Sir Francis Peto) had commanded *M-2* (when equipped with her 12-inch gun) from 1923 to 1924: in 1918, his confidential report remarked that he was 'very zealous, especially at working out new inventions' and that he was 'very clever on a lathe'—which was, perhaps, unusual for an old Etonian. Since the Peto is also the name of an Australian fish, often called the Wahoo, there seems to have been a good enough basis for christening the little aircraft accordingly.

The first model of the folding two-seater, with a 135-engine, had a total range of about 150 miles at 70 knots with a maximum speed of 100 knots at sea level or 94 knots at 5000 feet (taking eleven minutes to reach that height). It is not clear how the seaplane was to be used in war, nor what was to happen to

Soon after World War One, the US Navy began to consider the possibility of basing floatplanes, capable of being used for observation or scouting, on submarines. Late in 1923, the 800-ton S-1 was given this ability. The first floatplane used on S-1 was the small Martin MS-1 but, although quite quickly dismantled, it took four men four hours to reassemble. In 1926, a Cox-Klemin XS-2 was adopted instead and it proved much easier to knock down and put together again, but the project was abandoned in 1927 because the Secretary of the Navy held that the disadvantages of carrying aircraft on submarines outweighed the advantages. The Japanese came, in due course, to the reverse conclusion!

When S-1 surfaced, with XS-2 in its watertight cylindrical pod abaft the conning tower, the handlers leaped into action, dragged out the aircraft and assembled it while the pilot (Lt D C Allen) climbed into the cockpit. The submarine then partially submerged until the aircraft floated free, whereupon it commenced a normal water take-off. Trials from July to October 1926 showed that the time taken from S-1 blowing tanks at periscope depth to the XS-2 starting its engine could be as little as twelve minutes: recovery and stowage in ideal sea conditions took only a minute longer.

the unfortunate aircraft if the weather deteriorated while it was in flight: the endurance was no more than two hours at best. It had to land on the sea and be picked up by the special derrick on the submarine. Landing and recovery in anything stronger than wind force 2 was reckoned to be impossible: the Beaufort scale describes force 2 as a light breeze and the accompanying sea has 'small wavelets with glassy crests which do not break'. With practise, however, a slight—very slight—sea proved manageable.

The launching operation involved ten men

crowding themselves into the tiny hangar while waiting for the giant door to open. It would have been prudent to shut the pressure hull hatch behind them for the safety of the submarine, but it must have been tempting to leave it open with a claustrophobic atmosphere building up and a flow of orders from the control room which might have been difficult to interpret on the telephone. Then, too, there were probably bits and pieces of equipment to be passed up at the last minute.

Speed in launching the aircraft was clearly

important. The pilot and observer were briefed by the captain well beforehand and some time before surfacing the pilot ordered the electrical oil and engine heaters to be switched on. With a warm engine and lubricating oil, the engine started much more readily when the moment came, shortening the time spent on the surface.

The crew concerned with launching the machine wore long waders and sea-boots because, when the hangar door was opened, water was bound to wash into the hangar, and the casing itself would certainly be wet.

Italian 1788-ton (submerged) *Ettore Fieramosca* laid down August 1926 at Taranto. Originally intended for minelaying and scouting with a seaplane, the submarine never used its aircraft, stowed in a deck hangar, in war.

HMS *M-2* off Southsea c. 1929.

A high coaming around the hatch leading down into the boat prevented too much water finding its way below when the hatch was reopened.

As soon as the boat was on the surface, the Captain ordered the hangar door to be opened. This fell down flat in front of the hangar, ready for rails to be laid over it connecting the hanger to the ends of the cata-

pult rails on the fore-casing. The aircraft was then pushed out onto its catapult trolley where the wings were unfolded and secured.

It was a team event and the crew took pride in carrying out the drill with precision and speed; but it is all too likely that over-enthusiasm eventually cost the ship's company their lives.

The Captain, as in any other aircraft carrier, turned into the wind at sufficient speed for the wind gauge in the conning tower to register enough air speed over the casing—10 or 15 knots—to ensure a clean take-off. The intrepid pilot then opened the throttle fully and, when he was as happy about things as he was ever likely to be, raised his hand so that the Captain could order the launch.

The man who actually pulled the catapult lever was a Stoker but, true to the British tradition demanding that the upper deck must always have the final word, he took his orders from a Seaman who was in turn directed by the Captain on the bridge. The acceleration on the catapult was rapid and, said a contemporary article in *Flight*, 'there was no wavering or drop whatsoever . . . this was somewhat amazing when it was realised that the impetus given by the catapult was so great as to reach this speed (about 60 knots) in such a short space. Of course, in doing so

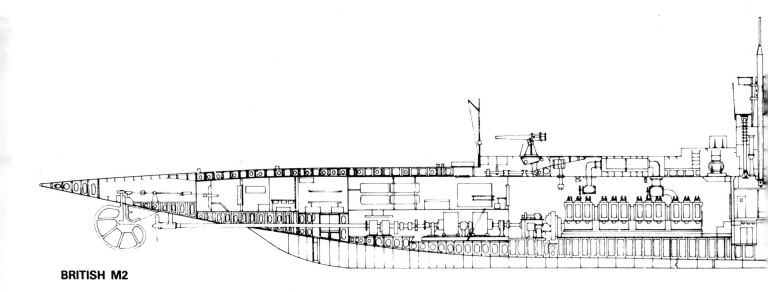

BRITISH M2

M-2 off Malta. Her motto was PER MARE PER COELUM.

both the pilot and the observer are naturally banged against the back padding in their cockpits.'

The Commander-in-Chief Atlantic Fleet, with aviators on his staff, pointed out[1] that 'as weight is such an important factor in submarine-borne aircraft crews should be specially picked.' There was no shortage of volunteers with flying and submarine pay both allowed. The first two pilots, Lieutenants Byas and Keighly-Peach, were well-qualified and apparently came within the weight specifications, although there was a standing joke (possibly founded on fact) about the pilot having to wear gym shoes instead of flying boots if the observer, sitting in the front cockpit, wanted to take any additional equipment like a camera or binoculars.

Unfortunately, the Admiralty forgot the C-in-C's advice later on and sent *M-2* a massive pilot together with an observer who weighed in at a healthy eighteen stone. It was probably this substantial crew that brought about one of the three crashes sustained by Peto seaplanes.

One day on trials in the Solent with a new machine, the pilot never succeeded in gaining height after launch. The little Peto made its wavering way towards the smart seaside resort of Lee-on-the-Solent a mile or so away while the pilot struggled with full throttle to clear the obstructions ahead. His best efforts failed: the starboard float demolished one of the bathing huts, revealing to public gaze a distinguished local citizen inadequately clad in a small pink towel.

The aircraft simply flopped down on the shingle. Nobody was even bruised. The two airmen climbed out and surveyed the irate citizen and the wrecked fuselage with equal dispassion. There was nothing to get excited about in the pilot's view and he would have enjoyed a quiet cigarette if one of the gathering crowd of spectators had not pointed to a stream of petrol pouring out of the tank.

A furious complaint was laid before RA(S) by the beach-hut inhabitant but the affair was smoothed over in the normal naval way. Lee-on-the-Solent was used to submarine encroachments although in the past these had usually been in the form of misdirected torpedoes charging up the beach. Anyway, it was all the Admiralty's fault for sending the wrong size aviators.

By March 1930, the drills for launching and recovering the Peto were perfected. Trials off Gibraltar showed that, starting

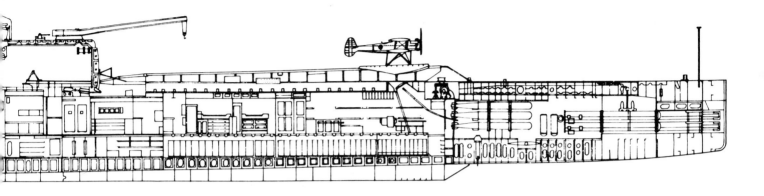

with *M-2* at periscope depth, the aircraft could be airborne in a little less than twelve minutes. Some of the actions were concurrent, but, breaking down the evolution, from the order 'Open hangar door', it took two minutes to spread the wings, three minutes twenty seconds to get the engine running, four minutes ten seconds to secure the catapult trolley in the firing position and seven minutes 50 seconds to fire. A full minute was lost between the Captain opening the conning tower hatch and deeming it safe, with minimum freeboard, to open the hangar door when the submarine had ponderously achieved sufficient surface buoyancy. It was a minute grudged; and the grudge was to prove fatal in the end.

Recovering the aircraft was a little quicker—ten minutes 50 seconds from the Peto landing to the submarine regaining periscope depth with the aircraft safely housed. This time depended, however, on ideal weather: if a lee had to be made, the operation could take much longer.

Whatever may be thought nowadays about *M-2*, there were some splendid contemporary claims made for her performance. It was noted with regret by Their Lordships that the size of the submarine was limited by treaty and this in turn limited the size of the aircraft and hence its potential. Submarine protagonists at the Admiralty replied by pointing out that surface aircraft-carriers were exceedingly vulnerable because their bulk made them such an easy target:

it would, they said, be folly to place an aircraft carrier ahead of the fleet (where aircraft were needed as scouts), unless the ship was contained within the protective radius of the fleet itself. A submarine, on the other hand, could proceed at a considerable distance ahead of the fleet and need not surface to launch her aircraft unless and until enemy units were seen to be clear. It was also pointed out that a high cruising speed for the submarine would be necessary: how high was not specified.

But events in the anti-submarine air world were moving significantly. Could a submarine afford to surface to launch and recover an aircraft in wartime? Would the aircraft itself survive? Submariners were beginning to doubt it; and, following one fateful newsflash, public opinion, too, started to weigh heavily against submersible aircraft-carriers.

On the night of 26 January 1932, the Admiralty announced:

News has been received this evening that HM Submarine M-2 dived at about 1030 this morning off Portland, and since then no further communication has been received from her . . .

The submarine was located a few hours later, three miles west of Portland Bill, lying on the bottom in seventeen fathoms. Salvage craft and divers were sent to the scene but it was too late. The Captain, Lieutenant Commander John de M Leathes, and his entire crew of 60 officers and men had perished.

What happened can only be conjectured; but divers were to find that the hatch leading up to the hangar and the hangar door were both open and an eye-witness, Captain Howard of the china-clay coaster *Tynesider*, reported seeing the submarine surface and then dive stern first with her bows out of the water. He asked whether this was usual: indeed it was not.

Leathes was an exceptionally talented and dedicated officer. He was devoted to making *M-2* efficient in all respects and doubtless he was anxious to cut the time of launching, which would have increased the possibility of a mistake being made. But when submarine disasters occur, they are very seldom due to one thing going wrong by itself. Almost always it is the combination of two things going wrong at the same time which spells disaster: submariners know this, all too well, as Murphy's Second Law.

It can only be guesswork, but two mistakes were quite possible. First, the main (ballast) vents may not have been shut on surfacing when air was blown into the tanks. This has happened in plenty of submarines at one time or another, although the drill has been made virtually foolproof since the last war. The result is that, although the boat surfaces initially, the open vents allow the air to escape again, quickly destroying the positive buoyancy that has been gained. Alternatively, telemotor (hydraulic) pressure might have been lost at the critical moment, possibly with similar results and with

the added effect of losing hydroplane control while the boat was more or less hanging on planes while coming fully to the surface. If eager to open the hangar door and beat the clock, the Captain might easily have given the order prematurely in the belief, from all appearances, that the boat was buoyant when, in fact, it was anything but. With the hangar so close to the waterline on surfacing, flooding into the hangar and down the hatch would have been immediate and uncontrollable. It has also been suggested that there may have been a misunderstanding of orders. In particular, 'close' could sound like 'open': 'close number four' (main vent) might have been interpreted as 'open the hangar door'. Whether or not this was true, the word 'close' in British submarines was forbidden from then on: hatches, valves or whatever were either 'open' or *shut*'.

Lessons were learned in *M-2*, but some of them were learned the hard way. Ironically, it was Japan, Britain's future enemy, who gained most from them.

M-2 at Gibraltar in 1930, with the hangar door open, Commander A S Hutchinson in command.

At the London Naval Conference of 1930, the Japanese delegates fought for a larger submarine arm than the other major powers. The size and number of capital ships and aircraft carriers were limited by the Conference, but the building of submarines was thereby unintentionally stimulated.[2] In the end, Japan had to accept submarine parity with the United States and Britain (although, as will be seen later, midget submarines hugely swelled the numbers from 1934 onwards); but, with the vast area of the Pacific to cover, the Japanese decided to include in their underwater fleet a number of aircraft-carriers.

For many years, Japanese submarine designs were based upon proven foreign types, especially the British L-class. Officers of the Imperial Navy were given access to naval dockyards and installations in Europe and they gained, without resource to spying as such, all the essential information about the submersible aircraft-carriers with sealed hangars in other navies, notably USS *S-1* (SS-105, 1920), the Italian *Ettore Fieramosca* (1929), the French *Surcouf* and HMS *M-2*. They also probably noted a proposal, which was not in fact implemented, to use the door of a German pressure testing dock to shut off the hangar on *M-2* because the Japanese

submarine hangar doors turned out to be remarkably similar.

The Japanese Navy recognised, some ten years before the war with America which they regarded as inevitable, how important a scouting role was for their submarines: this role, they believed, could be furthered by the employment of submarine-based aircraft. The cruiser submarine *J-1* (type *I-5*) was therefore modified to carry a single seaplane, dismantled and stowed in two large cylinders to port and starboard abaft the conning tower; successful trials were carried out in 1932. The almost identical *J-2* (type *I-6*) was similarly equipped and was also fitted with a catapult aft for launching the aircraft. The need for a hangar was obviated by the cylindrical stowages but the components took too long to assemble for operational safety and the seaplane was eventually taken off *I-5* in 1940. However, *I-7* and *I-8* were of the much larger *J-3* cruiser type displacing 2231 tons on the surface and 3583 tons submerged: there was room not only for effective seaplane and catapult arrangements, but also for the command and communication arrangements necessary for these submarines to act as flotilla leaders controlling a number of submarines over a wide area. The type *A-1* and *A-2* boats were still larger and the modified A types, *I-13*, *I-14* and *I-15*, developed from the *A-2* type, were specifically designed as scouting submarines to replace the light cruisers traditionally employed on this task. In these big submarines, two aircraft were carried in a

hangar offset to the starboard side under the conning tower.

By the time that Japan launched her attack on Pearl Harbor in December 1941, the Navy knew a good deal about the potential and the problems of submersible seaplane-carriers. Under the Third Fleet Replenishment Law, three new types of submarines had been planned. These vessels, known as Type A (Headquarters Submarine), B (Patrol Submarine) and C (Attack Submarine) were derived from experience with Junsen and Kaidai types. Forming the spearhead of the Japanese submarine force, their production was continued, with various modifications, throughout the war. Both A and B types were equipped with seaplanes and their displacements varied between 2500 and 2900 tons on the surface and 3500 to 4150 tons submerged. They were capable of up to 23 knots on the surface and had a 90-day endurance with ranges between 14,000 and 16,000 miles at 16 knots. They were thus exceptionally well fitted for both reconnaissance and attack, either independently or in groups. In the event, when war came, the Japanese submarines were not generally used as originally intended and were, before long, largely diverted from offensive operations to defensive and supply tasks. But, whatever the submarines might be used for when it came to the test, Japanese designers had concen-

Opposite top
M-2 diving with the hangar door nearly submerged and the crane locked in the amidships position.

M-2 during conversion at Chatham with her 12-inch gun just removed.

Above
Parnall Peto hoisted out at Gibraltar.

Above right
M-class galley, which was in fact a great improvement
on the rudimentary arrangements in earlier boats, but
the occupants of the adjacent bunks can not have wel-
comed its proximity!

trated on producing war machines and gave
scant attention to habitability: poor living
conditions at sea and the inability to afford
the crews proper rest and relaxation after
their patrols was to contribute to the increasing weakness of the Imperial Submarine
Force as the war went on.

However, before the shift in operational
emphasis and before weaknesses started to
appear, the submarine seaplanes provided
important information from their reconnaissance missions over Allied bases; and, more
offensively, in August 1942, *I-25* despatched
her seaplane to start a forest fire in Oregon
with incendiary bombs. The latter operation
did nothing to affect the course of the war,
but it made American citizens realise that
the war was 'for real' and, in this sense,
the sortie was counter-productive to the
Japanese war effort.

With all this experience of submarine-
borne aircraft behind them, the Japanese
Navy, at the personal wish of Admiral
Yamamoto, issued an order in 1942 for the
building of eighteen giant submarines of the
Sen-Toku type, the *I-400* class. More than
400 feet long and displacing 5223 tons on the
surface, these monstrous multi-purpose
aircraft-carrying boats were the largest submarines that had ever been built, although
only three of them, *I-400*, *I-401* and *I-402*,

were actually finished, and *I-402* was converted to a supply submarine while still on
the stocks.

The *I-400*s were designed to combine the
principal features of the large A, B and C
type boats already in service in order to
carry out the duties for which these earlier
vessels were already being employed—
coordination and control of operational submarine groups, long range reconnaissance
and attacks on enemy warships. The original
design called for a submarine of 4550 tons
capable of carrying two bombers in a watertight hangar on the upper deck, but these
plans were later modified to include space
for three aircraft. This raised the displacement by about 700 tons and increased the
hangar length to 115 feet. In order to
achieve the degree of stability necessary for
surface operations and launching aircraft,
the beam-to-length ratio was enlarged by
forming much of the pressure hull into two
intersecting circles laid side by side, spectacle fashion, with a common longitudinal
bulkhead running between them, but the
two torpedo rooms forward were one above
the other in a vertical figure-of-eight. The
safe diving depth for this novel kind of hull
was 325 feet (100 metres).

The large hangar for the aircraft was sited
over the hull slightly to starboard for nearly
one-third of its length, while the conning
tower was placed to port. This arrangement
was similar to the *I-13* modified A type
which was ordered at the same time. The
Imperial Headquarters Staff were against
building either of these two classes because
large Japanese submarines were proving too

open to detection and attack and were beginning to suffer heavy losses, but Admiral
Yamamoto insisted on the programme going
ahead, partly because he firmly believed air
reconnaissance to be the key to success in the
Pacific and also because he was determined
to carry out a bombing attack on the Panama
Canal—an operation which, if successful,
would be a strategic master-stroke.

M-2's catapult, designed by R Falkland Carey and normally powered by compressed air although cordite
could be used instead.

Ready for take-off.

The moment of launch.

Take-off.

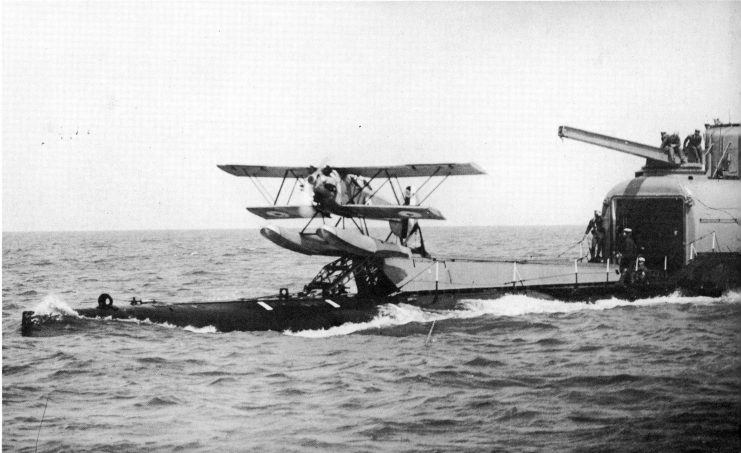

The Peto airborne.

It was usually a wet business. It is possible that Aircraftsman T E Shaw—Lawrence of Arabia—was a member of the hangar crew for a short period.

The Peto returning to *M-2*.

Coming alongside for recovery.

The last ship's company pictured at Chatham in about 1930.

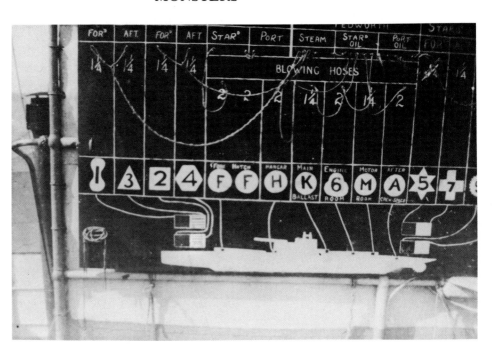

Above
Memorial Service for HMS *M-2* at Portsmouth Dockyard church.

Top right
The blowing indicator board on the diving vessel HMS *Tedworth* during the unsuccessful attempt to salvage *M-2* after the disaster in 1932.

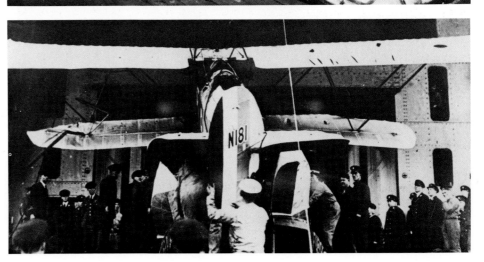

Some of the few items recovered from the wreck: the bridge steering wheel and lifebuoy.

The Parnall Peto N181 was salvaged. It is shown here being hauled aboard HMS *Furious*.

Submarines with a 90-day endurance and a range of 37,500 nautical miles at an economical speed of 14 knots (top speed 18.7 knots) could clearly not be inhibited by lack of torpedoes. Consequently, the *I-400*s had eight 21-inch torpedo tubes forward (arranged in two groups of four with the upper tubes staggered some three feet forward of the lower set) and twenty reload torpedoes were carried. The gun armament was no less impressive with one 5.5 inch gun sited on the after casing, three sets of triple 25 mm cannon arranged along the top of the superstructure over the hangar and one 25 mm cannon sited at the after end of the conning tower.

Although the full operational crew with a senior officer's staff embarked could number 21 officers and 170 ratings (a total of 144 was more usual but 213 men were on board when *I-400* surrendered), the size of the boat enabled habitability to be a little better than in other Japanese boats; but it did not compare with the excellent living conditions in US Fleet submarines and the Japanese were not good housekeepers. As in practically all World War Two submarines, water was in short supply: the total fresh water capacity was 1820 gallons, implying a ration, common to submarines in most navies, of one gallon per man per day for all purposes including cooking. There was, however, a shower room and space allowed such luxuries as an Engineer's and a Ship's Supply and Secretarial Office. Evaporators, using heat from the engine exhaust or electric heaters, could supplement the water supply but there is no reason to think that they were particularly reliable: 'stills' or 'evaps' were notorious world-wide (excepting some US models) for breaking down, inefficiency, electrical greed and wild heat.

Like the *I-14* class, external surfaces were covered with an anti-sound reflecting substance comprising a resilient foundation of synthetic rubber and sand with a thin cement or plastic covering. Whether this offered any real protection against Asdic (Active Sonar) transmissions on such a huge submarine is doubtful and there was no occasion in wartime when its value was either proved or disproved. Rivetting rather than welding was employed throughout and Allied experts examining *I-400* after the war reported a 'definite impression of careless construction'.[3]

For some reason which, from reports, the crews themselves did not fully understand, an automatic trimming control system was fitted which enabled the submarine to hover—normally at a depth between 130

and 165 feet. Noisy and not much used, it was presumably installed not only with the idea of saving the battery but also to help maintain a given position while the aircraft were in flight. Two airguard radar aerials, as well as a seaguard aerial, were fitted for defence and for locating the submarine's own seaplanes. Five pairs of very large 20x pressure-tight binoculars were mounted on the bridge but they offered a rather restricted field of view. The 43-foot W/T mast, raised by an electric motor, ensured adequate radio communications.

A rudimentary schnorchel was installed on the starboard side of the conning tower as an intake and exhaust for the auxiliary engines only. It extended twelve feet above the highest point of the periscope standards and was doubtless included in the design to avoid, when operations permitted, the *I-400* presenting its full profile: with the top of the bridge towering some 30 feet above the waterline when on the surface, she was an unhealthily large visual and radar target. The Japanese were painfully aware of the problem and, when in inland waters dummy funnels were occasionally rigged abaft the conning tower in an attempt to disguise the otherwise easily identifiable shape of the boat with its 85-foot long catapult stretching from the hangar door almost to the bows. The Imperial Navy absorbed and put to use every scrap of foreign intelligence, past and present, and had heard of the *Deutschland*'s artifice.

The catapult was worked by a compressed air piston (similar to that in *M-2*) and, when fired, the aeroplane carriage travelled forward a distance of 70 to 75 feet. Recovery was effected by a large derrick on the port side abreast the after part of the catapult and, worked by gearing and shafts from a motor inside the submarine, it could take a load of about five tons. The system was simple, satisfactory and not prone to malfunctions.

The aircraft chosen was the proven Aichi M6A1 *Seiran* Type bomber. A single-engine floatplane that was also used in the *I-14* class, it had a weapon load of one torpedo, one 800 kg bomb for level bombing or two 250 kg bombs for dive bombing. Twenty-eight machines were to be built before the war ended.

Training could not await commissioning: there was too much to be done and too little time to do it in if the submarines were going to play their part in a war whose tide was running strongly against the Empire by the beginning of 1944. During that year, when construction was well under way, aircraft

mechanics were chosen to become crew members of these new submarines and small groups of engineering mechanics were assigned to the building yards to familiarise themselves with the complexities of each boat. Meanwhile, in late 1944, the submarine Seiran Corps was formed under the command of Captain Tatsunoke Ariizumi, who would later become Flag Officer of the First Submarine Flotilla to which the *I-400* class submarines were eventually assigned.

During December 1944 and January 1945, the first two boats were completing with remarkable speed. Trials of the new aircraft and their launching equipment were carried out concurrently with the acceptance trials of the submarines themselves. When the launching system had been proven, the aircrews assigned to the Seirans learned for the first time of their intended secret mission— Yamamoto's long-planned attack on the Panama Canal, 6500 nautical miles distant from the Japanese mainland but the gate through which Allied forces from the West might be expected to flood into the Pacific and totally engulf the embattled Imperial forces. Training from then on had an edge to it.

Meanwhile, a much more terrible use was being proposed for the *I-400* Class seaplanes. The Top Secret 'PX Operation', put forward by Vice Admiral Jisaburo Ozawa, Vice Chief of the Naval General Staff, would see germ-carrying rats and mosquitoes released over the United States and American-held Pacific Islands with the bulk of their deadly cargoes being dropped over the larger cities on the American West Coast. Bubonic plague, cholera and typhus bacteria were apparently amongst those actively explored for the purpose. Fortunately, General Yoshijuro Umezu, Chief of the Army General Staff, put a stop to this plan in March 1945, saying that germ warfare would escalate to war against all humanity.[4] But the fact that it was very seriously considered and strongly backed by others is a chilling reminder of today's possibilities.

So far as the submarines were concerned, by the middle of April 1945 teething problems, notably experienced with the bomber engines, had been resolved; but the First Submarine Flotilla now found itself increasingly short of fuel because the American submarine blackade was beginning to bite. Sea-going exercises were being conducted out of the Kure Naval Base and, although this was one of the largest facilities of the Imperial Japanese Navy, its storage tanks were almost dry; priority for the remaining oil was naturally given to urgent

Above
Japanese ex-seaplane carrier *I-8* (Cdr Uchino) carrying raw materials from the Far East for the German war effort, arriving at Lorient in August 1943. The main components of the seaplane were originally housed in two large cylinders to port and starboard abaft the conning tower, but the aircraft was removed in 1940 when assembly proved too lengthy a business for operational safety.

Above right
I-8 entering one of the massive bomb-proof U-boat pens at Lorient.

Centre right
I-8 securing in the pen assigned for her stay, protected from British air attack. She was given a royal welcome with a guard of honour and had been escorted in from sea by three *Elbing* class destroyers: the Germans were anxious to make the best possible impression on their Axis partner.

Bottom right
Jollifications for the Japanese crew of *I-8* at a French Chateau included this conga led by a German U-boat officer accordionist. Some of these laughing sailors must still have been on board when, under the later command of (then) Cdr Ariizumi, *I-8* sank two ships totalling 14,118 tons near the Chagos Archipelago on 29 June and 2 July 1944: the survivors of the American liberty ship *Jean Nicolet* (bound from Los Angeles to Calcutta with army stores) were hacked to death or cut about, bound and left to drown—a stain which may well have contributed to Ariizumi's decision to commit suicide before surrendering his final command, *I-400*, at the end of the war.

I-8 cheering ship on sailing from Lorient for Singapore where she berthed on 28 November 1943. The twin 140 mm (5.5 inch) guns were presumably fitted especially for the voyage, replacing the single weapon usually carried. The submarine, by now equipped to carry *Kaiten* human torpedoes but on a standard torpedo operation, was eventually sunk by US destroyers off Okinawa on 31 March 1945.

Japanese *I-37*'s floatplane taken out of the hangar, rigged and positioned on the catapult: the crane arm for lifting the aircraft back on board after landing is on the right.

operational requirements. Captain Ariizumi was left no alternative but to find his fuel elsewhere so, disguised with funnels as a frigate, *I-401* was directed to Dairen in Manchuria where supplies of the precious diesel oil were still available. Unfortunately, while passing between the main Islands of Honshu and Kyūshū she hit a magnetic mine laid a few days earlier by American B-29 bombers. The boat was not critically damaged but it had to return to Kure for repairs where the dummy funnels were transferred to *I-400* who succeeded in reaching Dairen, returning with a full load of oil and supplies.

By this time, despite continuing shortages of fuel, the First Submarine Flotilla had been joined by the two smaller submarine aircraft-carriers *I-13* and *I-14*. It was during a voyage to Chinhae to replenish again that, for the first time, tactical training was conducted under operational conditions.

Repairs to *I-401* were completed in early May and the Flotilla sailed for Nanao Bay on the northern side of Honshu where training would be safer among the secluded coves than around Kure which was now practically beseiged by American submarines and aircraft. However, Nanao Bay soon became too confining for realistic exercises and the submarines were forced out into the open

Inland Sea where, happily, the marauding American boats did not molest them.

At first, almost an entire day was needed for the Seirans to be withdrawn from their hangar, assembled and launched, but after six weeks of intensive practising, this time had been cut to seven minutes for the first aircraft, and three seaplanes could be in the air in little more than 30 minutes after surfacing. Operational exercises began at 0200 in the morning because it would be in these early hours that the Seirans would be launched against their targets. Luminous paint was used at each attachment point to facilitate assembly of the aircraft in the dark.

The preparation of the aircraft for take-off was started while the submarine was preparing to surface. Warmed engine oil and coolant was pumped from tanks in the submarine's hangar to reduce the engine warm-up time while on the catapult—a variant of the arrangement for *M-2* a dozen years before. Once on the surface, the power-operated hangar door was swung open and the Seirans were rolled out in sequence on to the launching track. Here, the wings were unfolded and fixed and the seaplanes were made ready for launching. Ten men were needed to handle the attachment of the

floats alone, an operation that took two and a half minutes. Finally, with the aircraft ready and the pilot already briefed, the submarine's powerful catapult carried them down the fore-deck and into the air.

In July 1945, less two Seirans that had been lost during training, the First Submarine Flotilla returned to its home operating base at Maizuru confident of its ability to carry out an assault on the Canal. Ten Seirans were allocated for the operation: six were to carry torpedoes and four were to drop high explosive bombs. The attack was to be concentrated on the low-water side of the lock-gates, each weighing 600 tons, so that the massive pressure of water they were holding back would assist in their destruction.

No sooner had the Flotilla reached Maizuru than Captain Ariizumi was told that the plan to block the Panama Canal and hold back the tidal wave of Allied Forces now pouring into the Pacific as feared had to be cancelled, despite its importance. Imperial Headquarters believed that invasion of the Japanese mainland was near: all available forces had to be concentrated on defensive operations. Attack being the best means of defence, Ariizumi was directed to concentrate his Seirans on attacking, in Kamikaze

Japanese *I-29* (Type B1) arriving at Bordeaux 10 March 1944 under the watchful eye of the German navy. The seaplane hangar on this occasion was filled with materials much needed by Germany. With a range of 16,000 miles at 16 knots, this kind of large submarine was well suited for the task, but of four boats which attempted the passage from Japan to France, only *I-8* and *I-29* reached their destinations: *I-34* and *I-52* were sunk *en route*. Japan had acquired the U-cruiser *U-125* as a part of the victor's spoils in 1919, and submarines like *I-29* reveal something of the German ancestry. The crew are obviously still fit and alert after the long voyage: although the Japanese navy was modelled at the start on British customs, the sailors here are standing to attention with fingers extended in German style rather than clenched as in the Royal Navy.

JAPANESE I-400 CLASS

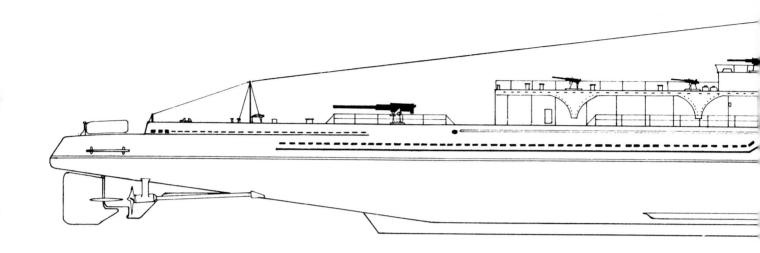

JAPANESE I-400 CLASS DETAILS

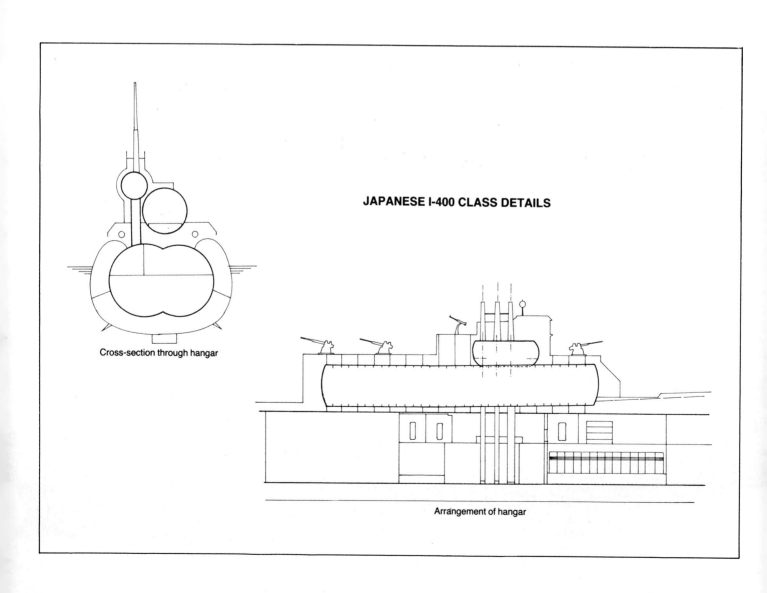

Cross-section through hangar

Arrangement of hangar

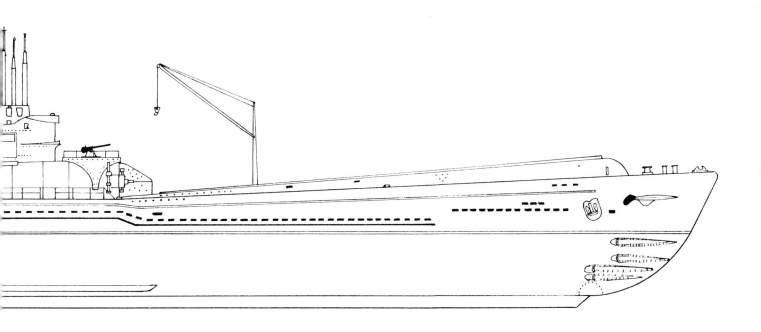

I-402 (converted to a supply carrier) at Kure in 1945. A submarine of the *I-400* class dived in 56 seconds. At the order 'clear the bridge' the lookouts dropped into the conning tower and then hurtled 25 feet down the tube to man their diving stations in the control room below. To cushion their landing, a three-foot thick canvas hassock was positioned at the bottom of the ladder.

The mess table in a large Japanese submarine (*I-169*). The Japanese navy made every effort to ensure that their submarines were provided with good food but it was not easy amidst wartime privations.

style, the American aircraft-carriers that were gathering at Ulithi Atoll.

On 21 July, *I-400* and *I-401* left Maizuru for Omineto Naval Base at the northern tip of Honshu and joined *I-13* and *I-14* which had embarked one land-based reconnaissance aircraft each. The attack upon the American carriers, code-named *Haikari*, was to involve these two reconnaissance aircraft being assembled at Truk Island and then flying westwards 800 miles to confirm that the American Fleet was still at Ulithi. The Seirans, in order to carry their full weapon load, had to be deprived of their floats (the aircraft having to ditch alongside the submarine on return) and Captain Ariizumi could not afford to send unrecoverable and irreplaceable aircraft to the Atoll only to find the Fleet no longer there. Accordingly, *I-13* and *I-14* sailed from Omineto two days ahead of *I-400* and *I-401*.

All four submarines came under heavy attack from American aircraft and anti-submarine surface ships on passage and *I-13* was sunk. *I-14* reached Truk safely after a particularly unpleasant 35 hours dived avoiding an American destroyer. Meanwhile, an electrical fire on board the flagship *I-401* left her unable to dive except, possibly, in an emergency, so Captain Ariizumi changed the rendezvous point with *I-400* to a remote position in the Pacific 950 miles from where the attack would now be launched. For some reason, *I-400* did not receive the new rendezvous signal and on 14 August was waiting off Truk for *I-401* to arrive. The operation was planned for the early hours of 17 August.

The attack never took place. On 16 August, *I-401* received the message that the Emperor had broadcast on the previous day informing his people of the Japanese surrender; the submarine was ordered to return to the nearest Japanese port. Despite

Centre right
I-400 (Cdr Utsunosuke Kusaka) leaving harbour, probably for her final aborted mission to bomb the Panama Canal locks—an operation cancelled in favour of attacking the US fleet at Ulithi Atoll on the Japanese principle that 'a man does not worry about a fire he sees on the horizon when other flames are licking at his *kimono* sleeve.' But fires more terrible than the world had ever dreamed of did more than lick at sleeves when two atom bombs on Japan put an end to all further resistance before *I-400* and her sister *I-401* could launch their aircraft.

Bottom right
Keep-fit class for the ship's company of a large Japanese submarine.

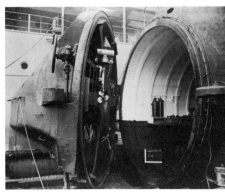

The hydraulically operated hangar door of *I-400* (very similar to *Surcouf*'s) showing the anti-sonar (Asdic) coating employed on external surfaces: this was 2–3 mm thick and consisted mainly of rubber and silica sand powder; it adhered better than the seemingly ineffective German equivalent.

The Japanese submarines *I-400*, *I-401* and *I-14* alongside the tender USS *Proteus* soon after surrender. The American officer first on board *I-400*, Joe Vasey (later Admiral), found the monster submarine 'incredibly filthy, with a layer of grease and left-over food on the decks ... the stench was almost unbearable, particularly near the (oriental style) heads where one of our party lost his breakfast as he was hovering over the sanitary tank opening. That well-known paper product was conspicuous by its absence ... but despite the unhygenic conditions the physical appearance of the crew was remarkably good. Everyone seemed to be lean and alert.' The Japanese said the complement was 187 but the Americans counted 213. Fumigation resulted in a dozen gunny sacks of dead rats.

the Emperor's message, Naval Headquarters merely ordered Operation *Haikari* to be postponed until 25 August but this instruction was countermanded on the following day when all submarines were called back.

On 20 August, Ariizumi was advised to destroy all offensive weapons and important documents. The last order in the Imperial Japanese Navy to fire torpedoes resulted in *I-401* discharging her tubes, reloading and firing again and again until no weapons were left. In the process, one torpedo circled and passed dangerously close to the submarine;

although the warhead was set to safe, it might have caused considerable damage if it had hit. The aircraft in *I-401* were launched, pilotless, into the sea where they quickly sank; but on board *I-400*, the aircraft were simply dragged from the hangar and, with their fuselages slashed, they were pushed over the side. All three remaining *Haikari* submarines were eventually intercepted by American naval forces on their way back to the Japanese mainland and were escorted to Yokosuka Naval Base south of Tokio.

Captain Ariizumi had no intention of surrendering himself and his first thought was to scuttle his flagship, *I-401*. With this privately in mind he ordered the boat to dive but on reflection he decided to ensure the safety of the crew. Surfacing, he set course for Tokio. Just before entering the bay he placed a service pistol to his head and shot himself. In a last letter, he expressed remorse for subjecting the men under his command to the shameful situation of surrender, which Imperial Navy men and ships had never before experienced.

After the war, *I-400* and *I-401* were taken to America. They were sunk as gunnery targets off the American coast in 1946. *I-402*, converted to a supply submarine, was surrendered at Kure and taken to Sasebo where she was sunk by the Americans off Goto Island in April 1946.

Thus, like so many of the monster submersibles, the giant *I-400* submarines never took part in any operation for which they were intended. Events overtook them, but there is little doubt about their capabilities: they were, potentially at least, by far the best submersible aircraft-carriers ever built in any navy.[5]

The Russian *Krab*, the first purpose-built submarine minelayer in any navy, undergoing trials at Sevastopol in 1915. The *Krab* was a failure in almost every respect, whilst the long line of small, early German *UC* boats, with sloping near-vertical mine chutes, which started to emerge in April of the same year, achieved notable successes: *UC-1*, alone, sank 59,000 tons of Allied shipping with her mines. Even the prototype minelayer *UB-12*, completed in March 1915, caused the loss of 22 ships totalling 10,234 tons.

Below
UC-2, by no means a monster at 168/183 tons but carrying twelve mines in six chutes.

Bottom right
UC-27, equipped with three torpedo tubes as well as six mine-chutes for eighteen mines, but not oversized at 410/490 tons. A crew of three officers and 23 men was sufficient for this very effective type of submarine. *UC-27* sent to the bottom, by one means or another, 52 merchant ships (67,471 tons) and one warship in 1917 and 1918; she herself survived the war.

Below
Loading a mine into one of the later and larger *UC* boats.

6: Great Minelayers

Practically every submarine since the beginning of World War One has been capable of carrying mines; and the Russian navy started much earlier than that. Submarines are excellent vehicles for mine-laying: compared with surface minelayers, they run little risk of detection and can be expected to lay substantial fields more accurately than aircraft. The disadvantages in using submarines are the time they take to transit to and from enemy inshore waters (although this is now overcome by nuclear power) and, usually, a sacrifice in the number of torpedoes that would otherwise be carried, with a consequent reduction in fighting power if called upon to attack targets directly during their missions. It is the latter point in particular which has tended in recent years to lead naval staffs in the west away from the concept of submarine minelaying. And, as a corollary, singularly little is said—publicly anyway—about the threat which submarines of potential enemies might pose in this way. Yet, it is not too hard to imagine what the effect might be of minefields laid covertly and anonymously around, say, the Falkland Islands or in focal areas anywhere during times of tension.

A few statistics from World War Two illustrate the devastating results that submarine-laid (and, therefore, secret) minefields can achieve. A total of 658 mines were sown by Allied, mainly USN, submarines in the Pacific where the minelaying effort eventually came to be concentrated. This resulted in 27 Japanese ships being sunk or damaged beyond repair; and another 27 were damaged but repairable. For each dozen inexpensive mines laid, therefore, one was successful at huge cost to the enemy. No submarines in the Pacific were lost while minelaying. On the other hand, submarines of all navies suffered heavily from running on to mines themselves. Between 1939 and 1945, twenty-six out of 75 British submarines lost (not including seven X-craft) are known or presumed to have been sunk by this hidden underwater menace—more than one-third of the total of losses.

There is reason to think that these figures have been forgotten; but the dangers today are considerably greater than they were 40 years ago. Firing systems sensitive to magnetic-field changes and acoustic or pressure influences as well as physical contact are extremely difficult to counter: it is impossible to believe that any ship or submarine can either be sure of detecting and avoiding mines or render itself entirely safe by any conceivable methods of self-protection. Yet, only a very few modern authoritative writers, notable amongst them the French Rear-Admiral Hubert Moineville,[1] have pointed out the immense influence which mines are likely to have on future naval strategy, observing that minelayers (which, of course, include submarines amongst their number) are spreading their potential areas of activity to deep water where an enormous extension of the threat can be exercised. Mine-warfare, Moineville predicts with convincing logic, will be employed in offensive operations as well as for establishing defences in one's own waters and limiting the enemy's strategic freedom of action in his surrounding seas.

It is, perhaps, as well to remember that Russian Tsarist and successive Soviet submariners have, from the earliest days, regarded mine-laying as a most important function; they have ample experience to build on now and in the future.

In contrast to the Soviet view, minelaying was emphatically not a popular diversion for the majority of United States and British submariners in the last world war. The results were not immediately apparent if, indeed, they were ever known—and Allied submariners disliked exchanging familiar torpedoes for clumsy mines which were difficult to handle and slow to lay. Furthermore, the specialised British minelayers of the *Porpoise* class, each carrying 60 standard Mark VIII moored mines, were, by the standards of the day, big boats, ill-suited to inshore operations where enemy anti-submarine measures were strongest. Memories of the losses incurred by submarines specifically designed to carry mines were probably another reason for turning attention away from this field of submarine activity after the war.

When submarine mines were specially constructed to fit 21-inch torpedo tubes, the requirement for purpose-built mine-layers in western navies was thought to have lapsed: but it seems odd that torpedo armament should willingly thereby have been sacrificed when it had proved entirely practicable to instal vertical mine-chutes externally with little or no loss of torpedo armament. For example, there were sixteen mines in the saddle tanks of half-a-dozen British E-class submarines built *ad hoc* during World War One at the marginal cost of two beam tubes; and HMS *Tetrarch* was similarly equipped, for a brief trial period, at the beginning of World War Two. There were similar but improved arrangements in German U-boats of both World Wars. The six French submarines of the *Saphir* class had one of the best systems with 32 moored mines in external wells: the best known of these, *Rubis*, laid 683 of these in a record-breaking 28 patrols between 1940 and 1944, claiming fourteen supply ships, seven AS vessel and mine-sweepers, and damage to one supply ship and a U-boat.

These capabilities must surely have been noted carefully by the Soviet Navy. It would not necessarily be obvious to an outside observer that any particular submarine was carrying mines in external, let alone internal, tanks or stowages. Nor need submarine performance be markedly affected, if at all, provided that a partial double hull was acceptable.

All in all, the lesson from two world wars seems to be that purpose-built submarine minelayers are unnecessary and that quite simple external modifications to incorporate mine-chutes could enable several types of diesel-electric submarines, and possibly some with nuclear propulsion, to carry a sizeable number of mines while retaining a full load of torpedoes. Furthermore, mine-chutes, unlike standard torpedo tubes, can be built to any size so as to accommodate various kinds of mine.

Two giant purpose-built mine-layers, HMS *M-3* and USS *Argonaut*, deserve attention because either of their quite different systems could form the basis of a multi-purpose minelayer today; *Argonaut*'s installation in a modified form might be included in a nuclear design without involving too much new technology.

USS *Argonaut* at Pearl Harbor, probably in early 1942, showing lines which recall the German U-cruisers of World War I. It was her wide-ranging Pacific role with two 6-inch guns as well as torpedoes, rather than her mines alone, which dictated her 3,046/4,164 tons displacement.

The *V-4* design which was to become USS *Argonaut* (*SM-1*, ex-*SF-7*, ex-*SS-166*) was drawn up between 1923 and 1925, and was unlike any other submarine built in the United States or elsewhere. With a length of 381 feet, *V-4* was the longest USN submarine ever—until the nuclear-powered and almost immediately redundant[2] radar picket USS *Triton* (*SSBN 586*) was laid down in 1956. *V-4* had, for the first time, the high flat-sided bow derived from World War One German U-boats which was to be a standard feature of all successive US submarines until after World War Two;[3] but the significant innovation was the mine-stowage aft for 60 Mark XI moored mines, each of which was 69 inches long and 40 inches in diameter, and two large launching tubes at the stern.

The stowage area aft was divided, rather pessimistically, into two compartments with watertight doors between them so that if flooding accidentally occurred through the launching tubes (which had hydraulically operated vertical doors), the submarine, which had an unusually large 21.8 per cent reserve of buoyancy, would remain afloat so long as only the aftermost compartment was flooded. However, it is doubtful whether she could have surfaced from any great depth in this condition (her maximum diving depth was 300 feet), and it is certain that she could not have remained controllable submerged.

A long tube ran along the bottom of both stowage compartments: this itself held eight mines and, when these had been discharged, it was used as a compensating tank to adjust the trim while successive mines were laid. Immediate trimming, and flooding and draining of the launch tubes, was accomplished by a WRM (Water Around Mine) tank roughly equivalent to the WRT tank used for a similar purpose with torpedo

Below left and right
When USS *Argonaut* was modernised at Mare Island in 1942, and before being converted for the Makin Island raid, two external stern torpedo tubes were added to the armament together with two storage tubes for reloads. The stated purpose was to enable the tubes to be reloaded at sea on the surface; but, like *Surcouf*, the intention must surely have been to seek shelter in some bay or inlet at one of the many islands involved in the Pacific War because it would have been totally impractical to carry out this evolution in the open sea in other than flat calm weather out of range of enemy aircraft.

tubes. There was a good deal of pumping and flooding to be done and the drill was by no means simple when dropping mines at the intended rate of eight in ten minutes. This rate, incidentally, was much slower than the British *Porpoise*-class with their external power-driven chain-conveyor system permitting a manageable dropping interval of 30 seconds. Assuming a submarine speed of not less than 2.5 knots, the minimum speed at which the hydroplanes could reasonably be expected to keep control of any boat while laying, this meant that *Argonaut*'s mines could be laid no closer than 312 feet apart, which compares with the denser fields laid by *Porpoise* and her sisters where the mines could be separated by as little as 120 feet.

The handling arrangements in *Argonaut* were difficult and it is questionable whether the crew ever had sufficient experience in peacetime to become fully proficient, because even exercise mines were expensive. The heavy, fat black cylinders were moved by hydraulically-driven worm shafts into rotating cages which offered up the mines to the tube inner doors. It sounds quite rational and there was nothing intrinsically wrong with the arrangement, but it was necessarily noisy and undeniably complex: the task of the team aft would not be envied by modern submariners, but doubtless a much quieter, simpler system could be produced today.

Whatever capabilities as a minelayer she might have had, *Argonaut* was never employed as such. Originally laid down in May 1925 and commissioned on 2 April 1928, *Argonaut* did not lay a single mine in anger. In 1942, she was hastily converted to a troop carrier in order to transport 120 Marines of the Second Raider Battalion in company with USS *Nautilus* who carried a similar contingent. The battalion was led by Colonel Evans F Carlson who had with him Major James Roosevelt, son of the President, and their orders were to carry out a raid on Makin Island which Admiral Nimitz hoped would divert Japanese forces from Guadalcanal. The Makin Island raid was held to be highly successful although the strategic results were probably nil: Carlson's raiders were widely acclaimed, even if the submariners were rather neglected in the general celebrations that followed.

At that stage of the war, it was the best use that *Argonaut* could be put to. The supposed success of Makin Island led to her being despatched to Brisbane with the sensible object of relieving the more operational fleet submarines from the special missions continually demanded by General MacArthur: these mainly involved carrying land-

ing parties and supplies to Japanese-occupied islands.

Unfortunately, Captain (later Admiral) 'Jimmy' Fife, who was in command at Brisbane, had formed a firm belief that the poor results of US submarines based there under his predecessor Ralph Christie had been due to over-caution. He was anxious for all his boats to prove that they could fight—and that included *Argonaut* now *en route* under Lieutenant Commander Jack Pierce. In this, Fife misjudged *Argonaut*'s ability to act as a standard patrol submarine. Pierce was a

The giant submarines *Nautilus* and *Argonaut*—hastily converted to troop carriers to transport thirteen marine officers and 198 marines to Makin Island—returning (less 30 of the original number) to Pearl Harbor after the raid in August 1942. Conditions on board for the troops were unpleasant. The marines suffered from heat and seasickness and the wardrooms had to be used as operating theatres for the wounded.

The extraordinarily successful but moderate-sized 762/923-ton Free French submarine minelayer *Rubis* being inspected by Admiral Muselier. The Admiral is in turn being inspected by the intrepid Bacchus who accompanied *Rubis* on her patrols and was awarded the Valiant Dogs' Decoration by the National Canine Defence League.

brave man and loyal. In unquestioning obedience to orders by radio, while nominally in transit but diverted to patrol in the hazardous area between New Britain and Bougainville south of St George's Channel, he directed his giant and cumbersome submarine towards an escorted convoy of five freighters on 10 January 1943. Perhaps unwisely, he went for one of the destroyers first and achieved a hit which was, by chance, witnessed by a US Army aircraft passing overhead. The two other escorting destroyers raced to counter-attack, dropping depth charges over a positive datum. The

aircraft overhead watched helplessly as *Argonaut*'s great bow broke surface. The submarine was obviously out of control and the forward casing remained visible at a steep angle while shells pounded into it. Then, in moments, it slid below the sea and disappeared from view. *Argonaut* went down with 105 officers and men, the greatest number lost in any USN submarine during the war.

It was a sad and, submariners might say, a needless loss. The huge boat never fulfilled her rightful role; and misemployment, the bugbear of submariners on all sides in too

Rubis (Capitaine de Corvette H. L. G. Rousselot DSO, DSC) stopped and unable to dive 40 miles off the Norwegian coast on 22 August 1941 after being damaged by her own torpedoes, fired too close to the target, following a minelay. The photograph was taken by a (fortunately) friendly aircraft and a strong escort brought her safely home to Dundee. *Rubis* carried 32 mines outside the pressure hull in four groups of four vertical wells, each loaded with two mines one above the other. She made a record-breaking 28 patrols, laying 683 mines which resulted in the sinking of fourteen supply ships (totalling 21,410 tons), seven A/S ships and minesweepers and damage to one supply ship and a U-boat. *Rubis* survived the war and was scrapped in 1950.

HMS *M-3* diving with her 12-inch gun before conversion to a minelayer.

M-3 alongside at Fort Blockhouse in about 1930.

Above left
M-3 from the port quarter showing the 'clam' mining door.

Above right
HMS *L-17*, completed 30 September 1918, carried sixteen mines. The holes in the starboard saddle tank are visible in this photograph from above in harbour; but it would have been very hard to detect her minelaying role in normal circumstances at sea—a significant point when considering the possibility that apparently normal submarines may carry mines now or in the future.

Left
Four of the six wartime British minelayers showing the bridges displaced to starboard to allow the endless chain and rack system carrying 50 mines to pass over almost the full length of the hull beneath the casing. From inboard: *Rorqual* (the only survivor in the war), *Grampus*, *Porpoise* (first of class completed in March 1933) and *Narwhal*.

Below
The *Porpoise* class minelayers were not immune to heavy rolling.

many circumstances, brought her brief but gallant wartime career to an end.

USS *Argonaut* was still completing at Portsmouth Navy Yard, New Hampshire when HMS *M-3* arrived in Chatham on 13 June 1927 for a major refit and a change of role that would rival the American would-be minelayer. *M-3* had not been operationally employed since the exercise in November 1925 during which her sister submarine *M-1* was rammed and sunk. While being the only sea-going boat in the Experimental half-Flotilla based at Portsmouth in 1926, her only notable task had been to help supply electrical power (together with *K-26* and *L-23*) to the Royal Victoria and Albert and the King George V London Docks from 9–14 May during the General Strike: it was an unpopular duty aptly titled 'Operation Blackcurrent'; but *M-3* alone kept four meat-refrigeration plants, two cranes and some important bilge and tunnel pumps going with up to 1500 amps at 480 volts DC—the equivalent of almost 750 hp.

On 15 October, *M-3* had been placed in reserve and now, at Chatham, her 12-inch and 3-inch guns were removed to make way for a vast free-flooding superstructure extending over about two-thirds of the submarine's length from the after bulkhead of the torpedo stowage compartment right aft to the stern, by-passing the bridge and conning tower.

Two sets of mine rails ran along the pressure hull inside this casing to carry 100 standard Type B contact mines on their sinker-trollies. The mines were laid, surfaced or submerged, by means of chain-conveyor gear through a single large door at the stern

Above left
His Majesty King Edward VIII inspects the minelayer
HMS *Narwhal* shortly before his abdication on
11 December 1936.

Above right
A mine being loaded on board HMS *Porpoise*. A great
advantage of the system in this kind of minelayer was
that standard mines could be used.

which slid up and over the waiting mines and into a recess. The original four 18-inch torpedo tubes forward, with four reloads, and four Lewis guns for mounting on the bridge were retained.

The conversion, which for political reasons was called a refit, was completed at the remarkably low cost of £10,235 on 8 October 1928 and *M-3* finished post-refit trials by the middle of November. Simplicity had won the day. Only 80 mines were carried initially but the remaining twenty were embarked later. The system immediately proved satisfactory in an experimental lay of 79 mines in December 1929 and the mines themselves functioned correctly with only two cases of depth error amounting to six feet in each case: what happened to the eightieth mine is not recorded. Sufficient was learned to proceed straight away with the construction of HMS *Porpoise*, the lead submarine of six new minelayers each of which would carry 50 Mark XVI mines.

M-3 herself was only regarded as experimental, and that was just as well because however good her minelaying gear might have been, her diving capabilities were grossly impaired by the slow-flooding mine casing which held 600 tons of water when it eventually filled. The diving time with mines embarked was ominously reminiscent of the K-boats; and certain other characteristics revived unhappy memories in the older officers and ratings. The least time to submerge in calm conditions was five minutes and it took thirteen minutes or more for her to get under if it was rough. In bad weather she had to start her dive head to sea until the casing filled; she then had to turn beam-on in order to submerge fully. In a sea state 3 and

above, or in any considerable swell, the submarine was 'definitely unreliable'[4] at periscope depth (33 feet). Control submerged could seldom be maintained below two and a half knots and, if steering a course bow or stern to a moderate sea, the minimum speed was about five and a half knots—a speed that exhausted the battery in four or five hours at best. Meanwhile, the submarine had to be trimmed heavy. If allowed to drift up above 30 feet with supposedly neutral buoyancy, she had an irresistible trick of continuing to rise until the bridge broke surface with an angle of four degrees bow down—a most uncomfortable and confusing situation for the officer-of-the-watch and the planesmen. Conversely, if just a touch too heavy, she went on sinking bodily when the depth gauge needle passed 35 feet.

Keeping periscope depth was an exciting business. The cause of these very serious limitations, leaving aside her trace of K-boat blood, was, according to the Director of Naval Construction (who ought to have foreseen the problem) 'the bad shape of the casing which is very susceptible to wave action when submerged and the wrong weight distribution due to most of the mines being aft which made *M-3* heavy by the stern till the mines became water-borne.'[5] A great deal of attention was paid to the casing-design of the *Porpoises*, and their mines were limited to a single row.

It is not surprising that the head of the Submarine Service (Rear Admiral Nasmith, vc, of *E-11* fame) was, by May 1930, 'definitely of the opinion that at present *M-3* is not efficient or reliable as a submarine and could not with safety be used in war.'[6]

HMS *M-3* was due to be scrapped in 1933

but, in light of these unfavourable reports, the date was brought forward and the Director of Navy Contracts informed Rear Admiral(S) on 19 February 1932 that she had been sold for breaking up to Mr John Cashmore, Great Bridge, Staffordshire.

Despite deficiencies in the submarine itself, the external minelaying gear was certainly preferable, at the time anyway, to the internal arrangements in USS *Argonaut*. The *Porpoise*-class, which directly resulted from experience with *M-3*, functioned very well. The six of them laid 2599 mines in all during the war, with *Rorqual*, the sole survivor by the end, laying 1284. The cost, however, was heavy: five of the minelayers were lost (HMS *Seal* actually being captured) during operations of one kind or another, but the reasons were not all related directly to minelaying. All that can be said is that these submersible minelayers were noisy and large, displacing 2117 tons dived, with a length of 293 feet; they were obviously vulnerable to detection and attack by anti-submarine forces in the shallow, inshore areas where they were sent. Moreover, their commanding officers were not tactically minded. It is hard to disagree with Nasmith's opinion of *M-3*: she could not have lasted long in the sort of war which British submarines were called upon to fight from 1939 to 1945.

PART 2
Midgets

Net-cutting exercise.

7: The Mock Turtle Midget

In July 1802, the *Naval Chronicle*, that extraordinarily well-intelligenced 'Monthly Register of Naval Events', reported an account by Monsieur St Aubin, a man of letters of Paris and a member of the *Tribunale*, giving an account of a certain *bateau-plongeur*—'a Diving-boat, lately discovered by Mr Fulton, an American'. St Aubin wrote:

I have just been to inspect the plan and section of the NAUTILUS *or Diving-boat, invented by Mr Fulton, similar to that [with] which he lately made his curious and interesting experiments at Havre and Brest.*

The Diving-boat, in the construction of which he is now employed [NAUTILUS *was launched in May 1800], will be spacious enough to contain 8 men and provisions enough for 20 days, and will be of sufficient strength and power to enable him to plunge 100 feet under water, if necessary. He has contrived a reservoir for air, which will enable 8 men to remain under water for 8 hours. When the boat is above water, it has two sails and looks just like a common boat. When she is to dive, the mast and sails are struck.*

In making his experiments at Havre, Mr Fulton not only remained a whole hour under water with three of his companions, but held his boat parallel to the horizon at any given depth. He proved the compass points as correctly under water as on the surface, and demonstrated that, while under water, the boat made way at the rate of half a league an hour, by means contrived to that purpose.

It is not twenty years since all Europe was astonished at the first ascension of men in balloons; perhaps in a few years hence they will not be less surprised to see a flotilla of Diving-boats, which, on a given signal, shall, to avoid the pursuit of an enemy, plunge underwater, and rise again several leagues from the place where they descended.

The invention of balloons has hitherto been of no advantage because no means have been found to direct their course. But if such means could be discovered, what would become of camps, cannon, fortresses and the whole art of war?

But if we have not succeeded in steering the balloon, and even were it impossible to attain that object, the case is different with the Diving-boat, which can be conducted under water in the same manner as on the surface. It has the advantage of sailing like a common boat, and also of diving when it is pursued. With these qualities it is fit for carrying secret orders to succour a blockaded port and to examine the force and position of an enemy in their own harbours. These are sure and evident benefits, which the Diving-boat at present provides. But who can see all the circumstances of the discovery, or the improvements of which it is susceptible?

Mr Fulton has already added to his boat a machine by means of which he blew up a large boat in the port of Brest; and if by future experiments, the same effect could be produced on frigates or ships of the line, what will become of maritime wars, and where will sailors be found to man ships of war, when it is a physical certainty that they may every moment be blown into the air by means of a Diving-boat, against which no human foresight can guard them?

This report, written three years before the Battle of Trafalgar, sums up pretty well the original concept of submarine warfare. It was all to do with attacking or defending harbours and anchorages. Hence, midget submarine warfare, of the kind practised during the 1914–18 and 1939–45 wars dates back a good deal further than underwater warfare in the open seas. Indeed, it is logical that it should do so: not only were submersibles incapable of venturing far afield until the advent of diesel power a few years before World War One, but concentrations of shipping in harbour were obvious targets for covert reconnaissance and attack while submersibles were also ideal blockade runners.

Disregarding altogether the dubious claims of submarine pre-history in the sixteenth and seventeenth centuries, the idea of what would now be called midget submarine operations belongs, however, not to Fulton, whose inventions are well recorded, but to David Bushnell, who constructed his tiny semi-submersible *Turtle* during the American War of Independence. Unfortunately, the tales about the *Turtle* and its use against the blockading British Fleet at New York in 1776 are a good deal less reliable than history of Fulton and his *Nautilus*. The stories were fostered by growing American national pride, and they have to be taken with a large pinch of sea-salt. What really took place during the first submerged attack ever attempted will never be known. Even with clearer hindsight, aided by modern physiological and engineering knowledge, together with recent (and hopefully objective) research, it still needs imagination to visualise what happened; but it is at least possible now to sift the legends and edge closer to the likely truth than most history books allow.

David Bushnell, the son of a farmer, was born in Saybrook (later Westbrook), Connecticut. His formal education as a boy in the one-room village school amounted to the three R's and little more; but he foraged books from his family and friends and over the years made himself proficient in the sciences and mathematics. He was 27 when his father died and, free of family obligations, he sold his inheritance so that in 1771 he could enter Yale University, where he became class-mate and friend of Nathan Hale, the future patriot-spy.

Bushnell was apparently unprepossessing in appearance and physically weak but he had a remarkably agile and inventive mind. While on the farm he built a harrow with springy teeth that passed over and around the heavy stones on the New England fields rather than breaking off as the rigid teeth on the standard implements were apt to do. He also devised a way of insulating the walls of the isolated family farmhouse with marsh-grass to keep out the damp, salt fogs of winter. At Yale, he enrolled in a divinity course but, finding this too narrow for his tastes, he applied his mind to subjects far removed from theology, amongst them the effects of underwater explosives.

It was the theory of the time, which Bushnell disputed, that an explosion in water would dissipate itself and do no damage. Even in October 1805, more than 30 years after Bushnell started experimenting, English spectators were still perplexed by the destruction of the brig *Dorothea* off Deal

Full scale seven-foot high model of the *Turtle* built by Scicon Ltd, a leading designer of modern submarine systems, on display at the Royal Navy Submarine Museum, Gosport. It is impossible to be sure what the original *Turtle* really looked like but the model gives a fair impression.

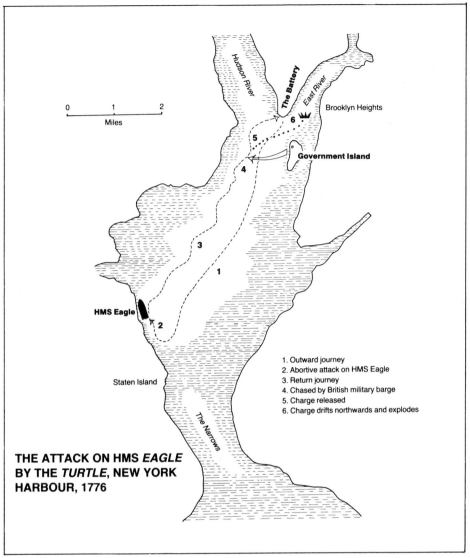

1. Outward journey
2. Abortive attack on HMS Eagle
3. Return journey
4. Chased by British military barge
5. Charge released
6. Charge drifts northwards and explodes

THE ATTACK ON HMS *EAGLE* BY THE *TURTLE*, NEW YORK HARBOUR, 1776

when a 'torpedo' (mine) was tested against the evidently expendable ship:

It is impossible to describe a more complete decomposition of a Vessel, or a more dreadful crash of materials. It was perhaps one of the most curious Experiments which has been made in modern times, for who would not have concluded that the powder would spend its force on the water, which is moveable, and not pass through the strong framed bottom of a Vessel? Why was the report arising from the explosion so inconsiderable, when the effect was so great?[1]

Bushnell had long ago discovered the answers to these questions, using small barrels of gunpowder and simple clockwork detonating devices. Although chiefly remembered for his *Turtle*, he was the originator of the naval mine as well as, in his own words, 'several other machines for the Annoyance of shipping'. It was, in fact, the possibilities of mines (or 'torpedoes' as they were called for many years) that led him to explore the possibilities of underwater craft to carry them.

Mines could be floated downstream towards an enemy fleet and might cause alarm—as they certainly did in the famous Battle of the Kegs when a string of them let loose on the British Fleet off Philadelphia at

Christmas 1777 generated enough annoyance to satisfy the most ardent Colonialist; but it was only by chance that they would do any damage, and they might even turn with the tide and endanger friendly vessels.

An 'infernal machine' or 'torpedo' had to be conveyed secretly and directly to its target, argued Bushnell. A rowing skiff was bound to be seen; and a diver's crude apparatus of the day would never manage the job in deep water at any distance from the shore. A submarine was the answer and Bushnell turned to the principle proposed by William Bourne two centuries before. Somehow he managed to keep up his studies while, over a period of four years, the *Turtle* took shape at the Saybrook Farm with the help of David's brother Ezra.

The difficulties of design and construction were formidable, but the fermenting unrest and eventually open warfare between 1771 and 1775 lent urgency and purpose to the

project even though it cost Bushnell the bulk of his father's legacy, the only money that he had.

There are various accounts of the *Turtle*, one being a lengthy description from Bushnell himself, but there are no contemporary drawings and Bushnell may have destroyed the original plans to avoid them being discovered by pro-British Tories. In a letter dated 13 October 1787, Bushnell described his submarine thus to Thomas Jefferson, then in Paris as American Minister to France:

The external shape of the Submarine Vessel bore some resemblance to two upper Tortoise shells of equal size, joined together ... the inside was capable of containing the Operator and air sufficient to supply him thirty minutes...

Nobody would claim that the models, one of them full-sized and about 7 feet high, in the

Above
The Irish-American John Philip Holland, the father of modern submarines, noted the supposed success of the *Turtle* and the real achievement of the Confederate *Hunley*, itself inspired by David Bushnell's invention, which sank the Northern ironclad frigate *Housatonic* during the Civil War in 1864. This is Holland's first 'submarine boat', launched 22 May 1878 and now at the Paterson Museum, New Jersey.

Right
Simon Lake was another inventor ultimately, if not consciously, indebted to David Bushnell. This is his *Protector* of 1902.

Above
USS *Holland* (SS-1) undergoing repairs in 1900.

Left
Torpedoes became the natural weapons for submarines in the latter part of the nineteenth century and the idea of screwing an explosive container to a target's hull or towing a charge beneath it was abandoned other than by midgets. However, J P Holland devised a novel weapon-system which anticipated submarine missiles for *Holland VI* (later USS *Holland*) with a bow Zalinski pneumatic gun. The six-foot projectile (top right hand corner) is being tested here at Perth Amboy, New Jersey in the spring of 1898. A similar weapon had been fired successfully from Holland's *Fenian Ram* in 1881. (R. K. Morris Collection).

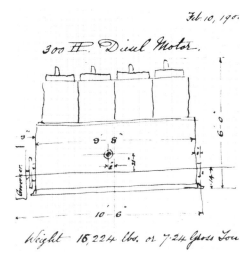

Feb. 10, 190.
300 H. Diesel Motor.

Weight 16,224 lbs. or 7.24 Gross Tons

Foot and hand-powered propellers gave way to steam plants, petrol engines and electric motors from the 1870s on; but J. P. Holland was, as usual, ahead of his time when he proposed a 'diesel motor' with this sketch dated 10 February 1900. He well understood the advantages of this engine over the petroleum Otto which powered most of his early submarines on the surface: a year earlier he had tried, unsuccessfully, to negotiate with Adolphus Busch, the American representative for the Diesel Motor Company, for engines of this type. However, diesels did not start appearing in submarines until about 1908. They proved to be the only safe engines for midgets.

Royal Navy Submarine Museum at Gosport are exact replicas, but they probably give a fair impression of what the craft was like.

In the early trials, the operator was Ezra Bushnell—David himself was not strong enough to do all that was needed. The *Turtle* was most probably propelled by means of a foot-pedalled two-bladed propeller whose blades were said to be constructed like the vanes of a windmill but only 12 inches long and 4 inches wide. Flat out, leg-work ought to have achieved a speed of 3 knots but it must have been desperately hard going. Some reports speak of a *hand*-cranked oar or 'an oar formed on the principle of the (Achimedian) screw' instead of a propeller (which did not publicly emerge in recognisable form until 1833–1836), but the 'vanes of a windmill' description is believable and could apply to a pitched pair of paddle-blades, a forerunner of Fulton's 'fly'. But, in whatever way the blades were shaped, it would certainly have been easier to use feet rather than hands for motive power.

A 200 pound mass of lead ballast, which could be let down on a 50-foot line to the bottom as an anchor or as a means of getting rid of weight in a hurry, kept the oddly-shaped vessel upright and, with the added weight of the operator, sank it low in the water so that little more than the upper hatch and the glass eyelet holes in the hatch-coaming were visible above the surface. More precise trimming was accomplished by

a kingston-valve, worked by one foot, to admit water to a chamber at the base of the craft and by a ballast forcing pump, worked by hand, to eject water when necessary. By this means, together with a vertical propeller (or screw-oar) and a rudder, it was possible, in theory, to submerge to a depth of several feet with a reasonable degree of control over the course, trim and depth. In ideal conditions and calm water, the system could conceivably have worked in practice, but a latter day midget submariner would view it with the gravest of grave misgivings.

Air was taken in through tubes passing through the upper hatch and fitted, like schnorchel masts, with shut-off valves. All inlets and outlets were carefully covered with perforated plates which admitted water or air but prevented them being choked by debris.

The weapon system consisted of a clockwork-fused 150-pound watertight package of gunpowder. This was attached by a lanyard to a detachable auger—a large, pointed screw that could be rotated from inside the craft so as to pierce a target's wooden hull from below. When the 'torpedo' was firmly fixed in place, the *Turtle* would retire.

In darkness or when below the surface, a faintly luminescent compass gave the operator a very rough indication of his course. A simple glass tube or 'watergage', 18 inches high and one inch in diameter, sealed at the top and open to the sea through a hull connection at the bottom, indicated the depth by means of a floating phosphorescent cork.

It was partly due to problems with the hand-operated piston ballast-pump and partly to an unexpected lack of phosphorescent material—just the sort of minor detail that has always bedevilled submarine building programmes—that seems to have prevented the *Turtle* from being sent against the British Fleet at Boston in 1775 after the first clash between British troops and the American militia which occurred at Lexington on 19 April. Fox-fire, the only source of phosphorescence available, came from rotten stump-wood and had a short life which evidently ended with the initial trials. In the autumn of 1775, heavy frosts extinguished further supplies. No more replacement material would be available until the next spring at earliest; and, because even Benjamin Franklin could not suggest any alternative illumination other than a candle—which used up precious air too quickly if kept lit—there was no choice but to abandon operations until 1776.

By the time that the essential fox-fire had

showed itself again, the *Turtle* itself was leaky and Bushnell's brother was badly out of practise. Caulking and repairs were put in hand and the *Turtle* was transported in secrecy down to New York where British ships were known to be and where there was a secure base at the Battery (at the southern tip of Manhattan) to operate from.

Practises were recommenced and a few days after 4 July 1776, when the Declaration of Independence of the United States was signed, Ezra Bushnell was ready for business. The prime target was soon obvious: HMS *Eagle*, wearing the flag of Admiral Lord Howe, freshly arrived from England to command the blockading fleet, had moored conveniently close to the north-eastern point of Staten Island on 13 July. The flagship was near enough for General Putnam's troops on the Brooklyn Heights across the Narrows to claim that they could smell the Englishmen when the wind was right.

Now bad luck struck again. Brother Ezra took a fever and, by August, he was still manifestly unfit for the planned operation. Generals Israel Putnam and George Washington held an urgent meeting to discuss the situation. Both were eager to send the *Turtle* into action against the enemy at the earliest possible moment and, accordingly, a volunteer was sought to carry out the enterprise in the place of the man who had the experience of five years behind him.

A brave soldier of good character, one Ezra Lee, a Sergeant from Old Lyme, Connecticut, duly stepped forward. Days and nights of arduous training followed in Long Island Sound; but it could scarcely be hoped, even after a month or more, that the sergeant would equal his predecessor's skill. Nonetheless, Bushnell was satisfied that Lee could do the job, and towards midnight on either 5 or, more likely, 6 September, with the moon full and the tide ebbing, a rowing boat put out from Whitehall Stairs at the Battery. The *Turtle* was secured alongside, bobbing gently with the waves, and the boat made off with muffled oars in the direction of the British flagship some five miles distant.

It is from this point, where Lee pressed on alone, that traditional versions of the world's archetypal submarine operation have to be questioned. But let them be questioned with respect and understanding—respect over the years for individual ingenuity, skill and bravery coupled with more recent understanding of how submarine operations are subject to gossip and rumour by ill-informed commentators and to exaggeration for the sake of propaganda, which is, after all, a perfectly legitimate weapon of war.[3]

Above left
One of the first operational schnorchels, which David Bushnell anticipated by more than a century and a half: the Netherlands submarine *O-19* trying out the device just before the outbreak of World War Two. The periscope is on the left, then the intake and exhaust aft on the right.

Above right
The first type of British 'snort' mast (postwar) seen through the search periscope in low power. The 'gefuffle' is from the submerged exhaust.

The sergeant said—or is reputed to have said—that he succeeded in cranking his way up to and under the 74-gun *Eagle* unobserved, although the tide at first carried him past and he had to pedal strenuously to regain position until the tide slackened. But once there, with the ship's stern above him, he could not make the auger bite home. It was thought that either he was unable to penetrate the copper sheathing (commonly fitted to prevent similar but much more devastating attacks by the Teredo worm) or that he kept striking the iron bars strengthening the quarter section and connecting the rudder to the hull. And, anyway, as the drill drove upwards, so the *Turtle* was forced downwards.

Lee's repeated efforts (the story continues) failed to attach the charge and, with day breaking and the tide flooding, he decided to abandon the attempt. On the way back he found himself being chased by a British military barge which had put out from enemy-occupied Governor's Island where soldiers on the parapet espied the strange object and crowded to watch with amazement as it drifted northwards on 'a very irregular zig-zag track' (no wonder) while poor Lee pedalled and strove, with his compass now 'out of order', to find the way home by opening the hatch at frequent intervals and peering out.

Lee, in desperation, released the explosive knapsack to decoy his pursuers: it was, anyway, hindering his frantic navigation. It drifted past Governor's Island until the one-hour delay ran out its time whereupon 'it unpinioned a strong lock resembling a gun

lock, which gave fire to the powder'. The gunpowder 'exploded with great violence' at the entrance to the East River where General Putnam and his Staff watched while 'large columns of water and pieces of wood that composed it' were blown 'high in the air'. Meanwhile, the *Turtle* was sighted from the Battery and towed back to Whitehall Stairs by a boat sent out to fetch the exhausted pilot. During the few days of good weather that remained to the autumn of 1776 two more attempted attacks were made on ships in the Hudson River above New York, but they, too, achieved nothing.

The considerations which argue against contemporary and subsequent reports have now to be stated, albeit with regret. They may as well be listed categorically. First, HMS *Eagle* was not copper-sheathed until several years after the *Turtle* affair, and, if iron straps were the obstruction, surely Lee could not continually have struck the narrow area that they occupied.

Then, charioteers and midget submariners of 1939–1945 vintage will know it is utterly unbelievable that any one man in wartime, in a tideway and at night, without mechanical assistance, could have pedalled and cranked and flooded and pumped and changed depth and steered and navigated and found the target and remained undetected and rotated the screw to fix the explosive. Sergeant Lee's reported performance simply was not possible. It is just conceivable that Lee could have managed to bump blindly up against the side of HMS *Eagle* before pressing the foot-pedal to flood the tank and submerge. But Viscount Howe's Marine sentinels, by

Standing Orders dated at Sandy Hook 12 July 1776, had, after sunset, to 'give the word "All's well" every ten minutes or quarter of an hour, beginning with the one on the starboard side of the poop, repeating it forward on that side, and round back on the larboard'. To prevent 'any misdemeanour or neglect of duty' they were to be 'regularly relieved before any punishment be inflicted on them on that account' (meaning, presumably, that they were to be relieved sufficiently often to ensure that they stayed alert). Nor were Marines 'to be forced to go aloft' like common seamen. It is clear that, under Howe and his captains, the Marines were trained and reliable guards and, largely, they escaped the frequent floggings in the squadron at New York. It is unthinkable that the *Turtle*'s approach and subsequent bumpings, scrapings, gurglings and bubblings would have escaped notice.

There is no record whatever in the logs meticulously kept on board HMS *Eagle*, in accordance with the Vice Admiral's unusually specific orders, of any noteworthy incident above or below water on or about the dates concerned.[4] The Captain, in his own journal, recorded minutiae such as the nature of the seaweed floating past. Surely he would have made at least a passing reference to a disturbance?

On Friday, 6 September the only note (by the First Lieutenant) was to the effect that Samuel Kingston, Seaman, was punished at five pm with twelve lashes for drunkeness and that the ship 'heard the report of several cannon'. At one am the following morning (7 September), 'several musquets were fire'd at the Guard boats'. Later that day *Eagle*, 'at half past ten made the signal for all Petty Officers. At noon sent a boat to meet a flag of truce'. Most of Saturday, 7 September was occupied in manning and launching 'Flatt Boats' but there is nothing to suggest that this or any other activity (which included a depressingly large number of floggings) during the month of September was in any way concerned with fears of an underwater threat or any 'infernal device'.

In particular, the assertion made several years afterwards that Admiral Lord Howe was so alarmed that he lifted his close blockade and sailed away to safer waters simply is not true. He remained moored off New York (with a short period from 13 to 15 December at single anchor only) until Monday, 13 January 1777 when *Eagle* moored between the Wharf and the Fly Market 'to avoid the ice'. The words 'off New York' were amended during December and January to read 'off the town of New York', which presumably implies that the ship was then lying even closer inshore.

Nor was there anything recorded about the effect of the detonation off Governor's Island of which an American journal[5] said that 'General Putnam and others who waited with great anxiety for the result [of Lee's expedition] were exceedingly amused with the astonishment and alarm which the secret explosion occasioned on board of the ship'. Although implicit, it is not sure that the despondency observed with glee by Putnam referred to the flagship; but no other British ship fits the bill and the report looks very like wishful thinking on the part of the Americans.

So where does the truth lie? There is no doubt that the *Turtle* actually existed and that covert attacks on the British Fleet were attempted. Moreover, Bushnell must be credited with anticipating midget submarine strategy and tactics. But the conflicting reports surrounding the *Turtle* were probably due not merely to making the best of a good story but also to Ezra Lee being overcome by carbon dioxide. The symptoms of confusion, anxiety and weakened physical resources which can be inferred from the various accounts are recognisable to submariners of succeeding generations. In British terms, Sergeant Lee would not have known whether it was Christmas Eve or the Marble Arch by the time that he reached his target. Add to this the great difficulties he must have experienced in propelling and controlling the *Turtle* (it was hard enough to position a four-man X-craft in 1943 with a reliable motor, compass and controls), and it is not surprising that the operation against HMS *Eagle* was abortive. In fact, the good sergeant probably only survived because, on the way back, with his compass not working, he had to open the hatch so often. The fresh air was his saving.

It is hard to avoid the conclusion that Lee never in fact reached the *Eagle* or any other ship; but that does not detract from a gallant and inventive effort—an 'effort of genius', as George Washington called it. Let Washington have the last word in his letter to Thomas Jefferson in Paris written on 26 September 1785 in reply to a question about 'Bushnell's experiments in submarine navigation during the late war', which, incidentally, implied a keen underwater interest in France:

I am sorry that I cannot give you full information respecting Bushnell's projects for the destruction of ships. No interesting experiments having been made, and my memory being bad, I may in some measure be mistaken in what I am about to relate. Bushnell is a man of great mechanical powers, fertile in inventions and master of execution. He came to me in 1776, recommended by Governor Trumbull and other respectable characters, who were converts to his plan. Although I wanted faith myself, I furnished him with money and other aids to carry his plan to execution. He labored for some time ineffectually; and though the advocates for his schemes continued sanguine, he never did succeed. One accident or another always intervened. I then thought, and still think, that it was an effort of genius, but that too many things were necessary to be combined to expect much from the issue against an enemy who are always upon guard.

That he had a machine so contrived as to carry him under water at any depth he chose, and for a considerable time and distance, with an appendage charged with powder, which he could fasten to a ship and give fire to it in time sufficient for his returning, and by means thereof destroy it, are facts, I believe, which admit of little doubt. But then, where it was to operate against an enemy, it was no easy matter to get a person hardy enough to encounter the variety of dangers to which he would be exposed; first, from the novelty; secondly, from the difficulty of conducting the machine and governing it under water, on account of the current; and thirdly, from the consequent uncertainty of hitting the object devoted to destruction, without rising frequently above water for fresh observations, which when near the vessel, would expose the adventurer to discovery and to almost certain death. To these causes I always ascribed the failure of his plan, as he wanted nothing that I could furnish to insure the success of it.

Bushnell withdrew from the field of underwater warfare after the *Eagle* affair and was formally commissioned in 1779 as a captain lieutenant in the Corps of Engineers of the Revolutionary Army. On 19 June 1781, he was promoted to full captain at the handsome salary of 50 dollars a month, which must have been welcome in view of his depleted funds. Later, it is probable that he emigrated to France, perhaps encouraged by Jefferson.

Finally, he returned to America and settled comfortably in Louisiana under the assumed name and title of Doctor Bush. There is no record of how his patients fared (if indeed he practised medicine), but both Doctor Bush and Ezra Lee, as in all good stories, lived happily ever after, both surviving to a ripe and respected old age. Why Bushnell sought anonymity is not known, but it could well have been connected with the *Turtle*'s failures.

The legend, for such it now appears in the main, did, however, have important consequences. It led to the successful (but suicidal) attack on the Northern ironclad *Housatonic* by the Confederate semisubmersible *Hunley* during the Civil War in 1864; and it inspired later inventors, including John Philip Holland—fairly reckoned to be the true father of modern submarines—who wrote (concerning the British-American War of 1812): 'American Turtles might have prevented the capture of Washington and rendered America invulnerable to England in 1812 had they been in hands accustomed to their management.'[6]

From the latter part of the nineteenth century onwards, submarine warfare directed at enemy harbours—or in defence of one's own—was pursued with vigour by France, Italy, Austria, Russia and Great Britain until the conclusion of World War Two. And it was onto Bushnell's early stock that minelaying and the singularly successful attacks by miniature submarines and human torpedoes were in due course grafted.

Above and below left

The Italian navy became very interested in midget submersibles before World War One for harbour defence and reconnoitring but not, apparently, for offensive operations. When war came it was presumably thought that midgets proper would not be able to penetrate enemy defences. These photographs, taken in July and August 1913, are of the *Alpha* whose construction started in 1912 at the Venice Navy Yard: the single operator seems to be enjoying his ride at the maximum surface speed (electric motor) of 8 knots! Neither *Alpha* nor the sister submersible *Beta* were formally commissioned but they served as prototypes for the more sophisticated and larger four and five-man *A* and *B* classes which were intended solely for a defensive role in the Adriatic.

The Italian *B1* with a crew of five and two internal 45 cm (17.7 inch) torpedo tubes, pictured in 1916. The craft was completed in July 1916 and patrolled to guard against attack outside Bari harbour.

8: Bareback Riders

Pedal-power and handcranks had mercifully been superceded by diesel-engines and electric motors by the time that the first major war involving submarines broke out in 1914. Submarine machinery was, however, heavy and bulky, and we have already seen that the calls for greater speed and endurance made submarines larger and larger. The technology of the day did not permit miniaturisation, but there was one important exception—the torpedo proper, which, by now, had been developed into a reasonably reliable, short-range miniature submarine. It was logical, therefore, for certain sneak craft to follow the pattern of Robert Whitehead's locomotive fish when the strengthening of harbour defences started to make raids by other means impracticable.

By 1918, the last year of the Great War, harbour attacks had become well practised in daring raids by the Italian Navy against the Austrians at the northern end of the Adriatic. Small, fast torpedo-armed motor boats achieved remarkable successes: more than 300 of these craft—MAS boats[1]—were built before hostilities ended, and many more were commissioned during the five-year period immediately following the Armistice. Their wartime operations culminated in the destruction of the old coast-defence battleship *Wien* by *MAS-9* in the principal Australian port of Trieste on the night of 9/10 December 1917; and then there was the sinking of the new dreadnought *Szent Istvan* by *MAS-15* in the open Adriatic on 10 June 1918, an event wrongly attributed to submarine attack and attended by panic on board the giant ship where only the Captain and the Chaplain kept their heads and dignity, the latter blessing the thousand officers and men as they crawled on all fours over the side as the ship began to capsize.

These were heavy blows at the Austro-Hungarian Empire's will to win the war; they saw the beginning of despair and the crumbling of optimism. Consternation followed and the navy had to face the nation's indignation: the sinking of the *Wien* was particularly bad for morale because, although heavy losses at sea may be accepted with resignation, a sinking in harbour is apt to be seen as a national humiliation.

The Austrian reaction to these disasters was to bottle up its remaining battleships in the heavily fortified port of Pola whose boom defences were impenetrable to assault craft, even if they were equipped as boom-jumpers, like the sledge-shaped *Grillo*.[2] This strange but imaginative vehicle was one of four *Barchini Saltatori*,[3] which were equipped with toothed chains like tanks, and it had clambered over three of the four barriers at Pola in May 1918 before being brought under fire and overcome.

Two Italian officers now came together independently (and without orders) to try to devise some kind of vehicle which could penetrate the seemingly impregnable defences and destroy the dormant menace of a fleet in being. They were tackling, as individuals, a strategic threat in a way that was to be repeated, with sundry variations, on several occasions a quarter of a century later during World War Two. Although when their craft emerged it could not properly be called a chariot (to use the 1939–45 term) and still less a midget submarine, credit has to be given to Major (later Colonel) Raffaele Rossetti from the Naval Constructor Corps and Surgeon Lieutenant Raffaele Paolucci for the first human torpedo.

Their device was similar in shape to a torpedo and it was based on an old 14-inch B57 bronze weapon. Known as *SI* or the *Mignatta* (Leech), the vehicle carried two 170 kg TNT charges at the forward end and was propelled, with a four-bladed 17.7 inch diameter screw, by a cold-air engine fed by compressed air at 205 atmospheres. The vehicle, which could be piloted and operated by two men sitting astride (or working alongside it in the water), had an endurance of about ten miles at between three and four knots. The mines were equipped with magnets (whence the advantage of a bronze body) and had clockwork-delay fusing mechanisms. The two inventor-operators were prepared to sacrifice their lives, but they had no intention of committing suicide with the Leech; although it could be trimmed right down the craft could not dive—at least not voluntarily. The pilots steered by paddling their hands in the water: there was no rudder, although the stabilising fins of a

standard torpedo were retained aft. This almost absurdly simple device worked well enough but perhaps only Italian senior officers, well used to sneak craft, would have given it credence and support.

Training began in July 1918. The two officers tried their skill against every possible obstruction that could be erected around the base at Venice. Four months of gruelling hard work and considerable hardship found them ready for an operation and on 31 October the *Mignatta* was lifted aboard a torpedo-boat which set off from Venice soon after midday under a cloudy sky with rain threatening.

Five hours at 15 knots brought the attackers close to the Brionian Islands, opposite Pola's harbour, where stone for building the Venetian Palaces had been quarried centuries earlier. Here the *SI* was lowered carefully into the sea together with a small motor boat which towed the craft, still unmanned, to within about a quarter of a mile of the solid Pola mole. The Constructor and the Surgeon climbed astride their craft and waved farewell to the motor boat as it disappeared quietly to the west. It was now about 2200 and the night was dark. Each operator wore a special light waterproof suit enclosing his whole body except for the face. The suits were coated with camphor to increase their water resistance because it promised to be a long business: the Austrians would undoubtedly be alert and searchlights were sweeping the water, so the final approach had to be made slowly and with caution. The two men could not expect to use the craft's full speed for more than a few minutes at a time; and when they did it threw up, tonight of all nights, an unusual amount of brilliant phosphorescence. And then there were the obstacles to be overcome.

The outer defence system, consisting of a string of large empty metal cylinders from which heavy steel wires were suspended, was reached at 2230. It was not difficult to push and pull the craft through this barrier but there were others ahead. These included a complex erection of heavy timbers and ugly spikes intended to defeat boom-jumpers: petrol cans were fixed on some of the protrusions to give a primitive but doubtless effective audible warning if intruders ran into them. Various obstacles of this kind were painstakingly examined before the gate in the boom was discovered. The swimmers had wrapped their heads with material so as to look, hopefully, like wine-flasks bobbing on the surface: Paolucci, more than once believing that a sentry on the main pier was staring at him while swimming away from the beach to reconnoitre, weaved his head about slowly to imitate the movements of a floating flask.

The gate, when they found it, was, of course, closed: the wires supporting it, which were slacked off for lowering, had been hauled up taut, but they managed to coax their machine over the half-submerged wooden beams.

Although they were safely inside the main defences, they now had to cross first a double and then a triple row of nets. Rain, darkness, a water-logged compass and time were all against them but with the *Mignatta* twisting clumsily against the current and twice capsizing, they at last succeeded in pushing and hauling the machine—with much splashing which was fortunately unobserved—through the last of the nets by 0300. The carefully planned timetable had to be forgotten: the attack was due to have been completed by now and the *Mignatta* should have been on her way back to the rendezvous with her parent motor boat. But all hope of the planned return had, anyway, to be given up because, after all the manoeuvring in and around the obstructions, the compressed air supply for the engine was more than half consumed. However, there was ample left for an attack—and six Austrian pre-dreadnoughts and three super-dreadnoughts lay ahead.

Meanwhile, the after immersion valve, used for trimming down in the water, had somehow cracked open and the *Mignatta* was in danger of sinking altogether. The valve was shut just in time and air was blown into the after compartment, but all this meant further delay.

It was 0415 before they came close to a giant *Tegetthof*-class dreadnought: it was the *Viribus Unitis*, flagship of the Austrian fleet. The idea was to stop the device 100 metres beyond the target, trim down, slip off alongside into the water and allow the ebbing tide to carry them down to the battleship's bows. That plan failed because an unexpected current swept them to one side, and they had to make their way upstream and start all over again. The rain had turned to hail, the waterproof suits were definitely not water-

proof despite the camphor and both men were nearing exhaustion. The prospects did not look bright.

Rossetti, physically the stronger of the two, loosed one of the mines when the *Mignatta* eventually came to some twenty metres from the *Viribus Unitis*, and then swam with it to his objective. Twenty-five minutes passed while Paolucci struggled with the machine which drifted with the tide and capsized. While Rossetti was attaching his mine, Reveille sounded in the battleship above

Anti-torpedo nets were frequently rigged during World War Two; and if the midget threat again develops (as seems likely), it is not inconceivable that some similar kind of protection may be needed in the future. For the moment, scare-charges are the first line of defence against covert attacks by underwater swimmers followed, as demonstrated recently by the Swedish navy, by somewhat heavier munitions! In this photograph, Lieutenant Leir (the Arch Thief—see Chapter Two) is superintending the evolution during pre-war exercises on board the battleship HMS *New Zealand* in 1908 while doing General Service time.

and, as the 'floating flask' reappeared (much to Paolucci's relief), a searchlight illuminated the scene. They were discovered.

Expecting to be fired upon at any moment, Rossetti swam to the *Mignatta* and opened the immersion valve while Paolucci actuated the second mine and set the vehicle in motion so as to ensure that, whatever happened, the secret craft would be destroyed in accordance with an oath which the gallant pair had sworn before starting out. In moments a motor boat shoved off from the battleship and made for the Italians who were partly blinded by the searchlight's glare.

'*Wer da?*' demanded the Coxswain. Paolucci saw no point in denying that they were '*Italienische Offizieren*', whereupon both men were plucked out of the water and taken on board the flagship where they arrived at 0555. The mine had been set to detonate at 0630.

The Italians found the battleship in an extraordinary state of chaos, not because of their activities but because on the previous day—31 October 1918—the Austro-Hungarian Empire had collapsed. Austria was in a state of revolution: a crew from Pola (with 'Yugoslavia' on their cap tallies) had taken over the ship, expelling all German and German-Austrian officers and locking up others below decks. There had been heavy drinking throughout the night and discipline was abandoned. This explained why the two raiders were able to force their way through the boom without being challenged; but they, of course, knew nothing of all this until they were informed, none too politely, on the quarterdeck of *Viribus Unitis*, that the Austrian fleet had been handed over to the Yugoslav National Council.

Captain Voukovitch, the new Commanding Officer, was, rather surprisingly, asleep; but Rossetti insisted on an immediate private interview at which he announced that the ship was 'in serious and imminent danger'. He urged that it be abandoned forthwith.

When Voukovitch passed this disturbing news to the crew, panic ensued. Men jumped half-clothed into the sea rather than be blown up and the Italians were allowed to follow them. However, confusion reigned and the word was next put about that the Italians were bluffing; their story was only a device to let them escape. So, as some of the crew climbed back on board, with the clockwork mechanism ticking away beneath them, Rossetti and Paolucci were also hauled back to confront a thoroughly angry and disenchanted crowd of damp sailors.

The set time of 0630 came and went while the frogmen were being stripped and searched; but at 0644 there came, according to Paolucci, 'a dull noise—a deep roaring, not loud or terrible but rather light. A high column of water followed.' Underfoot the deck vibrated, shook and trembled. Apart from the frogmen and Captain Voukovitch, the upper deck was empty; all the

Surgeon Lieutenant Paolucci's 'wine-flask' head-gear in 1918 was the fore-runner of various kinds of camouflage employed by swimmers and midget submarines during the 1939–45 war. This is a German midget *Biber* periscope (see Chapter Twelve) concealed by tufts of grass and straw in readiness for the unsuccessful attack on the Nijmegen Bridge in November 1944.

rest had leapt overboard once again to save themselves. The Captain himself, however, was in no hurry and nor were his prisoners. While Rossetti was calmly chewing a piece of chocolate, which he had saved from the pile of clothing at his feet, Voukovitch shook hands with the two men and pointed to a rope hanging over the side. The Italians took the hint and swam to one of the rowing boats that were milling around the stricken ship. Voukovitch stayed, climbing up and over the giant side of *Viribus Unitis* as the ship slowly turned turtle and sank. When the Italians last saw him he was standing erect on the massive keel; but he died while struggling to swim clear of the whirlpool when the battership finally vanished.

Taken to the accommodation and hospital ship *Hapsburg*, the frogmen were in poor shape. When the ship's doctor felt Paolucci's pulse he confined himself to a single ominous word—'*Funfzig!*' (fifty). It scarcely mattered: both men fully expected to be put to death. But four days later, on 5 November, Paolucci looked out of his cabin-prison scuttle and saw the Italian battleship *Saint Bon* entering harbour. The cabin door was not locked so Paolucci raced up on deck, seized a megaphone and shouted 'Admiral of the *Saint Bon*, long live the King!' Rossetti joined him and together they shouted again. Admiral Cagni, the Commander-in-Chief at Spezia, answered the salute himself: 'Long live the King!' Soon the adventurers learned that an Armistice had been signed and they were free.

The entrance to Portsmouth Harbour protected by a fairly typical boom: the photograph was taken from the submarine base, Fort Blockhouse, shortly before the outbreak of World War One.

The *Grillo*, one of four Italian 'Jumping Boats' commissioned in March 1918 as assault craft, fitted with caterpillar tracks like marine tanks, for clambering over harbour-defence barriers. These remarkable craft had a crew of four and could make four knots on their single 10 hp electric motors. *Grillo* nearly succeeded in penetrating the Pola defenses on 14 May 1918.

Three 'Jumping Boats' at the naval dockyard, Venice, in early 1918. Each carried two 45 cm (17.7 inch) torpedoes in side-cages. *Cavaletta* and *Pulce* (aft), after an unsuccessful attempt on the harbour, were both scuttled off Pola on 13 April 1918 but *Locusta* (left) survived the war.

Their achievements were rightly acclaimed and a wildly enthusiastic reception awaited them on their return to Venice. Rossetti had coolly calculated, before setting out on the expedition, that their chances of returning were six to four against; but here they were back safely, having destroyed not only the Austrian flagship but also the transatlantic Austrian Lloyd liner *Wien* (not to be confused with the battleship that had gone down earlier), which had been sunk by the second of the two mines propelled towards

the luckless vessel by the *Mignatta* when Paolucci had set it in motion and cast it loose before their capture. It was indeed a heroic and remarkable achievement. The attack came too late to have any effect on the war and was, strictly speaking, unnecessary, but it was not wasted for it inspired a new and powerful generation of human torpedomen when Italy again went to war in 1940.

When all had quietened down, the Italian Government awarded the newly promoted Colonel Rossetti—the senior partner—

650,000 lira in recognition of the feat; but Rossetti secretly and unostentatiously arranged for the money to be passed to the widow of Captain Voukovitch and other families bereaved by the attack. It was a gesture typical of the two heroes' gallant and chivalrous spirit—a spirit which was to be renewed by Italian frogmen riding their *Maiali* during World War Two a quarter of a century later.

9: Emergence of the Midgets

Although midget submarines did not come into use until World War Two, a number of small submersibles were constructed during the latter part of the nineteenth century in various countries with the idea of penetrating harbour defences and planting or attaching mines. Russia was particularly keen on the concept.

During the Russo-Japanese war of 1904–05, previous experience enabled the Tsarist navy to construct, quickly, a hand-cranked midget with a crew of three and a bow filled with explosives.[1] There is no record of the craft making an attack—which would necessarily have been suicidal—but it evidently had some interesting features. Small buoyancy chambers, one at each end, were housed in depressions in the hull. They were attached to wire ropes that could be paid out or hauled in from inside the submarine. When the craft was dived, by flooding a single ballast tank, it was held suspended from the buoyancy chambers at a depth determined by the amount of wire paid out, the chambers themselves being camouflaged with seaweed. There was no rudder but the propeller was mounted on a universal joint, similar to modern commercial mini-submersibles, which was moved by hand for steering. It was an ingenious design, probably copied from Goubet's first boat of 1885, but electric motors had been in common use for submerged propulsion for twenty years or more in Russia (and elsewhere) and reliance on a hand-crank in 1904 is incomprehensible.

A few years later, Lieutenant Godfrey Herbert, serving in HMS *Monmouth* on the China Station, with the lessons of the Russo-Japanese war fresh in mind and the area of operations not far distant, was struck in 1909 with the germ of a more imaginative scheme. Herbert was not a lucky officer: in October 1914 he was to have his new command *D-5* blown up beneath him by a mine in the North Sea; in August 1915, commanding the Q ship *Baralong*, he took the decision to shoot the German crew of *U-27*, which he had shelled, while they were escaping or attempting to hide in the SS *Nicosian*, a ship they had just captured—an action which earned him undying hatred in Germany (although the Admiralty put about a fictitious story that the name of the *Baralong*'s captain was William McBride); and in January 1917 his brand new *K-13* foundered on trials in the Gareloch—the most notorious of the K-boat disasters. In fact, looking back over Herbert's career, he seemed destined for disaster of one kind or another and if his plans for what he called the *Devastator* had come to fruition there is little doubt that nemesis would finally have overtaken him.

His first effort to persuade the Admiralty to adopt a high-speed midget submarine were politely turned down in the usual way: 'Their Lordships do not intend to proceed further in the matter at present'; but, at the same time, they gave a small hint of encouragement which persuaded Herbert, kicking his heels in the depot ship *Maidstone* after the loss of *D-5*, to pursue the idea further. He was doubtless anxious to do something to dispel the clouds that were hanging over him: they had gathered not only because of *D-5*'s loss but because, a couple of months before the submarine was mined, two torpedoes which Herbert had fired at the important German cruiser *Rostock* from a range of 600 yards had underrun their target.

It was not entirely Herbert's fault: proper allowance had not been made for the difference in weight between a warhead and a practice head, but the crew of *D-5* were quite sure that the failure was due to bad joss and that the trouble was caused by, of all things, a mascot teddy bear. One sailor knew the remedy; soon after the abortive attack, Herbert came across the man standing over a bucket in the fore-ends with the teddy bear in one hand and a knife in the other. 'I'll teach you to be *good* joss', the seaman muttered and then proceeded to slit the furry throat, letting the sawdust trickle out into the bucket below.

Unfortunately, the grizzly little ceremony did nothing to dispel the evil genius presiding over *D-5* but it typified Herbert's

The Tsarist navy favoured submarines for defence just as the Soviet navy does today. The first midget, designed by Drzewiecki, was laid down at St Petersburg in 1879. This boat and its immediate successors (50 were ordered) were foot-pedalled with two propellers but the later craft shown here at Vladivostok in 1904 was modified with one screw and an electric motor. Two 110-lb dynamite mines were carried in recesses on the upper part of the hull and, equipped with spikes, these were intended for releasing beneath a target where, hopefully, they would rise and be embedded, whereupon they were to be fired by electric current through a cable attached to the submarine. Not surprisingly, most of these boats were abandoned and used as buoys or pontoon-supports long before this photograph was taken during the Russo-Japanese war.

This Russian midget, said to be crewed by two men, was photographed in 1915 and appears almost identical to the *Drzewiecki* pictured in 1904. It may be the same or a sister boat carrying a charge at the bow (as evidenced by the spike) modified with a more practical, albeit suicidal, weapon—a system of the kind described in the text.

Another miniature Tsarist submarine, the *Pyotr Koshka*, launched in 1901 and shown here in 1903 with two drop-collar 18-inch torpedoes. Two electric motors drove twin propellers at a maximum speed submerged of 6 knots. Subsequent midget submariners in their various navies were not apt to wear frock-coats.

successor to the motorcycles which had long been his hobby.

At any rate, Herbert submitted improved plans to Commodore Keyes, the Head of the Submarine Service, who in turn made sure they went via the proper channels as a formal proposal to the Admiralty in 1915. Winston Churchill and Prince Louis of Battenburg—First Lord and First Sea Lord respectively—turned the idea down flat, observing (rightly) that it would be a dangerous weapon to develop, while reviving a criticism that had been applied by Britain to submarines as a whole at the turn of the century, namely that the *Devastator* would essentially be the weapon of a weaker power. The Admiralty official who conveyed this view to Herbert added that if England was in the position of Germany, he would certainly favour it, but at this time plans were going ahead at the opposite end of the size-scale for very large steam-driven submarines. These, of course, were to become the K-boats and Herbert, little knowing what was in store for him with *K-13*, said he trusted he should never be told to command such a submarine: he would rather have his 10-ton *Devastator*.

The *Devastator* was not a suicide weapon, although the chances of survival for the single operator would have been slim. The navigator was to be enclosed in a detachable buoyant compartment and, once the missile had been directed accurately on its course carrying a large explosive charge towards its

association with bad luck. However, he had exceptionally *good* luck in being great friends with the very successful Max Horton of *E-9* fame and Horton was much taken with the plans for the *Devastator* which had 'for its object to provide means of propelling against an enemy ship or other target a large quantity of high explosive, and of effecting this with great economy of materiel and personnel'. Reading between the lines of various papers, Max probably intended himself to drive the beast—a cross between a torpedo and a submarine—as an exciting

The Holland 'submarine boats', adopted by most major navies other than the French and German at the beginning of the century, are not normally classed as midgets but several of their features were apparent in the British X-craft that started to emerge in 1942. At the other end of the scale, the enormously larger fast nuclear hunter-killers adopted the same porpoise-shape from the 1950s. HM Submarine Torpedo Boat *No. 3*, shown here coming down Portsmouth Harbour from Fareham Creek in about 1903, has her whole crew plus one passenger on deck, but three white mice are keeping watch below, ready to signal the presence of carbon monoxide from the petrol engine exhaust fumes by squeaking or, *in extremis*, turning their little feet up.

target, he would release a clip and eject the chamber by means of compressed air. He was protected against the initial shock and subsequent buffeting in the sea by air cushions which lined the compartment, and, it was confidently hoped, a destroyer or some other vessel would then come along and hoist the whole chamber aboard like a modern space-ship capsule.

The *Devastator* was to be launched for its mission from a capital ship when the opposing fleet had been closed to about ten miles, at which range the great guns would be opening fire. It was, to say the least, an ambitious project, but Herbert's contemporaries believed it would be 'irresistible'. Several of them, probably over the depot ship bar, volunteered to man the midgets if ever they were built (knowing full well that the chances of this were minimal), but Herbert was determined to be the first to try out his invention in practice. He was never called upon to do so.

The *Devastator* anticipated remarkably similar Japanese midgets and human torpe-

does by some 25 years. If a number of these weapons had been built, and if they had performed even half as well as the inventor predicted, it is interesting to conjecture what their effect would have seen at, say, the Battle of Jutland in 1916. But there were too many 'ifs' and 'buts' about the idea at that time: trials, modifications and training would have occupied many months and it is doubtful whether the technology of the period was sufficient for success. Then, too, it was a touch too flamboyant for His Majesty's Navy: it smacked of the circus.

Nonetheless, the idea steadily gained support in the peacetime submarine service where boredom was setting in. In January 1923, Max Horton, by now Captain (S) of the First Submarine Flotilla, was again pressing Herbert's plans[2] 'for a small, very fast, submarine or man-guided torpedo, known as the *Devastator*.'

Horton admitted that, at the outset, the scheme appeared fantastic,

but once given the practical completion of such a craft then the various uses to which it could be put are fascinating to contemplate ...

a. *Limited size, not to exceed about ten tons.*
b. *Very high speed—45 to 50 knots.*
c. *Method of propulsion—hot-air driven engines of the ordinary torpedo pattern, enlarged.*
d. *Capable of proceeding either on the surface or submerged to 200 feet.*
e. *Crew of one or two officers.*

f. *Big explosive charge (one ton) built integral with the bow.*
g. *Radius of action—about 30 miles or as far as possible.*

Observation underway, continued Horton, would be 'by a short periscope or conning tower. When chased or fired at, the *Devastator* would dive deep and 'porpoise' for observation at intervals. Such craft could be carried by almost any surface ship, and even by another submarine. An M-class, without the 12-inch gun, could carry two or three on the upper deck.' Horton was very fond of the monster 'Mutton Boats' and was constantly looking for new ways to use them.

The weapon would be carried 'as close as possible to its objective, and then released or launched. With its great speed, no capital ship could avoid it if within its limited radius of action.' When the *Devastator* reached 'a suitable position about 200 yards from its objective, automatic steering and depth control gear would be brought into action, and the release cylinder would enable the crew to become separated from the craft before the latter exploded itself against the enemy'.

Horton believed that 'from a submarine point of view, the idea appears perfectly practicable, and for an experimental craft to be built would cost very little, since much materiel is available from surplus war requirements that could be used for this purpose—for instance, the engines might be two or three 21-inch torpedo engines coupled or geared to a shaft or shafts. 21-inch or

Lieutenant and Commander Max Horton with the crew of
Holland 3, January 1906. Horton was influenced by his
early experiences in the little Holland boats and became
a great supporter of midget submarines later in his distinguished career.

18-inch torpedo air vessels could be grouped
inside for the necessary supply of air.'[3]

On the outbreak of any future war, one or
more surface ships 'of high speed', carrying
Devastators, would be sent at once to a position close to the harbour where the enemy
was supposed to be concentrating. Arriving
there, the weapons would be launched and
would attack the enemy inside the harbour.
No nets, said Horton, or obstructions 'as at
present designed' could prevent the entry of
such craft, 'with their strong hulls of special
steel and fitted with sharp guards and cutters. Aeroplanes would also be ineffective,
except by the greatest good fortune or a
luckily dropped bomb on a target moving at
fifty knots, and only momentarily on the surface; gunfire would be similarly ineffective.

The fragile and vulnerable CMB [Coastal
Motor Boat] cannot be compared with such
a craft as the *Devastator* which is fit to work
in any weather in which the objective can be
seen ... capital ships could readily be made
fit to carry one or two *Devastators* to be
launched in a Fleet Action against the
enemy's line ... large submarine transpor-
ters could be constructed to carry *Devastators* on the upper deck, and to lie off the
enemy's port to await the exit of a suitable
target.'

Horton acknowledged that 'much of the
effect of this new weapon would be lost if it
was known to the enemy, and it is strongly
urged that one of the experimental craft
should be built and tried with the greatest
secrecy.'

A pencilled note by one of the Commander-in-Chief's Staff Officers against
the last point remarked 'this paper is not
marked Secret!' And, indeed, the ubiquitous
Japanese officers who were continually visit-

ing naval ports and installations in England
to gain, quite openly, information about
British submarine progress must have acquired a fairly complete knowledge of the
plans: some of the early Japanese midgets
which started to emerge in the mid-1930s
had characteristics reminiscent of Herbert's
ideas.

The Royal Navy, however, took the proposals no further. Despite Horton's protesta-
tions that 'the crew will have a fair chance of
being recovered', that 'the late war has
clearly shown how men, properly led, will
stand firm when ordered to fight to the last,
even when escape is possible', and that 'no
thought of the risk incurred in war should
prevent the use of so potent and decisive a
weapon', it still appeared to be too much of
a suicide craft for the Admiralty to include in
the Fleet. Furthermore, it really was too
much like hitting below the belt: some of the
Admirals were still inclined to the Edwar-
dian opinion that any kind of submarining

David Bushnell first perceived in the 1770s that an explosion underwater would be much more effective than in air: in the twentieth century small limpet mines proved his point as shown here. Midgets carrying explosive charges of one kind or another were rightly seen by a few early submariners as potent weapon systems.

was no occupation for a gentleman and damned un-English.

The Japanese had no such inhibitions but, as will be seen later, they greatly underestimated the practicalities and the degree of training required for midget operations of whatever kind.

Meanwhile, Robert H Davis of Siebe Gorman and Company Ltd (later Chairman of the famous firm which became best known in submarine circles for escape apparatus) had devised and patented, but not built, two midget submarines and two human torpedoes which were at least 25 years ahead of their time. One of the midgets, carrying two or three men, included a new type of 'emergence chamber' by means of which a diver could leave the craft and return to it on completion of his task. It was not a new idea because Simon Lake, at the end of the last century, had provided an exit and re-entry compartment in his *Argonaut*, but the Lake design was on the diving-bell principle with a trap-door in the bottom and had considerable limitations which restricted its use to working on the bottom, for which the craft was provided with wheels. The Davis chamber, on the other hand, had a hatch in the top and was totally flooded from tanks inside the submarine to which the water was returned when pumping out, thereby not upsetting the trim.

Like the *Devastator*, the Davis midget failed to impress the Naval Staff who saw no use for it in the Royal Navy and, along with the lingering prejudice against sneak craft, the cumbersome hard-hat diving equipment—all that was available between 1914 and 1918—militated against the project. The Japanese do not seem to have got wind of the Davis mini-submersible which was protected commercially and, hence, perhaps with more realistic secrecy than naval designs: this was just as well, because the X-craft which eventually followed in 1942, soundly based upon the Davis principle, were to prove more effective than the *Devastator* semi-torpedo types which the Japanese chose. At the same time, the human torpedoes which Davis proposed were far in advance of the Italian *Mignatta* used at Pola in 1918 but they, too, were rejected.

The Great Depression of the 1920s and the severe naval cuts imposed did little to encourage midget plans to advance, but one retired submarine Commanding Officer, Commander Cromwell H Varley DSC, who had been rated medically unfit in 1922 (much to the regret of the Submarine Service), doggedly persevered. When commanding HMS *L-1* in 1919, Varley had been reported as 'clever and capable and of a very inventive mind but somewhat lacking in a sense of proportion'.[4] The latter criticism was unintentionally apt because Varley had a predilection for very small submarines rather than the monsters which practically everybody else was concerned with at the time. 'Crom' Varley enjoyed scant encouragement until, as is the way of things, his help was suddenly and urgently required to solve a most serious strategic problem.

On 9 April 1940, the Germans invaded Norway. The occupation was virtually complete by June. From that time the enemy maintained naval forces, including capital ships, in Norwegian ports where they were well placed to break out into the Atlantic and in due course threaten Russian convoys. Their mere presence was sufficient to oblige most heavy units of the British Fleet to remain on guard in Scottish waters rather than undertake the offensive operations which were becoming increasingly desirable, first at home and then in the Far East. In short, the bulk of the battle fleet was rendered impotent by a threat which never fully materialised and which could not be countered by conventional forces. The harbours in which the German heavy units lay were strongly defended and often far from the open sea. Neither RAF long-range bombers nor carrier-based naval aircraft were available to attack them (and would probably have been shot down if they had tried), while ordinary submarines stood no chance of penetrating the deep Norwegian fjords. Something akin to the old fire-ships was needed—but what?

Fortunately, a few perceptive minds in the Admiralty remembered Varley and his suggestions. The answer clearly lay in midget submarines—or X-craft as they came to be known. Varley was told to go ahead with a prototype midget at his works in Hampshire. But, already, in the Mediterranean, a new underwater menace had been prepared for war by Mussolini's navy—a greatly improved and very practical type of manned torpedo.

10: Pigs and Jeeps

Human torpedoes were used with great effect by the Italian and British navies during World War Two. They were not independent units and can not properly be counted as midget submarines, but their purpose was much the same and it is well worth looking at their capabilities, even if all their operations are not discussed in full: most, but not all, of their deeds, in both navies, are recounted in various books.[1] There are indications that updated versions of the Italian wartime variety may reappear in the Mediterranean so these weapons are of more than passing interest.

It is, without question, Mussolini's navy that must be acclaimed, amidst a dreary list of wartime retreats and miscarriages, for perfecting the most successful manned torpedoes. But it was the Abyssinian campaign, launched in October 1935, rather than the entry of Italy into World War Two in 1940, that led to their development and to the creation of the Tenth Light Flotilla of assault craft; and it was the threat posed by the superior British fleet (which in the event did not actively oppose the Italian march on East Africa) which prompted the need for a new secret weapon which could be rapidly produced and instantly deployed to carry destruction into the enemy's camp at the start of hostilities and reduce the Italian disadvantage. Once again, as throughout history, it was the weaker power which turned first to covert underwater warfare.[2]

The example of Paolucci and Rossetti and their sinking of the *Viribus Unitis* in 1918 inspired two young submarine engineers, Lieutenants Tesei and Toschi, to design and construct a machine resembling Rossetti's *Mignatta* in some respects, but capable of complete submergence for a considerable period. Toschi wrote of it:[3]

In size and shape it is very similar to a torpedo but is in reality a miniature submarine with entirely novel features, electrical propulsion and a steering wheel similar to that of an aeroplane ... the crew (pilot and assistant), instead of remaining enclosed and more or less helpless in the interior, keep outside the structure. The two men, true fliers in the sea-depths, bestride their underwater
"aeroplane", barely protected from the frontal onrush of the waters by a curved screen of plastic glass ... at night, under cover of total darkness and steering by luminous control instruments, they will be able to aim at and attack their objective while remaining quite invisible to the enemy. The operators ... are able to cut nets and remove obstacles with special compressed-air tools and ... with long range underwater breathing gear ... can breathe and navigate underwater at any depth down to 30 metres and carry a powerful-explosive charge to an enemy harbour ... beyond the reach of the most sensitive acoustic detector, they will be able to operate inside the harbour until they find the keel of a large unit, fasten the charge to it and thus ensure an explosion which will sink the vessel.

Admiral Cavagnari, Chief of the Naval Staff, immediately seized on the idea and 30 technicians from the La Spezia Submarine Weapons Works were seconded to the project.

Starkly practical engineering and improvisation (the first engine came from an elevator in a dockyard block which was being demolished) resulted in two prototypes being ready by January 1936. The initial trials, in decidedly chilly water, were satisfactory but gave the two young engineers 'extremely novel sensations' when their 'submerged bodies stiffened convulsively' as they were carried along by the machine which they themselves had created. They 'felt a thrill of delight in the dark depths of the sea which the tiny human torpedo was penetrating so obediently'.[4] A further demonstration in one of the large docks at La Spezia, in the presence of Admiral Falangola and Senior Officers from the Ministry, was sufficiently convincing for the Admiral to authorise a number of operational units to be built forthwith. The final vehicles, 6.7 metres long with 300 kg of explosives in a detachable head, were officially known as SLC[5] Human Torpedoes but they were almost always called *Maiali* (Pigs or Swine): they were christened with this unflattering name after an incident during the early trials with one of the first when Tesei had to abandon his sinking craft. The inventor's first words on
being fished out were: 'that swine got away again!' The name stuck.

As it happened, there was no opportunity to use human torpedoes during the Abyssinian campaign and the weapons were stowed away secretly while the trained volunteers to man them were drafted to other posts. However, in July 1939, when it became obvious that war in Europe was imminent, the First Light Flotilla, commanded by Commander Paolo Aloisi, was reformed and expanded under the general supervison of Admiral Goiram, and at the beginning of 1940 the original pilots, while still attached to their ships, began to resume training together with half a dozen officers who were new to the 'pigs'. The latter included Sub-Lieutenant Luigi de la Penne and Aloisi himself. A year later, in March 1941, the Special Weapons Department of the Flotilla was detached and formed into two divisions, one underwater and one surface, under the original cover name of the Tenth Light Flotilla whose exploits until September 1943 were to result in four warships and 27 merchant ships being sunk or damaged, totalling 265,352 tons. The Tenth was commanded by the Duke of Spoleta (later Duke of Aosta) whose personal influence greatly facilitated the acquisition of supplies when these were short elsewhere.

Surface units—one-man explosive motor boats (E-boats)—rammed the British heavy cruiser *York* in Suda Bay on 26 March 1941 but the subsequent loss of this important ship was publicly attributed by the British Admiralty to German bombing in order to maintain the belief that Italian naval operations were ineffective. Torpedo craft also had some significant successes in the Black Sea; but it was the Pigs that were responsible for the bulk of the remarkably high tonnage that fell to the Flotilla. Nor were these successes purely tactical in nature; when *Maiali*, led by de la Penne, crippled the British 30,000-ton battleships *Valiant* and *Queen Elizabeth* in Alexandria Harbour on 21 December 1941, the balance of naval power in the Mediterranean was radically changed in the space of a few minutes.

Winston Churchill was understandably annoyed by all this activity in the Mediterra-

The Italian submarine *Sciré* equipped with containers for *maiali*. It was this submarine (camouflaged to look, on the surface, like a trawler going in the opposite direction!) which took three teams of 'pig-men' to their launch position off Gibraltar in the early hours of 20 September 1941 where they destroyed a tanker and two cargo vessels totalling about 28,000 tons. Exactly three months later, *Sciré* despatched three more teams, led by CC de la Penne, against Alexandria where they severely damaged the battleships *Valiant* and *Queen Elizabeth*, the destroyer *Jervis* and a valuable tanker, the *Sagona*.

Aerial reconnaissance photograph of Alexandria Harbour where *Maiali* made their attack with serious strategic consequences for Britain.

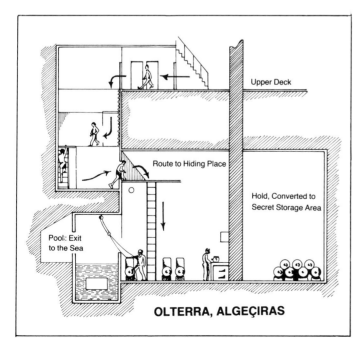

Upper Deck

Route to Hiding Place

Hold, Converted to Secret Storage Area

Pool: Exit to the Sea

OLTERRA, ALGEÇIRAS

The Italians used the half-sunken merchant ship *Olterra* at Algeçiras as a secret base for *maiali* raids on Gibraltar. A similar ploy could be used today (Drawing by David Hill.)

The controls of a *Maiale* human torpedo, also showing
the detachable 300-kg explosive charge forward.

nean by a navy which British propaganda insisted had no fight in it. On 18 January 1942, the Prime Minister sent a note to General Ismay for the Chief of Staff Committee:

Please report what is being done to emulate the exploits of the Italians in Alexandria Harbour and similar methods of this kind.

At the beginning of the war Colonel Jefferis[6] had a number of bright ideas on this subject, which received very little encouragement. Is there any reason why we should be incapable of the same kind of scientific aggressive action that the Italians have shown? One would have thought that we should have been in the lead.

Please state the exact position.[7]

The demand was rapidly passed down the line to Admiral Sir Max Horton, Flag Officer Submarines, who sent for an old acquaintance, Lieutenant Commander W R (Tiny) Fell who had joined submarines in July 1918 and thought his underwater days were finished when he relinquished command of *H-31* in August 1939. He had subsequently spent an exciting time commanding a particular kind of Q-ship—an unarmed trawler manned by fishermen towing a submerged submarine. It was a revival of the moderately successful World War One ploy but the trap was never sprung before Fell was transferred to Cloak and Dagger operations in Scottish 'puffers' supporting the Army in Norway, where he was promoted to

Commander and awarded the Distinguished Service Cross (although nobody told him at the time). He next found himself commanding the Combined Operations Infantry Assault Ship *Prince Charles* during Operation 'Archery', the attack on Vagsöy in December 1941 and a second raid in January 1942, code-named 'Kitbag' at Florö. Fell was thus exceptionally well experienced in raiding operations, but the extraordinarily exacting and sometimes frustrating nature of this work left him tired and restless. He was casting about for some means of rejoining the Submarine Service when Horton summoned him.

The task which Max assigned to Fell was totally unexpected. 'Go away', said the Admiral, 'and build me a Human Torpedo ... I'm busy, but get on with the job right away, and report as soon as you have got something. Goodbye and good luck.'[8] Max was never a man to waste words on somebody he trusted.

Meanwhile, another veteran submarine captain, Commander Geoffrey Sladen, had set to work at Siebe Gorman's constructing a flexible diving dress supplied by oxygen, and in a few days he joined Fell at Fort Blockhouse where Stan Kerry, the Engineer Commander, was turning a log of wood, twenty feet long and nearly two feet in diameter, into a prototype weapon broadly similar to a *Maiali* that had been captured after an abortive attack at Gibraltar. The beast enjoyed a variety of names—at first the Kerry Mark II or 'Cassidy' and then 'The Chariot'. For the operational models which followed it was the last name that went down in history; but submariners who carried the craft sometimes referred to them as 'Jeeps' after the rodent-like creature which emitted a series of 'Jeep-Jeeps' in the Popeye strip cartoons.

Fell and Sladen, who had previously commanded *Trident* with great success (torpedoing the German heavy cruiser *Prinz Eugen* amongst others), formed a powerful team. Sladen had immense physical and mental energy while Fell, 45 years old, had a personality that instantly attracted the loyalty and affection of subordinates. Both officers were experts at sizing up a man's character and made no mistakes in selecting the Charioteers, the first ten of which arrived at Blockhouse in April 1942 to join what was called the Experimental Submarine Flotilla. After a few days training with DSEA (Davis Submerged Escape Apparatus) which was to supply oxygen to the operators, Lieutenant 'Chuck' Bonnell, a Canadian RNVR officer, and Stoker Petty Officer 'Jim' Warren were made ready to

ride Cassidy in Horsea Lake at the top end of Portsmouth Harbour.

Fell and Sladen had already tested the machine in the experimental fresh water tank at Haslar but they forgot to adjust the trim for the salt water in Portsmouth Harbour. Cassidy obstinately refused to dive until pounds of lead had been nailed all over him, but eventually the prototype submerged, taking Bonnell and Warren slowly and safely down to the muddy bottom. Some of the other trainees, practising independently with their diving suits and tended by a line, fared less well. The Wrens who received the water-logged and exhausted bodies were notably unsympathetic ('we thought you were supposed to be tough'). One young officer, suffering from a flooded suit and oxygen poisoning, was tragically drowned before he could be hauled out.

The construction of operational chariots did not present any great difficulties. They were simple and, properly handled, they seemed to be reasonably safe—but the dangers of oxygen and carbon dioxide under pressure were not fully appreciated, any more than they were by the Italians who could certainly not operate safely for any length of time at 30 metres, as claimed by Toschi: 10 metres was nearer the mark.

Sladen's drive was such that the first powered Chariot (for Cassidy had no propulsion) was ready in early June. It was christened 'The Real One' and, painted green, was similar in size to a normal 21-inch torpedo with a detachable head containing 600 pounds of explosive. The 60-volt lead-acid battery, comprising 30 chloride cells in two rows, supplied the 2 hp electric motor which propelled the craft at 4 knots for four hours or at 2.9 knots for about six hours, giving a nominal range of 18 miles. It also supplied the ballast and trim pump motors. Four forward and two astern speeds were available to Number One, the pilot, sitting forward astride the main body behind a breast-high screen on which was mounted a depth gauge, compass and clock. The pump-control and main motor switches were at the bottom of the screen and a joystick between the pilot's legs operated the rudder and hydroplanes. Number One's back rested against the main ballast tank which served as a protection for the Second Diver straddling the after part of the machine where net cutters, magnets, ropes and two spare breathing bags were stowed in a locker which in turn provided a backrest for Number Two.

The 'Real One' behaved perfectly but it was hard to catch a trim—that is to say

Above left
An early back-to-back British Chariot awash.

Above right, and left
Trials of Mark II Chariot

achieve neutral buoyancy—while under way submerged. The Charioteers learnt that balancing was most easily accomplished on the bottom and it was best to trim the Chariot a trifle light while the divers made themselves a little heavy. Once that was done, the Charioteers could start to enjoy the sensation of slipping silently through the underwater world on their steeds, which responded lightly and accurately to the controls—once Number One had got the hang of it. In the early stages of training it was by no means always like that and there were unexpected hazards in store.

Portsmouth was no place for operational training. HMS *Titania* ('Tites' to her friends from the time she first became a submarine depot ship in 1918) was allocated as a

support and accommodation ship for the Chariots when the group moved to Scotland. *Titania* had previously been based at Rothesay on the Island of Bute with all its amenities at the mouth of the Clyde estuary: her Captain, Commander Robin Conway, did not welcome the move to Loch Erisart on the Island of Lewis where the base, known as Port D, was to be established in the wilds; and nor did he approve the setting up of a small private navy which he considered unlikely to achieve its object.[9] The party which the prospective charioteers decided to hold *underneath* the Glasgow train at Euston before departure did nothing to allay Conway's doubts when he heard about it. Fell had, perhaps unwisely, left his team to their own devices for two hours in London and, with

typical enthusiasm, they had made the very best of this short breathing space.

It was sheer bad luck that the First Lord of the Admiralty, accompanied by Max Horton, elected to take the same train north—to find the Stationmaster, dressed in frock coat and pin stripe trousers for the VIP's benefit, being forcibly persuaded to take part in the subterranean celebrations. As the Right Honourable Albert Victor Alexander CH MP came abreast the mêlée at the platform's edge he, too, was invited to join the fun. At this point Sir Max took charge. The Admiral had a power of command second to none and the simple order to 'stop everything' was instantly obeyed. Alexander was not noted for his sense of humour but Horton contented himself, after becoming involved in a rugby match in the corridor, with telling Fell that he 'seemed to have picked the right sort of types, but I wish you would not let them attack the First Lord when I am taking him to inspect the submarine flotillas in Scotland.'[10] The next morning, on board *Titania*, the charioteers were fallen in—sober—and inspected by the head of His Majesty's Navy in absolute silence. It was not an auspicious start, and Conway was less than pleased with his new charges. He turned over command to Fell in June 1942.

Erisart proved an impossible place for training and Fell remembered only half a dozen days there when the wind was blowing less than 30 knots. Loch Corrie, near Oban, offered more hospitable weather for a while before 'Tites' moved to the more sheltered Loch Cairnbawn where HMS *Bonaventure*, a 10,000 ton converted Clan Line ship, lay awaiting the X-craft soon to be on their way. This final training ground for chariots and midget submarines (whose preliminary training base was still at Rothesay) was code-named Port HHZ and *Titania* was preceded there by the subsidiary depot ship HMS *Alecto* and the drifter *Easter Rose*.

Titania was the target for the charioteers during the initial training period, but the two-man teams soon got to know her and the netted course too well. A more difficult and better protected target was needed and this was supplied by no less than the battleship *Howe* (with, at the time, totally unrecalled memories of the *Turtle* and the *Eagle*) which anchored close inshore and surrounded herself with a series of nets which were deemed impregnable. They were not.

The first three out of seven chariots on the first exercise penetrated or avoided the defences and attached dummy charges to the huge hull without trouble. Number Two in the fourth chariot ripped his breathing-bag on a jagged piece of wire while passing through the outer net and his Number One wisely decided to retire and return at top speed to 'Tites' where Sladen saw to it that the Number Two, who was in bad shape by this time, was revived with whisky, a hot bath and a pat on the back. Even this mishap was not spotted by the 'enemy'. Nor was the fifth team, whose chariot, which had a mechanical failure, was actually taken alongside *Howe* on the surface to fix magnets on the ship's side although it was impossible to attach the warhead itself. The sixth craft had a compass failure and hit a patch of fresh water which caused it to drop like a stone,

rupturing the divers' ears; feeling far from fit and obeying the strict instruction not to risk giving the game away, they reluctantly turned around and headed back. The last machine (the chariots were despatched at fifteen minute intervals) was piloted by 'Jock' Kerr who had been a Second Lieutenant in the Highland Light Infantry five months earlier; he made a perfect attack, sneaking under the battleship's stern from landward, where nets had not been laid.

So, in a thoroughly realistic exercise against an alerted and very well defended target, four out of seven chariots had placed their charges and none of the attackers had been detected. On the following night, four chariots repeated the attack and all attached magnets secured to pellet buoys (to point the way and make things easier for *Howe*'s divers), but two machines were seen making their way back.

On the third night tragedy struck. Sub-Lieutenant Jack Grogan, a South African Number One, took his machine deep on the run in and succumbed to oxygen poisoning underneath the 35,000-ton battleship whose draught exceeded (as is now known) the safe limits for breathing neat oxygen. His Number Two, Able Seaman 'Geordie' Worthy,

Dressing a charioteer in his 'clammy death' suit.

King George VI inspecting charioteers on board HMS *Bonaventure*.

Charioteers training and safely tethered.

took control by putting his arms around Grogan to grasp the controls. He steered the chariot out from under the target and brought it to the surface, but by then Grogan was dead.

Frankly, the failures and one death had to be considered par for the course: they were more than balanced by the success of the exercises. Nobody doubted that a price would have to be paid during any actual operation; but nor were there, any longer, doubts about how effective the chariots would be when given their chance. It was not long in coming.

The first operation, in October 1942, was aimed at the 42,000-ton German battleship *Tirpitz* anchored far up Trondhjemfjord, by now the greatest single threat to shipping arising from the German occupation of Norway. In September, Fell had reported to Flag Officer Submarines that four chariots were fully trained and ready for work. In the middle of October, a little 45-foot Norwegian fishing boat motored slowly into Loch Cairnbawn to take two teams to their destination. The *Arthur* was captained by a man who was to be acclaimed as Norway's national hero for his many exploits—Lief Larsen.

The tiny, weatherbeaten vessel scarcely looked warlike—but that was all to the good. She could carry two chariots on deck, concealed by tarpaulins and fishing gear, and she was equipped with a derrick to hoist them out and secure them more secretly beneath the wooden hull when sheltered waters inside the Norwegian fjords had

been reached. But, when the time came, those waters were not sheltered enough: the chariots broke adrift when the weather worsened a bare half a dozen miles short of the target. The Norwegian securing hawsers on *Arthur*'s keel were strong enough: the British bolts on the chariots were not.

It was a heartbreaking and unnecessary failure for Larsen, his crew and the charioteers after skilfully negotiating a dangerous passage. The *Arthur* had to be scuttled and, in two parties, the men set off on foot to cross Norway towards neutral Sweden. Apart from Able Seaman Bob Evans (a Number Two), they all reached the border safely; but Evans was wounded by a German bullet a few hundred yards short of the frontier: when he had recovered, the Germans shot him as a spy.

Tirpitz would have to wait for the attentions of larger and more independent underwater craft, but improved chariots were constructed and cylindrical containers were designed to hold them on the casings of parent submarines which could transport them much more securely and secretly than the little *Arthur*. Training was now concentrated on these lines and, on 26 November, 26 charioteers under Commander Sladen were despatched to Malta. Fell stayed behind to train more chariot crews to replace expected casualties in the Mediterranean. He also took the opportunity of interviewing Italian *Maiali* prisoners-of-war in a camp near London and learned much of interest about their methods and the problems which the enemy had encountered.

By December 1942, eight teams and three submarines—*Trooper*, *Thunderbolt* and *P-311* (another T-boat)—were ready. The boats sailed for Operation 'Principal' from Malta at intervals on 28 and 29 December. Captain SM 10 received a signal from *P-311* at 0130 on 31 December giving her position, but nothing more was ever heard from her: she probably ran onto a mine in the Straits of Bonifacio. Intelligence indicated a concentration of shipping, including a cruiser, at Palermo in northern Sicily and, on this information, both *Trooper* and *Thunderbolt* were directed to launch their attacks at that port rather than split the attack between Cagliari and Palermo as originally planned.

Owing to the relatively large silhouette and general unhandiness of chariot-carrying submarines, the passage through the Sicilian Channel was considered to constitute almost as great a risk as the operation itself. There were close and frequent enemy patrols in the area and, because of these, *Trooper* and *Thunderbolt* were held to the south of Pan-

tellaria until the afternoon of 31 December when Axis patrol activity had subsided for the time being. They were then ordered to proceed. By dawn on New Year's Day 1943, they were safely north of the most dangerous area; the attacks were now ordered for the night of 2/3 January.

The two T-boats launched five chariots off Palermo harbour just before midnight and then withdrew, leaving *Unruffled*, who had followed, to act as recovery vessel. Three of the machines ran straight into trouble. One had to abandon the attack owing to a defective breathing-bag and was picked up six hours later at 0425 on 3 January by *Unruffled*. Another suffered a battery explosion (a not uncommon event) which flooded one of the buoyancy tanks and sent the machine rapidly to the bottom. One man was drowned but the other bailed out at 95 feet with oxygen poisoning: he managed to swim ashore and was taken prisoner. The driver of the third team was suffering severely from the effects of sea-sickness experienced in *Trooper* and, to make matters worse, it seems that he ripped open his diving suit while struggling through the nets. His Number Two continued to control the craft and ran it on the rocks where the pilot scrambled off but drowned—probably because, grossly affected by nausea and unable to breathe easily from his set, he opened the visor and then stumbled. Number Two scuttled the craft in deep water and was eventually captured after swimming ashore.

However, the remaining two chariots, *XXII* (Lieutenant R T G Greenland and Leading Signalman A Ferrier) and *XVI* (Sub Lieutenant R G Dove and Leading Seaman J Freel), were more fortunate. They were able to use their skill and courage with devastating effect.

Greenland and Ferrier had wriggled into their suits with the assistance of their dressers by 2200 when *Thunderbolt*'s navigator gave Greenland the magnetic course for the entrance to Palermo harbour. There was an offshore force 4 wind, the submarine had been rolling throughout the day even at periscope depth and waves were now breaking over the casing. The weather always looks worse from a submarine low down in the water at night and it was pitch dark. Conditions were far from ideal, but it was now that the vigorous exercises in Scotland, in even worse weather, started to pay off. The handlers, prepared to get very wet, climbed up the conning tower first, down the side of the bridge and onto the comparatively broad catwalk covering the external torpedo tubes amidships; the charioteers followed them

more slowly, taking care not to snag their dresses on the way while the handlers opened up the containers abaft the bridge.

The submarine was extremely vulnerable at this point: the captain, Lieutenant C B Crouch, could not dive during the launch period and could only hope that he would not be surprised by anti-submarine units. The ship's company were, of course, at diving stations and there were three lookouts, besides the Captain and officer-of-the-watch, on the bridge. The Asdic operator kept a listening watch in the starboard forward corner of the control room but the chances of hearing anything were slight against the background of sea-noise and the quenching of the Asdic dome beneath the bows. *Thunderbolt* had no radar but some enemy units and shore stations were known to be equipped with fairly effecive search devices. The submarine was at a decided disadvantage.

It was an anxious time for Crouch. The next stage of the drill involved flooding some of the main ballast tanks to trim down and bring the containers awash. In this condition, of course, the submarine lost much of its stability and, with the stern lower than the bow, it was trimmed in the worst possible way for a sudden dive, but, anyway,

diving was unthinkable with so many hands on the casing. As *Thunderbolt* settled down into the water, the 'Jeeps' rose off their chocks and were pulled out of the containers, bucking as they came clear, while the riders flung themselves astride their mounts. Greenland circled the submarine once, hoping to join up with XVI from *Trooper*, but, not surprisingly, he saw nothing and, as he turned his machine to head by compass for Palermo and his prime target—a *Regolo* class cruiser—the faint irregular shape of *Thunderbolt* was quickly lost to sight in the blackness astern.

Running on the surface in a lumpy sea was uncomfortable until XXII came under the lee of the land with the harbour light ahead. Greenland felt behind him for Ferrier's hand and told him by tapping in morse (which the signalman had taught him) that he was going to stop, dive and catch a trim: in these circumstances they could not do so on the bottom. Surfacing again, Greenland continued towards the light only to find, very close inshore, that he was heading for a street lamp, but he correctly guessed which way to alter course and soon came across a breakwater which guarded the harbour entrance. It was no surprise to find a barrier of heavy netting, spiked and supported by buoys, sealing off

Charioteers in the later model, both facing forward, handling the craft with confidence. Even on the surface there was not much showing of this potent weapon.

the entrance. The nets, like over-sized curtains, hung all the way down to the bottom, where they lay in folds. The two divers could not lift the pile of wire mesh manually so Greenland wormed the nose of his machine under one of the folds and, hopefully, blew ballast. This manoeuvre, rather to his amazement, worked: the net and the chariot rose together to the surface while Greenland slid himself beneath the machine to avoid getting speared. Concerned only with getting past the obstacle, he forgot to give Ferrier the tip to do the same, but luck was with XXII and neither man was spiked, snagged or bruised while they pulled and pushed the machine clear and into the harbour.

For some reason, however, the net had caused the compass to deviate wildly. Fortunately, this was obvious. Greenland knew that he could not trust the instrument but it meant that the approach could no longer be made blind: they would, for most of the time, have to keep their heads above water. As it happened, this did not matter much because there was no discernible hostile activity in the harbour. They had to find the target in almost total darkness and fre-

Artist's impression (D. A. Rapkins) of the attack on the Italian cruiser *Ulpio Traiano* in Palermo Harbour.

been expected but an Italian report suggests that the safety pin in each limpet was not removed. If this was true, it was a simple mistake in the drill and readily understandable.

At any rate, Greenland determined to get out of the harbour and let nothing stand in his way. He threw caution to the winds and charged full-speed at the nearest net. The chariot miraculously cleared the hurdle without faltering but ran straight into a darkened merchant ship. Even then, the enemy was not alerted although the noise seemed deafening to the two charioteers; but the compass, which had shown signs of recovery, was now totally upset and Greenland found himself going round in circles. *Thunderbolt* was not going to wait past 0430 and that time was fast approaching. There was no hope of making the rendezvous and, with oxygen nearly exhausted, the sensible thing to do was to scuttle the craft and wander off on foot into the apparently deserted dockyard, hoping for the best.

While all this was going on, *xvi* (Dove and Freel) had also penetrated the harbour and placed their charge under the 8500-ton liner *Viminale*, which was being used as a troop transport. They were too exhausted to distribute their limpets but, like the others, they managed to sink their chariot in the harbour and make their way ashore.

The attack caught the Italians completely by surprise. It was not until the charge under the *Viminale* exploded at dawn that they were aware that anything untowards was occurring. Even then, there was great delay in reporting this attack. Then, at 0800, before any action could be taken, the other charge exploded under the bows of the *Ulpio Traiano*: while still free men, Greenland and Ferrier were treated to a magnificent spectacle as the Duce's newest cruiser blew up with a shattering roar. The charge fixed to the *Viminale* severely damaged the ship aft but did not sink her, but she was further damaged, while under tow, by two torpedoes from HMS *Unbending* on 23 January and was finally sunk on her way to Naples, after repairs at Messina, six months later. The smaller vessels attacked by *xxii* were not hurt.

All the surviving charioteers were, rather tardily, captured and sent to Germany at the express wish of Adolf Hitler. Having stripped off their Sladen suits, they were not well dressed for a formal meeting with the Führer if the occasion should arise but this did not worry them overmuch. Before matters progressed that far, Ferrier performed a final

quent looks would have been necessary even if the compass had been reliable.

The next obstacle was an anti-torpedo net extending down to 50 feet below the surface as expected; they nosed down and passed beneath this without difficulty. Coming up again, they found, right ahead and now very close, the vast, unmistakable bulk of the brand new cruiser *Ulpio Traiano* with her 13.5 cm (5.1 inch) guns outlined against the faint lights on shore.

In moments they were alongside with the motor stopped and in perfect trim. Hand-paddling took the machine down to the keel where they unbolted the charge, clamped it to the hull and set the clockwork fuse with a two-hour delay. It was a copybook operation, but the two divers were not yet

satisfied. They still had four five-pound magnetic limpets in the locker aft, and the anti-submarine vessels and merchant ships anchored close by looked inviting.

Moving unhindered and undiscovered from ship to ship they fixed limpets to the destroyer *Grecale*, the torpedo boat *Ciclone* and a small merchant vessel, the *Gimma*. Feeling, at last, that two men had done enough damage to the Italian navy for one night Greenland headed seaward at maximum revolutions with a following wind and the sea astern. He and Ferrier were both tired and had been breathing oxygen for a long time, some of it under pressure: their judgement must necessarily have been impaired to some extent. They had accomplished much more than could possibly have

Top and centre left
The Welman midget designed and built for the Army from June to August 1942 at 'The Frythe', a commandeered hotel outside Welwyn (one man submersible built at Welwyn—Welman) with the well-named Colonel Dolphin in charge. The original idea was to attack targets with a mine which could be released from inside the craft but no operation of this kind was actually carried out.

in May and June 1943 in preparation for Operation 'Husky', the invasion of Sicily, but Captain(S)10 (Captain G C Phillips) mournfully commented in his report following these operations:

It is hoped that these reconnaissances are of real value to the planners. It has become clear from recent results that submarines engaged on reconnaissance work fall off in efficiency for offensive patrols ...

Offensive chariot operations in the Mediterranean were resumed after Italy capitulated. In June 1944, an extraordinary joint British and Italian operation was mounted against the Italian cruisers *Bolzano* and *Gorizia*, which were under German control at La Spezia. Operation 'QWZ' was originally planned wholly against German U-boats at Muggiano in the Gulf of Spezia but, owing to the changing military situation, it was directed chiefly against the two cruisers to prevent their use as block-ships in the port of Spezia itself.

The Italian destroyer *Grecale* (the same ship that had escaped limpet attack in the previous year) and MS (MTB) *74* conveyed two MTSMs (fast assault craft) and three assault swimmers—under the orders of the renowned de la Penne himself in *Grecale*—and two British chariot crews from the Corsican port of Bastia, sailing on the evening of 21 June. It was a weird, uneasy combination of forces: the British ratings heartily disliked the idea of being embarked in an 'Eytie' ship and the Italians were taking the assorted teams to attack two of their own cruisers in their own *Maiale* base. Strangely enough, the mission was at least partly successful.

Welman charge.

miracle: he produced from his hip-pocket a small bottle of Navy Rum which he and Greenland shared while being watched by the envious Carabinieri who were languidly guarding the prisoners. The tots went down exceedingly well.

Only one chariot was recovered out of the five machines that had been launched, but Operation 'Principal' had been a resounding success. The price paid was, in any sense, extremely low. However, the Admiralty flatly refused to credit the charioteers im-

prisoned at Marlag Camp in Germany with anything more than their General Service pay from the day that they were captured: the extra money for special duties was stopped. This piece of parsimony saved the nation, by the end of the war, some £1300.

'Principal' was by no means the last chariot operation but it was arguably the most valuable. Chariots embarked on board the submarines *Unrivalled*, *Unseen* and *Unison* were employed for beach reconnaissance

Welmans underwent various modifications by the army. 150 were ordered on 23 February 1943 but the order was reduced to twenty by the Chief of Combined Operations (Vice Admiral Lord Louis Mountbatten) in October when FOSM outlined their main handicaps which, compared with Chariots, were their inability to pierce nets and very poor vision for the driver. Unfortunately, production could not be halted until 100 were built! Four Welmans were sent to attack Bergen on 20 November 1943 where they had no luck: *W.46* piloted by a 23-year old Norwegian midshipman was captured intact by the German patrol vessel *NB.59* in Westbyfjord on 21 November and an army officer from another craft was taken prisoner; but two other army officers escaped and were recovered in February 1944. Success in Norway was left to midget submarines proper—the X-craft (see Chapter 11): CCO said on 15 February 1944 that he had no employment for Welmans and three days later FOSM advised that 'they be dropped and no attempt should be made to "find" a use for them'. The German comment on examining the captured Welman was that 'the enemy continues the mini war with ever new ideas'.

MS-74, with the Senior British Naval Officer on board, arrived off La Spezia at 2340 and lowered her two British chariots into the water through the specially cut-away stern: the charioteers reckoned that the Italian MTB was the best means of transportation yet devised. *Grecale* had stopped well short of the coast and her two MTSMs, one of them with three Gamma men on board, had already sped off in the direction of the bay, the limpeteers being dropped over the side 300 metres from the breakwater. While the Italian frogmen were attaching their charges to a U-boat at Muggiano, the British chariots were negotiating the main harbour defences. Both teams were aggrieved to find that the run-in distance appeared to be considerably greater than they had expected: later they were to claim that they had been dropped six or eight miles out, but it seems that the real distance was almost certainly the correct two-and-a-half miles. If it

seemed longer it was probably because the machines' batteries were not fully charged and the chariots themselves were ploughing along at reduced speed. One chariot developed faults and had to be abandoned. The other, manned by Sub Lieutenant M Causer and Able Seaman H Smith, succeeded in finding gaps in the three lines of nets, but negotiating the defences took much more time than planned.

The 10,000-ton *Bolzano* was easily sighted and Causer took his machine deep to 25 feet when a cable's length off the target's beam. Soon the vast bulk loomed darkly overhead and he turned sharply to starboard while coming up to 20 feet. Almost immediately the machine was scraping the underside of the hull so he stopped the motor and hauled the chariot along by means of magnets which he attached as handholds. When Causer, a perfectionist, reckoned they were amidships and below the boiler-rooms the pair fastened

the warhead to the hull with more magnets. Causer set the fuse for two hours so that the charge would detonate at 0630. Finally, he pulled the release gear that freed the warhead from the chariot and steered for the breakwater where, with the battery extremely low, there was no choice but to abandon the craft.

The explosion came at 0623. The charioteers—all four of them—were able to watch from an excellent vantage point in the wooded hills some two miles north-east of the dockyard, where partisans were busily making them welcome. The effect on the Italian cruiser was dramatic. Heavily down by the bows she capsized and sank in little more than an hour. Her sinking robbed the enemy (the Germans, that is) of a valuable blockship and, as the official historian of the war at sea[12] remarked: 'Considering the very strong defences of Spezia, the principal naval base of Italy, the exploit was among the

Above
The Welfreighter, built by Shelvoke and Drewry Ltd at Letchworth, was a submersible motor boat with an endurance of 600 miles at 8 knots on the surface. It was designed to carry stores and agents: three men could be embarked. It was proposed that six craft could put half a section of commando troops ashore on an enemy coast at dusk and bring them off just before daylight, thus avoiding the time limitation of a surface craft which had to approach and leave the coast in darkness. A single Welfreighter was considered ideal for landing and recovering a two-man reconnaissance party: but the craft never saw operational employment. It could well be useful today for clandestine operations: production craft took only seven days to build.

Left
Welfreighter, cockpit looking aft.

Opposite top left
Welfreighter, cockpit looking forward.

Opposite top right
Welfreighter, conning tower controls.

Opposite centre
Welfreighter, shallow periscope depth.

Opposite bottom left
Breaking surface.

Opposition bottom right
Hoisting out.

One of the crude instruments of torture designed to measure the performance of frogmen and take them to the limit in comparative safety on dry land!

most notable of the Submarine Service.' The only thing wrong about this statement is that chariots were not really a part of the Submarine Service: they were proud to swim on their own.

It might be thought that the men who took part in these daring exploits would only remember the excitement and the successes they achieved and the decorations they so richly deserved—Italians and British alike. But, for men of the Royal Navy at least, it is memories of the Sladen suit, commonly known as 'Clammy Death', that linger foremost in the minds of many. To quote one experienced operator, George Fagence:[13] 'Photos of frogmen only remind me of the numbing cold of the suit, and shallow-water diving courses, and chattering teeth and red, raw eye-sockets . . .'

Italian *Maiali* men evidently felt just as strongly about their own equipment, judging by prisoner-of-war interrogations.[14] One captured frogman thought that the Italian gear (with something described as waterproofed silk for the suit) was immeasurably better than the British but it was clumsy and he did not want anything to do with Oxygen any more as he had no desire to ruin his health. 'Oxygen', he said, 'makes your tongue and gums go white and your teeth ache as though they would fall out.' A British expert[15] considered that the Italians were 'badly trained psychologically' with regard to oxygen but this was not true: they were simply more aware of the dangers as a result of some singularly ruthless experiments.

Carbon dioxide poisoning was another hazard, if the gas built up in a breathing set. The (surprisingly) popular RNVR medical officer principally concerned with research and training for underwater swimmers of all kinds, Surgeon Lieutenant Commander Melville Balfour, instituted a series of tolerance tests known as Balfour's Blackout Pa-

Top right
Sleeping Beauty MSC (Motor Submersible Canoe) on trials in 1942 with Major H. G. Hasler, RM, at the controls.

Above
Sleeping Beauty trimming down. The one-man craft could carry six limpets and personal assault equipment: it could dive to 40 feet.

Frogmen attaching demolition charges to an underwater obstacle. (RN Commando Association).

rades. The subject (usually a Royal Marine) was made to walk up and down wearing a breathing set from which the Protosorb CO_2 absorbant had been removed. Thereby he was slowly poisoned until he approached insensibility whereupon he was disconnected from the apparatus and revived.[16] The idea was for individual divers to recognise their own particular symptoms in order to take action early enough.

It may not be apparent today, when SCUBA diving is a common hobby, why a closed-circuit oxygen re-breathing set was used in preference to a simple, and much safer, normal compressed-air supply with a free exhaust. The reason, of course, was that no tell-tale air bubbles could be allowed to escape to the surface. The same consideration would necessarily apply to any modern covert frogman operation. If chariots or their like are indeed used for warlike operations in the future, their riders will do well to read reports from the last war with care and caution. Charioteering will never be a comfortable or easy business.

MK1** Canoe agent's kit muster! (RN Commando Association)

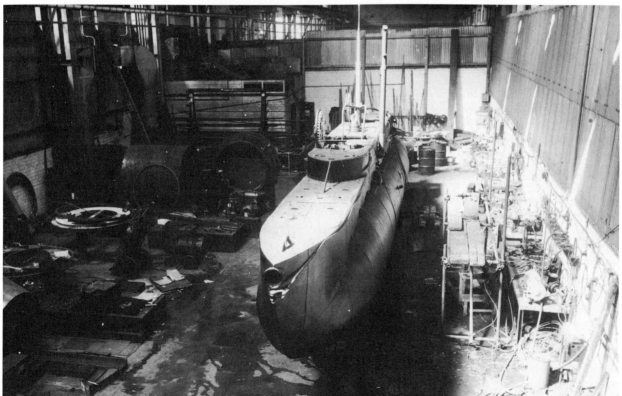

X-Craft building in early 1944 at Thos. Broadbent's yard, Huddersfield. The other builders of production craft were Vickers, Markham (Chesterfield), and Marshall (Gainsborough), but more than twenty other firms supplied parts and equipment. The induction mast shown raised here has not yet been fitted with the 'Hezlet' safety rail. The so-called night periscope forward of the principal periscope could not be raised: it was used mainly when shut down on the surface and for watching the diver submerged.

11: Midgets Magnificent

On 13 February 1943, Prime Minister Winston Churchill, ill with pneumonia in North Africa, dictated another irritable minute to the Chiefs of Staff in London about what he usually called The Beast:

Have you given up all plans for doing anything to TIRPITZ *while she is in Trondhjem? We heard a lot of talk about it five months ago, which all petered out. At least four or five plans were under consideration. It seems very discreditable that the Italians should show themselves so much better at attacking ships in harbour than we do ... It is a terrible thing to think that this prize should be waiting and no one be able to think of a way of winning it.*

Some very special submariners had, in fact, been planning to win this particular prize for the best part of two years already, but it took a long time to build midget submarines along the lines proposed by 'Crom' Varley and train the crews. Three different

ship-builders constructed the bow, centre and tail-sections; and more than twenty firms contributed to the internal 'gubbins'. It was a formidable jig-saw puzzle to assemble, and a frustrating period for Lieutenant Willy Meeke[1] in command, Lieutenant Don Cameron,[2] First Lieutenant, and Chief ERA Richardson.[3] As the First Lieutenant grimly remarked, it seemed that the policy was 'not to let the right hand know what the left hand undoeth.' There was much testing to be done ashore before concentrating on the craft itself, especially in devising a method of using the 'Wet & Dry' chamber safely for the diver's exit and re-entry.

Before the war, the boat-builders on the River Hamble leading down to Southampton Water launched a succession of the most graceful yachts that the world had ever known, and now the river was full of fast MTBs which had a certain grace and beauty of their own. But His Majesty's Submarine *X-3*[4] had nothing graceful or beautiful about

X-Craft bow showing the towing cable slip which was released from inside the craft. Side cargoes are attached.

X-Craft with side cargoes from below. The arrangement of the rudder, hydroplanes and propeller guard was remarkably similar to that of the Holland boats at the turn of the century.

her when she eventually slid down the chocks in secrecy at 2300 on the night of Sunday, 15 March 1942 at the Varley Marine Works, Sarisbury Green. However, she took the water at full surge and, to everybody's relief, remained afloat. To maintain security, she went under her own power (what other submarine has been able to do that at launching?) to a tarpaulin-covered articulated pontoon moored in mid-stream, within whose confines she discreetly hid herself. The pontoon was forthwith christened the Art Wot-Not and seagulls from Southampton helpfully hastened to whiten and disguise the modest sanctuary.

Frankly, *X-3* was fat, black and ugly: her face was not her fortune. In that, she resembled HM Submarine *No. 1* (*Holland 1*) which had founded the Royal Navy's Submarine Service at her launch on 2 October 1901, more than 40 years earlier: this archetypal 'submarine boat', which was salvaged in 1982 and put on display at the Royal Navy Submarine Museum, Gosport, can now be seen to have several features subsequently adopted for the first mini-monster and the craft which followed her.

An operational X-craft had glass viewing ports with screwed-down deadlights, almost exactly the same as the Irish-American John Philip Holland's scuttles at the turn of the century and, because of the low profile shared with *Holland I*, an air intake tube was fitted to supply the engine when the craft was on the surface with the hatch normally shut: this also served as a (rather inefficient) voice-pipe.

The pressure hull, however, was not the porpoise-shape of *Number One* because there were no torpedoes: the primary weapon system consisted of two Amatol side-cargoes—delayed action mines—which had to be fastened (with quick release gear) on either side of the hull. These, when in position, resulted in an excellent length-to-breadth ratio not too far removed from the nearly ideal 5.4 to 1 conceived by Holland. An alternative kind of side-cargo, looking externally the same, could act as a suitcase for a number of limpet mines, and limpets could also be stowed beneath the casing, if required, together with net-cutting gear.

Overall, *X-3* at about 50 feet was some 13 feet shorter than *Holland I*, and had only 35 feet of useable space internally including the Wet and Dry (W & D) compartment which also contained a hand-pumped WC. The rudder, hydroplanes and propeller guard made up the remainder of the length and were very reminiscent of *Number One's* configuration. There was barely four feet six in-

ches of headroom. The crew of three (increased to four in due course) had joined from normal submarines and were volunteers for hazardous service. Even during trials, and long before X-craft were despatched on operations, the service was indeed hazardous. There were many unknowns; but Varley, the inventor, in his thick tweed suit amongst the naval uniforms, was meticulous and surprisingly little went wrong with the first midget so far as seaworthiness was concerned. However, the whole tribe of X-craft was to be plagued with defects of a minor nature.

Delays were due chiefly to finding suitable auxiliary equipment but simplicity and rug-

Side cargo containing 3,570 lb of Amatex (Amatol plus 9 per cent RDX to give complete detonation) in the central section with buoyancy tanks top and bottom. Handwheels on either side inside the craft opened the flooding valves and freed the charge which, with the aid of a spring-plunger, then fell away to the sea-bed rounded side down. Detonation was pre-set from within the craft at 30 minute steps up to six hours. Cameron (*X-6*) said that the charges were not sufficiently powerful to sink a battleship with a fair depth of water under the keel.

A modest launch party for one of the operational X-Craft.

gedness were the key words for the hull and major components. The Perkins diesel engines in *X-3* and some of the others were trustworthy and later craft had equally good Gardner engines which properly belonged to the London bus fleet: they proved just as reliable at sea as they were on the streets of the Metropolis. Problems only arose with the more finicky bits and pieces, like the electric periscope-hoist motor: practically everything had to be miniaturised and it came to be said that taking command of an X-craft was like being given a toy train set for Christmas.

HM Drifter *Present Help*, commanded by Lieutenant 'George' Washington,[5] was attached as tender and made very comfort-

X-Craft control room with Captain at the periscope—a posed picture. The helmsman's seat and wheel are at the bottom left, with starboard charge release-wheel behind and bunk bottom right.

Induction mast (with Hezlet safety rail) through which orders were shouted down to the helsman; when the engine was running and sucking down air, it was hard to hear orders correctly and mistakes were not infrequent. The tiny periscope is fully raised: vision through this masterpiece of miniaturisation by Barr & Stroud was good provided the instrument did not mist up, flood or bend when hitting floating debris, and it was possible to range fairly accurately with the graticules. The projector-compass tube is raised on the right. One of the two lateral side-ports, with its protective anti-depth charge cover which could be slid across from inside the craft, can be seen amidships. There was a similar port overhead.

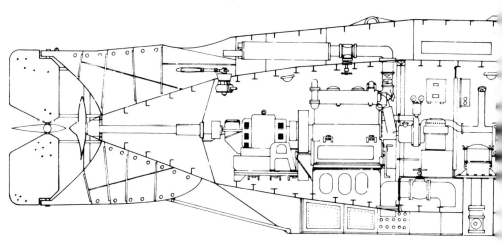

BRITISH X CRAFT

BRITISH XE-CRAFT

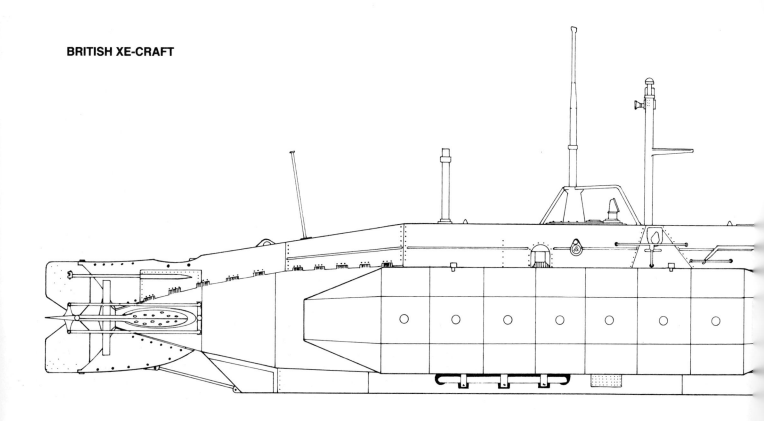

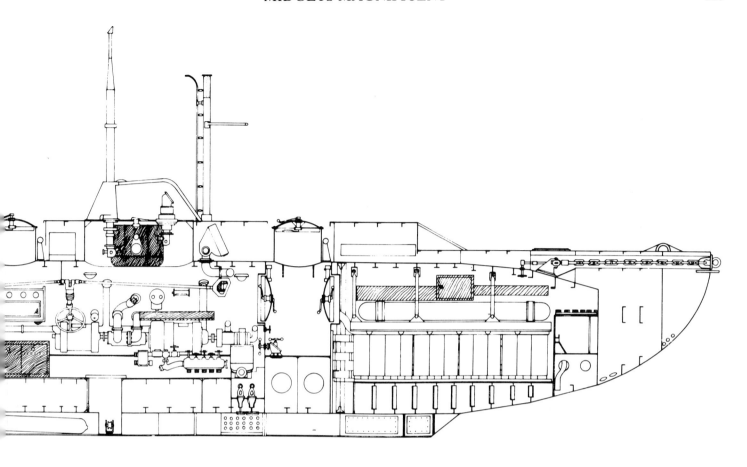

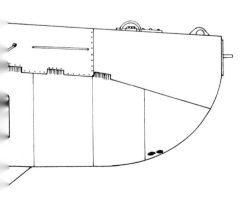

able; when not occupied in the Solent with W & D and side-cargo trials, she lay moored alongside the Art Wot-Not. Commander 'Tissy' Bell[6] had joined the unit to take charge of training shortly before the launch: Varley and Bell were to be jointly commemorated in the name of the first X-craft Shore Base, HMS *Varbel* at Port Bannatyne on the Isle of Bute. Formal training classes of officers and men started to assemble from May 1942 onwards; they included Australians and South Africans (all of whom excelled), and there was much to learn, for many of the new arrivals had little or no experience in normal submarines.

Once waterborne, *X-3* was rapidly put through her paces. The first dive at the end of March 1942 off Lee-on-the-Solent, with Varley on board (hopping about and upsetting the trim), was made very gingerly; but the craft hit the bottom at 30 feet with a heavy thud. Pumping brought her up easily enough and the crew quickly learned how to control her. Soon they were stopping, going astern submerged, changing depth with no headway and manoeuvring without difficulty

while Cameron, who reported that the boat did not make *too* much water, controlled the hydroplanes and trim.

X-3 proved to be a thoroughly handy little boat although it was already evident that the control room forward and battery compartment amidships ought to be changed round: crawling, usually in wet clothes, across the top of the battery cells to reach the engine was altogether too invigorating. In June, the prototype was towed to Portland where Meeke carried out a dummy attack on an anchored oiler. To make things easier for observers (mainly from the Army), *X-3* towed a buff to mark her progress and Meeke showed plenty of periscope. She was not spotted by the battery of military binoculars: 'It makes you think,' said Cameron, 'but our soldier friends were looking for us astern of the buff.'[7]

On 26 August 1942, *X-3* was taken to Southampton Docks where a crane lifted her onto a railway wagon bound for Faslane in Scotland. Cameron and Richardson, supported by an electrical rating and two stokers, formed the guard and Richardson rode chief shot-gun, armed with a revolver and a large supply of bullets. A six-compartment coach was converted into a Wardroom, ERA's Mess, Seamen's Mess, Rec Space and Galley. Cameron did rounds 'pusser-like' at 2100 each evening. Travel by rail thereafter became a popular way of getting an X-craft from one place to another: it was a great deal more comfortable than being towed at sea and the railway folk took good care of the crews, providing hot water and stopping at the most convenient places (near suitable hostelries) *en route*.

The craft was unloaded at Faslane and taken in tow by the antique depot ship *Alecto* down the Clyde estuary to Loch Striven where *Present Help* soon arrived to relieve her. Operational training was now started in earnest.

X-3, with the induction mast hull-valve jammed open, sank accidentally in 100 feet of water with a temporary crew on board in November: Murphy's Law decreed that the wheel-spanner needed to open the main ballast blowing valves should drop into the bilges at the critical moment. Everybody escaped but the craft had to be shipped back to Portsmouth while *X-4*, built in Portsmouth dockyard and next in line with Lieutenant Godfrey Place[8] replaced her for further training.

The performance of *X-3* and *X-4* was good enough to convince the Admiralty that midget submarines were well worth building in quantity. On 4 May 1942, a contract was placed with Vickers for six operational craft embodying improvements suggested by the initial trials. Most notably, the Control Room was placed conventionally amidships and the battery was repositioned right forward. The construction of *X-5* to *X-10* proceeded at full speed and the craft were delivered in the middle of January 1943. Cameron took *X-6* which he named *Piker II*, and Place *X-7* which he christened *Pdinichthys*.

The exercises grew steadily tougher and in March the first three operational craft moved to Loch Cairnbawn (Port HHZ) for a month for some very strenuous practising before the second division—*X-8*, *X-9* and *X-10*—took their place alongside HMS *Bonaventure*. These six craft, together with the chariots, now formed the Twelfth Submarine Flotilla. Captain Willy Banks[9] operated the Flotilla with charm, sympathy and great efficiency from HMS *Varbel* (which had been the Hydropathic Hotel) at Port Bannatyne; Capain P Q Roberts,[10] another famous submariner, commanded *Bonaventure*. The Twelfth was a very strong team.

X-Craft main engine affectionately christened *Gozo II* by a Maltaphile.

Although he felt that staff officers were over-optimistic about the projected attack on *Tirpitz*, Cameron's notes on the final work-up suggest considerable confidence in *Piker II*:

1. Night entrance to HHZ in the face of "stiff" opposition. We did this trimmed down—sitting on the casing with sound-powered handset—the water up to my middle. Very damp but good fun.
2. Sunday morning attack on MALAYA *[battleship] with Flag Officer Submarines [Admiral Barry] on board. This was quite funny as the gyro was misbehaving but it gave the old boy a thrill and his signal to* MALAYA *"Inspected your bottom at 1000 today" made the Captain of* MALAYA *(Captain O'Donnel) a trifle annoyed.*

3. "Operation Landing Agent" by day in Loch Nigg. The sight of Willy Wilson[11] in his birthday suit floundering through the shallows to the beach carrying his gear on his head amid the resounding cheers of the female population in the surrounding crofts, the scouts sent out to intercept him wiling the hours away in the pub at Drumbeg.

It had been the Naval Staff's intention to mount an operation against the *Tirpitz* in the spring of 1943, but, unfortunately, 9 March was considered to be the latest date suitable

Italian *CB (Caproni B) 9*. Between 1941 and 1943, 22 of this class of four-man midgets were built. Each craft carried two external torpedoes (or two mines as shown here) and was a complete submarine in miniature with a surface range of 600 miles at 7.5 knots and a maximum speed submerged of 6.3 knots for just over one hour. The diving depth was 50 metres. There were several other types of Italian midgets and some were extremely advanced although they did not see war service.

Italian CB midgets, photographed probably in late 1942, with stern-firing 45 cm (17.7 inch) torpedoes.

for an attack in Norwegian waters because from then on the hours of daylight were too long. So, much to the disappointment of the crews who could not possibly complete the necessary exercises in the few weeks available after the craft themselves were ready, serious operations had to be deferred despite the urgency of the task that lay ahead. Banks and Bell were fully supported by both Flag Officer Submarines and the Admiralty in their insistence on complete and realistic training. It would be worse than useless to send the midgets before they were ready: they simply had to work and wait. When the time eventually came, their crews had reached a peak of efficiency that was arguably unequalled anywhere else in the submarine service.

A great deal of thought had gone into planning the raid, particularly with regard to taking the X-craft to their destination. They could, conceivably, go under their own power but the crews would be exhausted before they got there; or they could be towed by Norwegian fishing boats, like *Arthur*; or they could be carried by *Bonaventure* (which was fitted with adequate derricks); or they could be towed submerged by normal submarines. It was the last suggestion that, beyond question, seemed the best: detailed preparations were made accordingly.

Timing was critical: the weather had to be good and the right balance of daylight and darkness was important. This limited any reasonable chance of success, 300 miles

north of the Arctic Circle, to the March and September equinoxes with a further restriction imposed by the phases of the moon implying, in the autumn equinox, the period 20–25 September. 'Operation Source' was therefore delayed until the early autumn, and the sense of this soon became apparent in other respects. During exercises in Loch Striven, one diver, Sub Lieutenant David Locke, was lost while cutting through a net: each crew was thereupon increased to four (at Cameron's urging) by recruiting a diver from the chariot teams. Meanwhile, three-man passage crews, who would be 'caretakers' in each craft during the long tow north, were assembled and trained during the summer of 1943.

At the end of August, six towing submarines—two T-boats and four S-boats—arrived at Loch Cairnbawn. All leave was stopped on 1 September. The submarines were equipped with guide-tubes and slips for the towing hawsers which were made of hemp or nylon with a telephone cable laid in the core. Cameron in *X-6*, due to be towed by *Truculent* (Lieutenant Robbie Alexander[12]), made sure that his rope was nylon; it was less likely to break than hemp and he believed, with subsequent justification, that a heavy, parted rope might drag a craft to the bottom together with its passage crew—especially since it was necessary to trim a craft a little heavy under tow to make sure it did not break surface.

Aerial photographic reconnaissance and clandestine messages from the Norwegian resistance movement revealed *Tirpitz* in Kaa

Fjord together with the 32,000 ton *Scharnhorst* and, close by in Lange Fjord, the 12,000 ton *Lutzow*. *X-5* (Lt H Henty Creer, RNVR), *X-6* (Cameron) and *X-7* (Place) were assigned to *Tirpitz*; *X-8* (Lt B M McFarlane, RAN) to *Lutzow*; *X-9* (Lt T L Martin, RN) and *X-10* (Lt K R Hudspeth, RANVR) to *Scharnhorst*.

The parent submarines, led by *Truculent* with *X-6*, left Loch Cairnbawn in pairs at two-hour intervals, starting at 1600 on 11 September. *Sceptre* with *X-10*, given the least circuitous route, did not sail until 1300 on the following day.

The X-craft were towed, dived, at an average speed of between eight and ten knots for the first four days. The passage crews broke surface at six-hourly intervals to 'guff through', changing the stale air by raising the induction mast and running the engine for ten minutes or longer if the battery and air bottles needed re-charging. In a rough sea this was an especially miserable period but the weather, in the main, stayed fair.

On passage, time ceased to have much meaning. Any real sleep was impossible. One man remained on the hydroplane wheel while the craft oscillated gently up and down, sometimes through 100 feet or more, while the planesman tried to determine whether the oscillation was normal or whether it signified that the trim or hydroplanes were wrongly set. For much of the

HMS *Titania*, seen through an X-Craft periscope, with towing submarines alongside shortly before the *Tirpitz* operation. Horizontal as well as vertical graticules could be used for estimating range.

X-5 on deck of *Bonaventure* before being hoisted out for Operation Source in September 1943.

Five of the six X-Craft commanding officers (Henty Creer absent) on board *Bonaventure* before Operation Source. Left to right: Martin, Hudspeth, McFarlane, Place and Cameron, the latter wearing RNR rings that invariably denoted above average expertise in navigation and seamanship.

HMS *Thrasher*, with *X-5* in tow, leaving *Titania* at Loch Cairnbawn on 11 September 1943. The tow rope, 600 feet long and black nylon in this case, represented 20,000 pairs of nylon stockings—rare and highly negotiable articles in wartime!

time the two men off watch had to work hard but at least this helped to keep out the cold—a damp, grey almost tangible variety that no kind of clothing could protect against. There were electrical insulations to be checked; equipment (including the vital periscope) to be tested; bilges to be dried; machinery to be greased and oiled; the whole craft to be kept scrupulously clean (a matter of particular pride); and food—such as it was—to be prepared.

There was, of course, no galley. A carpenter's glue-pot in the control room served as a double boiler; an electric kettle provided hot water. For the first 24 hours of a long tow some attempt was made to cook meals. That is to say, the first four tins which came to hand were emptied into the glue-pot, stirred and heated. The resulting potmess was then eaten with spoons out of soup plates. It was not an attractive meal but its memory remained until the next guff through: its smell pervaded the boat and condensation trickled drearily down the inside of the pressure hull. Appetites dwindled rapidly after the first day: cooked food, sardines, cheese, biscuits, oranges, apples, coffee, tea and fruit juice were rejected one by one—generally in that order. However, Lieutenant Peter Philip,[13] the stalwart South African passage CO of *X-7*, enjoyed gargantuan feasts—amongst them tomato soup, lamb's tongue with green peas and loganberries with tinned milk for a sweet: Able Seaman Mick Magennis (later to win the Victoria Cross in *XE-3* at Singapore) was an excellent chef. A generous government also provided, even in those days of strict food rationing, a large tin of barley sugar but that too soon sickened.

The passage crews did not have the excitement and the rewards of an attack (and nor were they faced with great dangers), but they were vital to the success of a mission. It was their task to hand over the craft to the operational crew in perfect condition after enduring days of appalling discomfort, boredom and weariness.

But dangers of a kind there were. At 0100 on the morning of 15 September, the telephone line between *Seanymph* and *X-8* failed and the tow parted three hours afterwards. It was 36 hours before *Seanymph* rec-

'The Beast'—an aerial reconnaissance photograph of the 42,000 ton battleship *Tirpitz* lying protected by nets at the head of Kaa Fjord: the boat gap is obvious from the air.

Place and Cameron (right) immediately after liberation from Marlag-Milag Nord prisoner-of-war camp in Germany. Both men were awarded the Victoria Cross, gazetted on 22 February 1944. Rear Admiral Barry concluded his report on Operation Source:
'It is clear that courage and enterprise of the very highest order in the close presence of the enemy was shown by these very gallant gentlemen, whose daring attack will surely go down in history as one of the most courageous acts of all time.'

XE-1, XE-3 and *XE-4* on the deck of *Bonaventure* at Labuan in July 1945. The first two were assigned to attack the Japanese heavy cruisers *Nachi* and *Takao* at Singapore and *XE-4* was to cut the seabed telephone cable off Saigon. The two craft on the right are fitted with limpet carriers and the one on the left with normal side cargoes. *Bonaventure* was an ex-Clan Line freighter capable of carrying locomotives to South America so she was well equipped for hoisting midget submarines in and out: seven X or XE craft could be embarked.

overed her lost sibling and resumed the northward passage, transferring the operational crew to relieve the passage team who were totally exhausted. The telephone cable between *Syrtis* and *X-9* also failed and then her cable, too, parted on the 16th. *X-9* was never seen again.

On the same day, *X-8* was again in trouble. This time the starboard side-cargo was leaking and McFarlane had to jettison the charge. He set the timing mechanism to safe but the mine exploded a few minutes later. No damage was done. When the port side-cargo developed similar symptoms, he set the fuse with a 2-hour delay before releasing it, reckoning this would be less dangerous. The explosion duly came nearly two hours later when *Seanymph* and *X-8* were more than three miles away, but, because of some unexplained freak of nature, *X-8* was badly damaged. The craft had to be scuttled.

Four craft remained. Three of them had nylon tow ropes. The tows that failed were hemp: Cameron had been right.

At dawn on 20 September, all four units were off the Norwegian coast. The operational crews paddled across in rubber dinghies and took over. Between 1830 and 2000 the craft slipped their tows and set course on the surface for Soroy Sound across the known German minefield. They were on their own—bound, as Godfrey Place noted in *X-7*'s log, for the Great Adventure.

Don Cameron in *Piker II* kept a full and very private kind of diary. It was a way of writing to his young wife Eve: the chances of ever seeing her again were not high. 'If I were a true Brit,' he wrote, 'the job would be the thing, but I can't help thinking what the feelings of the next-of-kin would be if I make a hash of it.' From time to time he felt in his pocket for Bunjy—a little wooden dog, Eve's first present to him—and was reassured. He envied John Lorimer, his First Lieutenant, Sub Lieutenant Dicky Kendall, the diver, and Nigger Goddard,[14] the ERA, who had learned his engineering with Rolls-Royce. They seemed so confident: for himself he admitted (for Eve alone) a 'just-before-the-battle-Mother' feeling. Looking at the moon rising above the mountains and brushing them with silver as *Piker II* surged up Kaa Fjord late on the evening of the 21st, he 'felt very homesick indeed' and wondered if Eve would be watching it too, far away at

Sub Lieutenant 'Robbie' Robinson at the hydroplane and trimming controls of *X-24* at about the time of the second attack on Bergen in September 1944. The ubiquitous cooking pot is by his left foot.

Lee-on-the-Solent. The diary continued: 'the elation of sitting in the middle of the enemy's fleet anchorage vied with the feeling of a small boy very much alone and wanting to go home and be comforted. Was not conscious of fear, just of wanting someone to talk to ...'

Although they all kept their thoughts to themselves, nobody, in any of the craft, had any illusions about the dangers ahead. If things went wrong it would not be a matter of pottering back with a shrug to friendly old *Bonaventure* for a gin.

Piker II's starboard side-cargo was flooded and the port charge's timing mechanism would only accept a two-hour

Sub Lieutenant Britnell on *X-24* flying her Jolly Roger at Port HHZ after the attack on Bergen when Max Shean sank the 7,500-ton *Barenfels* in mistake for his real target, the floating dock.

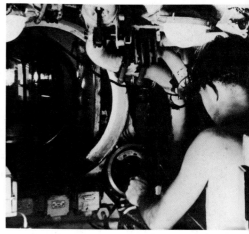

XE-Craft distinguished by her continuous flush casing from an X-Craft.

Helmsmen of an XE-Craft looking forward through the Wet and Dry compartment to the battery space: main vent hand levers above.

setting. A list to starboard had to be corrected by ditching food (which went against Cameron's Scottish sensibilities) and moving stores over to the port side. No. 1 main ballast blow was leaking and emitting a steady stream of bubbles. Worse, the periscope was letting in drops of water and continually misting up; Cameron and Kendall had to strip it down six times in all during the approach and it never worked satisfactorily.

Place in *Pdinichthys* (*X-7*) had no serious defects, but Hudspeth's *Excalibur* (*X-10*) suffered a succession of mechanical faults. The periscope hoist motor burnt out, producing clouds of acrid fumes, and both the gyro and magnetic compasses failed. There was no way that *Excalibur* could continue without jeopardising the entire operation and it was clearly impossible to make any repairs before the charges from the other craft were due to go up at 0830 on the 22nd. Hudspeth therefore kept out of the way and, sadly, started to retire seaward at sunset on that day, having heard two very heavy explosions at about the right time in the morning signifying that one or more craft had attacked. The crew were eventually picked up by *Stubborn* and *X-10* was scuttled. It could well be that Henty Creer's *Platypus* (*X-5*) experienced mechanical difficulties as well during the run-in.

X-6 made her way up Alten Fjord with her periscope, to all intents and purposes, useless. Cameron 'might as well have had a beer bottle'; fuzzy and indistinct when she appeared around the corner at the top of Kaa Fjord, the *Tirpitz* 'looked like a great haystack'. Nearing the nets protecting the

inner fjord at 0445 on 22nd, he took a chance and surfaced, in the broad light of day, to pass through the narrow gate, at full speed on the diesel, astern of a small coaster. The risk—unimaginable in cold blood—paid off, and it was probably a lesser risk than sending Kendall out to cut a way through the netting with time growing short. The boom was shut almost as soon as *Piker II* was through and, incredibly, there were no indications that she had been sighted. From the surface, *Tirpitz* could now be seen, gleaming in bright sunlight less than two miles away. Cameron dived again, thankfully, at 0505. Conditions could not have been worse: the fjord's icy waters were glassily calm.

The battleship was enclosed within a double row of anti-torpedo nets with only a 20 metre gap to seaward on the port bow. This gate was guarded by hydrophones and a special guard-boat but, unwisely, the Germans stood down the guard at 0600. At 0700, Cameron, by expert dead-reckoning, slipped through the narrow entrance, keeping just shallow enough to see the surface through the glass scuttles in the pressure hull.

At 0707, *X-6*, blind, ran on to a rocky shoal and broke surface momentarily. The German lookouts thought she was a porpoise and took no action. But the shock made both compasses swing wildly and at 0715 she ran into a net 60 feet off the target's port bow. The motor, full astern, pulled *Piker* clear but she shot to the surface out of control. This time she was correctly identified but, for the Germans, it was too late. *X-6* was too close for the battleship's heavy

secondary armament to bear and Cameron disregarded the hail of machine gun bullets and grenades that greeted him as he scraped along the giant grey hull abreast B Turret: 'not lethal but made a helluva noise like a rivetters' shed.' Goddard and Kendall grabbed the mine release wheels. As four tons of high explosive slid down to the bottom, the crew wrecked all the equipment they could reach and opened valves and vents to sink the craft. Cameron himself, ensuring that Bunjy was still safely in his pocket and with water rising to his knees, came last of course: 'Baled out just in time. Lost my pipe and tobacco—most annoyed.' He said a silent goodbye to the secondmost love of his life and climbed without haste up the little ladder through the hatch into the fresh air and dazzling light knowing that certain imprisonment or, very possibly, a firing squad awaited. Mercifully, he was wrong about the firing squad: 'Taken on board to meet reception committee. Reception lukewarm. But they didn't think we had completed our attack at the time and were quite cock-a-hoop.'

Place, in *X-7*, was releasing his sidecargoes at about the same time as Cameron—between 0723 and 0725. *X-7*, like *X-6*, had passed through the outer de-

Opposite top
Posed photograph of XE-Craft looking aft with Lieutenant Verry at the periscope, chart table on right.

Opposite bottom
XE-6 (Lieutenant Enzer) in 1945 at the USN base, Subic. Enzer and the First Lieutenant of *XE-3*, 'Dave' Carey, were to be lost, almost certainly due to oxygen poisoning, while experimenting in methods of cutting seabed telephone cables at depths between 40 and 45 feet.

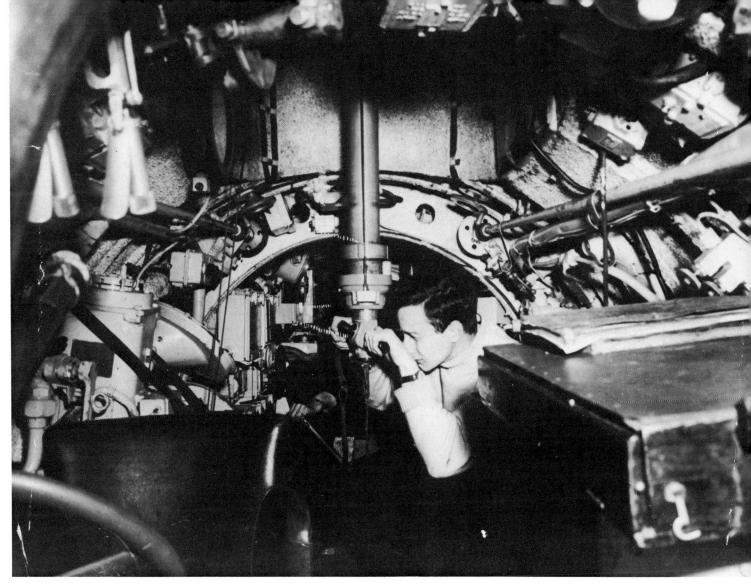

The Japanese heavy cruiser *Takao* crippled by *XE-3* at Singapore when her charges detonated at 2130 on the 31 July 1945, tearing a 60-foot by 30-foot hole in the hull. The United States Navy was set against X-Craft operations partly because X-Craft were wrongly thought to have the same limitations as the Japanese midgets and partly because the United States was determined to win the war by orthodox methods (a determination which was to be broken dramatically by the dropping of two atom bombs). However, Admiral Fife, USN, was eventually persuaded in their favour and the wrecked *Takao* was one result. The cruiser was no longer the sea-going threat shown in this 1939 photograph; but in the last few weeks of the war her 8-inch guns could have seriously imperilled Allied troops advancing along the Singapore Causeway.

Limpet mine of the type used, together with a standard side-cargo, to attack *Takao*.

fences unobserved but accidentally became entangled in a rectangle of nets protecting the empty berth intended for *Lutzow*. It took Place an hour to get free: his exertions put the trim pump out of action for a while and the gyro started to wander. *Pdinicthys* broke clear at 0600 and Place planned to go deep and slide beneath the final barrier of anti-torpedo nets rather than try to find a gap. Intelligence suggested that the nets would only extend to 60 feet below the surface, but the reports were optimistic; the secondary net hung down, at least in places, to the bottom and *X-7* was twice entangled. She broke surface briefly, with the gyro tem-

porarily off the board, and was not noticed before Place found to his surprise that the craft was actually inside the defences: the target was 30 yards ahead. Fortune had again favoured the brave.

Going deep to 40 feet, *X-7* hit *Tirpitz* below B turret where Place released one cargo below the keel before changing depth to 60 feet where the First Lieutenant, Bill Whittam,[15] caught a stop trim. Then, manoeuvring astern under the length of the target for an estimated 180 feet, Place released the other charge below 'C' Turret—the equivalent to 'X' Turret in British ships.

At 0740, endeavouring to find a way out,

Pdinicthys again became caught in the nets and broke surface, coming under small arms fire until Whittam regained control. Deep and blind, the craft once more hit netting off the target's starboard bow and here, at 0812, two gigantic and almost simultaneous explosions shook her free. The pressure hull was still intact but the internal damage was such that there was no hope of escape.

Place surfaced the craft alongside a battle-practise target and climbed out waving his white submarine sweater to signify surrender. The ballast tanks were leaking badly and at 0835 *Pdinicthys* sank beneath him with the remainder of the crew on board.

FE24-71/A16-3   UNITED STATES NAVY   12a/fg
Serial 00180-A   24 August 1945

From: The Commander Submarines SEVENTH FLEET.
To: The Commander in Chief, UNITED STATES FLEET.
Via: The Commander SEVENTH FLEET.

Subject: H.M.S. SPEARHEAD - Report of Special Mission -
           (Operation "SABRE").

Enclosure: (A) Subject Special Mission.

1.   Operation "SABRE", carried out by H.M.S. SPEARHEAD
commanded by Lieutenant Commander R. E. YOUNGMAN, R.N.R., with
XE-4 commanded by Lieutenant M. H. SHEAN, D.S.O., R.A.N.V.R., in
tow was conducted in the SAIGON Area.

2.   The Operation of cutting the SAIGON Cable was
faultlessly carried out and Lieutenant SHEAN showed sound
judgement throughout. The two lengths of cable brought home by
the divers provided most satisfying evidence of a job well done.

3.   The Force Commander congratulates Lieutenant
Commander R.E. YOUNGMAN and Lieutenant M.H. SHEAN, and the
Officers and Crews of H.M.S. SPEARHEAD and XE-4 upon the success-
ful completion of their assigned mission.

                              JAMES FIFE.

DISTRIBUTION:
CNO
Vice CNO
ComSubPac
Capt (S) 14 SubFlot
File

J. B. MILLER,
Flag Secretary.

COMMANDING OFFICER
15 NOV 1945
H.M.S. "BONAVENTURE"

Whittam coolly passed round the DSEA escape sets but only Sub Lieutenant Bob Aitken,[16] the diver, made it to the surface three hours later.

Half an hour after the explosions, at 0843, *X-5* was sighted 650 yards off *Tirpitz*'s bow. Cameron, from the battleship's quarter-deck, saw her too, 'showing lots of peri-scope'. Heavy and light AA guns opened fire as the periscope disappeared and two minutes later a destroyer dropped a pattern of five depth charges over the spot. Cameron was convinced that Henty-Creer's *Platypus* was destroyed at this time. *X-5*'s position suggests that Henty-Creer had been delayed and that he was waiting for the next 'safe-to-attack' period designed to prevent mutual interference: this was to commence at 0900. Nothing can be certain, but the evidence tends towards *X-5* not having dropped her

XE-5 (Westmacott) at Subic Bay setting off, towed by *Selene*, on 27 July 1945 to cut the Hong Kong-Singapore submarine telegraph cable in the Hong Kong approaches west of Lamma Island.

side-cargoes under the target. There were only two, not three or more explosions, as might have been expected if she had; and it would be surprising for her to be sighted where she was if she was on the way out be-cause she would surely have been closer still—very dangerously close—when the charges had gone up.

The fate of *X-5* is unsure, but there were three sightings which could conceivably have been her on 23 September in the vicinity of Stjernoy Island at the mouth of the outer fjord. If (and it is a big 'if') *Platypus* could still be controlled after being counter-attacked, it would have been logical to retire—past the position where the sup-

Left
X-23 (George Honour) coming up to HQ Ship *Largs* at 0930 on 6 June 1944 after acting as a navigational beacon for amphibious DD tanks of the Allied Invasion Force landing at SWORD Beach, Ouistreham. The package on the casing is a collapsed rubber dinghy. The special mast carrying the navigational beacon has been taken down.

Above
Photographs of Lt George Honour (X-23) given to him for handing to the French Resistance to make up a false identity card in case the Normandy beach-landing operation had to be abandoned. It is inconceivable that any Gestapo officer would have failed to recognise this photograph as anything other than a British Naval officer on an illicit run ashore in France!

posed sighting of a periscope and a possible X-craft on the surface were in fact made. She was not, incidentally, discovered during a search of Kaa Fjord itself in recent years. What happened after reaching Stjernoy Island—assuming the less than likely possibility that she got so far—can only be conjectured. Henty-Creer had said that he would try to make for the Kola Inlet in Soviet Russia if he had to escape, but Stjernoy Island was a bad starting point and the crew would have experienced great and probably insurmountable difficulties with winter drawing on.

Eight men, in two fragile craft with half-inch pressure hulls, has disabled a 42,000-ton battleship sheathed in 15-inch armour with a crew of 2500 officers and men. It was to be more than a year before *Tirpitz*, in a new berth off Haakoy Island, was finally destroyed by 12,000-pound 'Tallboy' bombs dropped by Lancaster aircraft on 12 November 1944; but 'The Beast' never put to sea again after the attack by *Piker II* and *Pdinichthys*. Cameron and Place had done precisely what was required of them and no two commanding officers ever more richly deserved their Victoria Crosses, simply inscribed 'For Valour'.

Much encouraged by this magnificent success, other X-craft went from strength to strength. *X-24* (Lieutenant Max Shean RANVR[17]) sank the 7500-ton *Barenfels* at Bergen in April 1944, mistaking her for the rightful target, a floating dock;[18] but the same boat with Lieutenant Percy West-

macott RN[19] in command put the mistake right in September. In the Far East, *XE-3* (Lieutenant Ian Fraser RNR) crippled the Japanese cruiser *Takao* at Singapore in July 1945 and Victoria Crosses were awarded to Fraser and his diver, Leading Seaman J S Magennis. *XE-4* (Maxie Shean again) cut the Saigon-Hong Kong and Saigon-Singapore telephone cables at about the same time. *XE-5* (Percy Westmacott in his new craft) searched for the Hong-Kong—Singapore cable for three and a half days and came back saying he could not find it; but, in fact, his grapnel, or perhaps the craft itself, did put the line out of action. And in the European theatre, two craft, *X-20* (Hudspeth, safely back from Operation 'Source') and *X-23* (Lieutenant George

Honour who had trained crews up at Rothesay)[20] had a vital task at D-Day in June 1944 when they preceded the invasion fleet by 48 hours to mark 'Sword' and 'Juno' beaches for the incoming amphibious tanks and landing craft.

All of these invaluable operations were accomplished at remarkably little cost in terms of either men or materiel. The expression had not been coined in World War Two, but X-craft must have been the most 'cost-effective' submarines ever built. Their capabilities were well summed up by the motto below the crest which Eve Cameron designed for *Piker II*: PISCIS MINIMUS MAXIMORUM ADPETENS—a little fish with big ideas.

The D-Day invasion fleet: it was preceded by two midget submarines.

12: Midget Mortality

The Japanese and the Germans did not exploit the potential of underwater swimmers to anything like the same extent as the Italians and British during the 1939–45 war, nor did they ally them to the concept of human torpedoes. The sneak craft and mini-submersibles in both navies fell, for the most part, between two stools: they were neither as independent and powerful as X-craft nor as simple and flexible as the *Maiali* and Chariots.

Most of the swimmers employed by the Japanese approached a target on the surface with their heads under overturned boxes and other debris; but, during the last year of the war, an underwater attack unit was formed known as the *Fukuryu* (crouching dragons). A crouching dragon's mission was to walk along the bottom of a harbour or coastal invasion area, in a self-contained loose-fitting wet diving suit, armed with a 10-kg lunge-type mine on a long pole. When under an enemy landing craft, he would thrust the mine against its bottom and fire it either by

contact or trigger action, thereby sending the victim to the bottom and the diver to *Tengoku* or *Jigoku*, Heaven or Hell, as appropriate. It was planned for any one man in three lines of defence to guard, for a period of ten hours, an area of 390 square metres with concrete underwater shelters to take refuge in, particularly during a pre-invasion bombardment. This was a hopelessly optimistic assessment of a diver's ability using oxygen rebreathing sets at depths around 15 metres (50 feet) and fatal accidents during necessarily hasty training were common. Some 1200 crouching dragons were ready and another 2800 were still in training when the atom bombs dropped on Hiroshima and Nagasaki brought the war to an end, but the *Fukuryu* force does not seem to have accomplished anything worthwhile. This little known underwater 'special attack' unit is only mentioned because of its idea of substituting stationary refuges for mobile midgets.

Japanese midget submarines were con-

ceived in the Spring of 1933 and the first two experimental Type A submersibles were constructed in 1934 at Kure naval yard amidst great secrecy. Various code-names were used before the Type A went into full production in 1939 with 59 operational craft coming off the lines: references to 'Type A metal fittings', 'targets for anti-submarine attack' and, for the production models, *Ko-hyoteki* (Target A) concealed the identity of these exceptionally fast 46-ton boats. Electrically-propelled with maximum surfaced and submerged speeds of 23 and 19 knots respectively, they had a limited range of about 15 miles at full speed or 80 miles at two knots: they had no self-recharging capability for the batteries. Each boat carried a pair of 17.7-inch (457 mm) Model 2 torpedoes with a range of 3000 metres at 40 knots and was manned by a crew of two.

It was not originally intended that the craft should be used against defended harbours or on extended operations. Rather, they were to be flung into battle (from the seaplane carriers *Chitose* and *Chiyoda*) during a general fleet engagement which the Imperial Japanese Navy expected to be decisive in a long-term strategic plan involving a hopefully exhausted American fleet. Nor were the midgets to be suicide craft: Admiral Isoroku Yamamoto himself insisted on that. But when their (still top secret) role was changed to harbour-attack in 1940, the navy, at lower and more realistic levels, recognised that *Ko-hyoteki* crews had only a one-way ticket. This was not regarded, as it would have been in European navies, as any great disadvantage because all Japanese fighting forces had been imbued since 1882 with the idea that 'duty is more weighty than a mountain; death is no heavier than a feather'.[1]

Ways by which the little submersibles could be recovered by parent submarines after an operation were investigated by Yamamoto's staff and, on the basis that

Ensign Sakamaki's Type A 'fly' stranded on Oahu Island after its attempted attack on Pearl Harbor, December 1941.

Ha-21 salvaged after the attack on Sydney Harbour in May 1942.

this was practicable, the Admiral approved their inclusion in the surprise attack on Pearl Harbor: indeed they were to lead the way.

In the early hours of Sunday, 7 December 1941 the large submarines *I-16, I-18, I-20, I-22,* and *I-24* submerged slowly, a few miles off the American base, to allow the midgets to float off their chocks abaft the conning towers. The midget crews, wearing white *hachimaki* head-bands and anointed with perfumed oil in the tradition of Samurai facing death, set course at about 10 knots on the surface for the guarded harbour entrance 8 or 10 miles distant. There was plenty of time in hand because attacks were not to be launched until after the initial air strike, timed for 0800. It must have been a little disturbing to know that bombs would be raining down on the harbour while the midgets were inside but the risk was, apparently, discounted.

Each craft was equipped with serrated steel net-cutters at the bow and conning tower and a jumping wire to deal with obstructions but there was no intention of cutting a way through the nets. It was known that American ships were constantly passing in and out of the gate and the obvious thing to do was to follow close behind one of them: the midgets' speed, although now reduced to 14 knots at best by the removal of a battery section to make room for more compressed air and oxygen, would easily allow them to keep up.

The arrangements for control submerged, with the hydroplanes worked by compressed air, were excellent and included a degree of automation linked, if required, with an echo-sounder, although the latter would have been an acoustic give-away at close quarters. The electrically-raised periscope in the tiny control chamber—which had a stubby conning tower on top—was adequate and there was room for a small chart table, so navigating in a confined harbour was entirely practicable. A radio set with a raiseable mast was also provided.

Thus, so far as weapons, equipment and means were concerned the five Type A Captains and their Petty Officers approaching Pearl Harbor on that Sunday morning could

Ha-69, a type C 50-ton three-man boat capable of 6.5 knots for 350 miles on the surface and 18.5 knots for one hour or 4 knots for 30 hours submerged. Fifteen *Hei-Gata* craft were built. This one is shown in August 1944 on board its carrier, *Transport Number 5,* from which it was launched on rollers, stern-first, down a ramp at the stern.

Kaiten on board an I-46 type submarine.

be confident. Hopes were high but the problems of actually penetrating the defences and delivering torpedo attacks were not underrated. Moreover, although a Japanese midget submariner's regard of death, whether deliberately sought or not, was very different from that of British and Italian midget submariners' and human torpedo teams', the almost certain prospect of losing one's life in decidedly unpleasant circumstances must have weighed on the *Ko-hyoteki* crews to some extent.

The later *Kamikaze* aircraft attacks on US carriers required relatively little skill and were conducted at exhilarating speed in hot blood—although this in no way lessens the bravery of the pilots—but it was another thing to manoeuvre precisely and formulate torpedo tactics with accurate fire-control in cold blood over a period of several hours in a pocket-sized submarine in very restricted waters. Hence, it is reasonable to suppose that the Type A Captains, while gallant in the extreme, found it even harder than their counterparts in Allied navies to apply themselves single-mindedly to the exacting calculations and navigation demanded by the task.

However that might be, and arbitrarily assigning numbers to the individual midgets, Number 1 passed safely through the Pearl Harbor channel gate at about 0500 and settled on the bottom to await the air attack. Her periscope had been briefly sighted by the minesweeper *Condor* but contact was not established.

An hour later and two hours before the air attack was due, the conning tower of Number 2 was seen by the destroyer *Ward*'s

helmsman following close astern of the old ex-freighter USS *Antares*. The United States was not yet, of course, at war but *Ward* very properly went to general quarters and closed at full speed, calling in a PBY patrol plane to assist. Opening fire, *Ward*'s second round of 4-inch hit the midget which rolled over and disappeared in 200 fathoms, where she still lies.

At 0835, with bombs still falling on the crippled US fleet, the destroyer *Monaghan* noticed, incredulously, that the seaplane tender *Curtiss*, moored off Ford Island in the centre of the harbour, was flying a signal indicating the presence of an enemy submarine. This was Number 1 whose Captain had come shallow to choose a target amidst the appalling damage inflicted by the 350 Japanese torpedo-aircraft, dive bombers and

Above
I-370, with *Kaiten* and their crews on deck wearing the traditional white *hachimaki* and waving their swords as the submarine sails on 20 February 1943 to attack concentrations of US invasion shipping. *I-370* was sunk six days later with the *Kaiten* still on board.

Left
A *Neger* being hoisted out with the pilot in position.

fighter aircraft. Number 1 duly selected the *Curtiss* but missed, hitting a dock at Pearl City instead. A second torpedo was then discharged at the fast approaching *Monaghan* but this, too, missed and exploded on shore, allowing *Monaghan* to ram and sink the aggressor. The crew were accorded a military funeral when the midget was raised, but the craft itself, far from damaging the United States Navy, was ignominiously

used as filling material for a new pier, thus becoming a solid part of the very base she had hoped to destroy.

Number 3, commanded by Ensign Saka-maki, had gyro trouble and was late on task, only arriving off the harbour entrance at 0700 in the full light of day when US naval units had been alerted. Detected by the *Ward*'s sound detection equipment and heavily depth-charged, Number 3 filled with smoke and Sakamaki himself struck his head, temporarily losing consciousness. His assistant, Petty Officer Inagaki, pressed on regardless and when the Captain recovered he found that *Ward* had lost contact astern. Unfortunately, he ran straight on to a coral reef but, in the confusion, he was not spotted. The bows were forced out of the water and one torpedo was damaged but Sakamaki managed to get clear using full astern power. Again the craft hit a reef and by now the two men were ill from fumes and almost exhausted. Superhuman efforts succeeded in moving the trimming ballast strung over the

Top
The dome of a *Neger* being admired for the benefit of a German propaganda photographer.

Above left
The rudimentary cockpit of a *Neger*: depth and pressure gauges in the centre; breathing apparatus and inclino-meter left-centre; firing, steering and depth controls on the starboard side.

Above
A *Neger* at normal operating level with the aiming spike visible.

batteries, which gave off powerful electric shocks, and the craft slipped clear but now the torpedo firing apparatus refused to function and Number 3 went out of control. Battery gas and smoke fumes choked the operators.

The situation was hopeless. Petty Officer Inagaki lapsed into a stupor and the craft drifted out to sea throughout the day with both men insensible. At nightfall Sakamaki came to and found land close ahead. Once more the boat ran onto a reef where the Captain endeavoured in vain to explode the scuttling charge. The fuse failed to ignite and Sakamaki's apparently lifeless body was dis-

covered washed ahore at Waimenalo Bay, 60 miles from Pearl Harbor, on 8 December. The brave but luckless Ensign became the first prisoner-of-war. In Japanese terms, Petty Officer Inagaki was much more fortunate: he drowned.

Sakamaki's boat was, of course, thoroughly investigated by the United States Navy before being carted around America on a trailer as part of a drive to raise War Bonds. His chart, however, confused the intelligence experts because it showed a pencilled track around Ford Island which led them to believe that Number 3 had successfully penetrated the harbour a day or more

before the air attack. Sakamaki himself, desperately shamed by his unwilling survival, was saying nothing; but after the war he admitted that the track represented no more than his intention: he had never passed through the entrance channel.

Neither did Number 4 gain entrance. Its shattered hull was discovered, accidentally, just outside the harbour in June 1960 and eventually taken back to Japan where it rests close to the Memorial Hall at the Maritime Self-Defence Force Service School. There was no trace of the crew but the conning tower hatch was unclipped from the inside, suggesting that the two men escaped from the craft. They were presumably drowned, very possibly of their own accord in a final and honourable act of sacrifice.

Number 5 has never been found but there is no reason to believe that her crewmen were any more successful than the rest. A signal was received by *I-68* (not one of the carrier submarines) at 1850 on 7 December from an unidentified midget reporting 'I have succeeded' but what this meant is not clear. Perhaps it was from Number 5 simply

Biber Number 55 with the hatch open (and imprudently unattended). A *Biber* could make 6 knots on the surface for 130 miles and 5 knots submerged for about one hour and a half. They carried two 21-inch (533 mm) electric torpedoes underslung and drew air for the petrol engine, in the normal shallow state, through a simple intake mast with no head-valve. The foremost stubby mast housed a projector compass.

Captured *Biber* in Chatham dockyard, 16 May 1945, showing the external torpedo recesses.

indicating that he had penetrated the harbour, for there is no evidence to show that any of the first special attack group caused significant damage: it was the massive, unwarned air strike alone that generated the slogan 'Remember Pearl Harbor'.[2]

When the second special attack group took to the water in the spring of 1942, their 'flies', as the Japanese navy had come to call them, were improved by substituting hydraulics for compressed air controls, thereby eliminating a number of high pressure air bottles and making room for the original outfit of batteries which restored their underwater speed to 19 knots; and they were also fitted with sledge-like runners at the bow to facilitate a passage through anti-submarine nets.

Admiral Yamamoto planned two simultaneous raids for the new group to take place at the end of May 1942—one on British warships anchored in Diego-Suarez Bay, Madagascar (until very recently controlled by Vichy French Forces) and the other on Allied warships in Sydney Harbour. Rear Admiral Ishizaka, who had organised the Eighth Submarine Flotilla for the tasks assigned, directed the intensive training necessary, which was started none too soon at the end of April.

The attack on Diego-Suarez Bay, a vital base for operations in the Indian Ocean now that the Allies had been driven from their Far Eastern positions, was mounted by three 'flies' carried by I-16, I-18, and I-20 with Ishizaka controlling the group from his flagship I-10, specifically designed as a headquarters submarine. I-10 carried a seaplane which, after a number of negative reconnaissance flights over British bases along the South-Eastern African coast, reported a 'Queen-Elizabeth'-class battleship and a cruiser at Diego-Suarez on the night of 29 May. This sighting report alone justified the carrying of aircraft on Japanese submarines. The battleship was in fact the 'Revenge'-class Ramillies. The reconnaissance aircraft was sighted and thought to be Vichy French, so Ramillies weighed anchor at 0500 the following morning and remained underway in the Bay over the dawn period during which a Vichy submarine attack appeared most likely to materialise, but she anchored again at daybreak when anti-submarine air patrols commenced.

Meanwhile, the parent submarines closed to positions 10 miles north of Diego-Suarez at the northern tip of Madagascar. The midgets were floated off during the early hours of 30 May but the motor in I-18's 'fly' obstinately refused to start and one of the remaining pair, probably the one from I-16, evidently sprang a leak or had a battery explosion on the way in and sank. Circumstantial evidence strongly suggests that it was Lieutenant Saburo Akeida with Petty Officer Masami Takemoto in the third midget, from I-20 (Commander Yamada), who alone successfully navigated the long, narrow and treacherous channel leading to the inner anchorages. Akeida had been involved with the Type As almost from the start and was far and away the most experienced officer in the group: training for the others had been lamentably short.[3]

The night was dark, the sea was calm and the British ships were not expecting a sneak-craft type of attack. There was no netting. These factors favoured the 'fly' in the night attack but the task was still fraught with danger and difficulty. The Captain had to con cautiously and with painstaking accuracy for about sixteen hours before coming within range of his primary objective.

At 2025 on 30 May, a torpedo struck HMS Ramillies on the port bulge just forward of 'A' Turret. The bulge plating was holed for 30 feet by 30 feet and the outer bottom for 20 feet by 16 feet. There was extensive flooding, including 'A' and 'B' Turret magazines and shellrooms, the forward 4-inch magazines and adjacent compartments up to main deck level. All lighting and power forward of 'B' turret failed. The damage assessment was that fighting efficiency was 'seriously impaired'[4] and Ramillies was not patched up sufficiently for her to steam to Durban for repairs until 3 June. The battleship was out of action for nearly a year so the 'fly' had a major strategic impact on Allied operations in the Indian Ocean.

A few minutes after the Ramillies was hit, the 6993-ton tanker British Loyalty went down to the midget's second torpedo. For skill and persistence the dual attack was hard to beat in any theatre of war.

The two crewmen abandoned their boat but, for some reason, did not explode the scuttling charge. The midget drifted on to a reef badly damaged, probably by corvettes which plastered the bay with depth-charges. The Captain and his assistant were shot on shore when they refused to surrender to a Royal Marine patrol.

The British believed, until the midget's crewmen were discovered some time after the attack, that a Vichy submarine had been responsible for the torpedoes; no warning was therefore passed to other commands before a group of three 'flies', directed by Captain Hanku Sasaki in I-21, set off from their carrier boats, I-22, I-24 and I-27, seven miles east of Sydney Heads at dusk on 31 May, less than 24 hours after the attack on Diego Suarez. A fourth carrier-submarine, I-28, had been sunk by USS Tautog, a fleet submarine, on 19 May off Truk.

The boom strung across Sydney Harbour entrance was not closed and there was no physical obstacle in the way of the midgets; but one (Ha 14) strayed off course and became inextricably tangled in the western end of the net. The Captain lit the fuse on the demolition charge and destroyed the craft, himself and his assistant. The magnetic loop, to seaward of the boom, proved, on subsequent analysis, to have registered the crossing of Ha-14 and, indeed, the other 'flies', but the traces were not distinguished at the time from those of friendly vessels passing in and out of the harbour.

The Australian authorities and the ships at Sydney were very slow to take action in response to a report at about 2030 of the midget trapped in the nets. The alarm was not raised for some two hours and it was later still—close to midnight—before a total blackout was achieved over the harbour. By then, a second midget, commanded by Ensign Katsuhisa Ban, had found its way round, surfaced, come under fire from the heavy cruiser USS Chicago, dived, surfaced again off Garden Island and discharged two torpedoes at Chicago nicely outlined against the dockyard lights. One fish ran ashore and failed to explode but the other, missing Chicago, ran underneath the Dutch submarine K-IX and hit the elderly ex-ferry accommodation ship Kuttabul. The magnetic loops recorded what may have been Ensign Ban's midget on the way out but the craft thereafter disappeared for ever.

The third 'fly', Ha-21, was, at some stage, caught in the nets and, while struggling to get free, either the new sledge-like runners or the fixed net-cutter at the bows, or perhaps both anti-obstruction devices, were bent around the torpedo tubes. When it came to the moment for firing (the captain, Lieutenant Keiyu, probably attained the inner harbour) the torpedoes would not leave their tubes. Forced to retire, Ha-21 came under heavy depth-charge attacks in the vicinity of Taylor Bay, a mile inside the boom. Keiyu and his assistant shot themselves with pistols after opening valves to sink the boat. Intact parts of Ha-14 and Ha-21 were salvaged and reassembled into a single craft which, like the Pearl Harbor midget in America, was trailed around Australia to raise money.

In October 1942, a more self-sufficient experimental Type B midget was launched.

A *Molch* in war-paint and fully armed being hauled ashore in 1944.

A *Molch* awash in harbour showing how easily such craft could operate in tight spaces.

This type had a 40 hp 25 Kw generator for propulsion on the surface and for recharging the batteries—a process that took an unacceptably long eighteen hours. This was followed by fifteen similar Type C models, *Ha-62* to *Ha-76*, intended for local coastal defence; eight were lost in the Phillipines towards the end of the war while endeavouring, unsuccessfully, to assist in slowing down the implacable American amphibious forces.

The Type D *Koryu* (Dragons-with-Scales) were more advanced, and, with the first, *Ha-77*, emerging at Kure at the beginning of 1945, orders were placed at eleven yards for 570 boats to complete by the end of September and a further 180 boats per month thereafter. This massive programme was aimed primarily at the defence of Okinawa,

bases in the Phillipines and, in the last resort, the Japanese islands themselves. B-29 bombing raids slowed down production, but about 110 *Koryu* were completed before Japan capitulated and many more were still under construction.

A Scaly Dragon could make 16 knots submerged for 40 minutes or 2.5 knots for 50 hours. The surface range was 1000 miles at 8 knots. The armament was a pair of 17.7-inch (450 mm) torpedoes or, when torpedoes became scarce, a 600-kg suicide warhead. The crew varied from two to five men depending on the mission. With a diving depth of 330 feet (100 m) and some excellent equipment, including in some cases a periscopic radar mast, the 60-ton *Koryu* were outstanding in the midget range, but their great potential was never exploited and the gigantic effort

made to produce them was wasted. There is no reliable record of them achieving anything worthwhile.

Smaller, 20-ton two or three-man *Kairyu* (Sea Dragons) were also ordered in very large numbers. They had proportionally lesser capabilities than the *Koryu* and practically all of them carried warheads rather than torpedoes; like all the Japanese midgets, they were, in practice, suicide craft. None of them appear to have seen active service—probably because of a shortage of crews.

Kaiten (stupendous, heaven-shaker or make a great change) human torpedoes (there were several varieties) were quite different from *Maiali* and Chariots. The pilot (often a trainee naval aviator) was fully enclosed with a periscope, gyro compass and good controls. In theory, the operator was supposed to make his exit, through a hatch beneath the cockpit, when certain that his vehicle would hit the target, which implies that he would have started to work his way out when, say, 100 metres distant and actually swim clear at 50 metres; but nobody took this means of escaping seriously. In any case, a man in the water so close to an explosion resulting from 1550 kg of TNT could scarcely expect to survive intact. However, the hatch had a more important function: it connected via a flexible tube with a hatch in the carrier submarine and so enabled the torpedo to be manned while submerged. A telephone line linked the pilot with the submarine's Captain until the last moment.

Top
Seehund Type xxvIIB miniature U-boats completing at Kiel.

Above
Seehund ready for service at Kiel.

A large submarine could carry four or sometimes six *Kaiten*; where four were embarked, all of them could be manned underwater by the pilots, who were almost invariably young airmen with no aircraft to fly. In a major fleet action it was reckoned that they would create havoc. The first *Kaiten* (Mark I) had engines similar to the Type 93 torpedo (so called because it was perfected in the Japanese year 2,593 and

otherwise known as the Long Lance) which was fuelled by petrol and liquid oxygen. Later models, which never saw service, had still more advanced hydrogen peroxide and hydrozine wakeless propulsion, but even the Mark I had speeds of 30 knots for 23,000 metres or 40 knots for about 10,000 metres. However, it was absurd for anybody to think that human torpedoes could career around at such very high speeds and have any idea of the situation on the surface although, if used by the parent submarine as ordinary torpedoes, they were released on a hitting track and had no need to see the target. When acting independently, they might go deep to make short fast bursts but

they would then be entirely blind with only a compass course to steer; and the slightest mistake on the controls might well have been fatal. At periscope depth they would be limited to slow speed—perhaps ten or twelve knots—if they were to view the target clearly before going to the requisite depth at high speed on a collision course. Even when going slowly the periscope wash would probably be sighted: indeed, it often was. The optimum depth during an approach was 15 feet in most circumstances.

As it happened, there were to be no fleet actions of the kind envisaged, but four *Kaiten* from *I-47* and one from *I-36* were launched off Ulithi Atoll between 0415 and 0454 on the morning of 20 November 1944 to attack the large assembly of US ships lying at anchor in the lagoon. The American gunners and anti-submarine patrol craft were ready: four of the human torpedoes—easily seen— disappeared amidst search-lights, shells and depth-charges almost as soon as they entered the harbour. Only one (Ensign Nishina) struck home, sending the oiler *Mississinewa* (AO-59) to the bottom with 150 of her crew.

The submarine *I-370*, bound for Palau on a similar mission at the same time, was sunk by two American destroyer escorts before her *Kaiten* were released. Five more carrier submarines took *Kaiten* of the Kongo Unit to Guam, Ulithi and New Guinea in January 1945: they accomplished nothing. The Japanese kept trying: successive *Kaiten* units were formed and transported in April, May and June to Ulithi, Okinawa, Guam and Saipan. They, too, failed in their missions and eight parent submarines were sunk or damaged.

One single success was scored, almost at the end. *I-53* (Lieutenant Commander Oba) *en route* to patrol off Luzon on 24 July, launched two *Kaiten* against the destroyer escort *Underhill*, the last from very close range—about 1000 yards. The first apparently failed. The second was immediately sighted and the destroyer opened fire—but not in time. It may be that *Underhill* rammed her attacker rather than vice-versa, but, either way, the *Kaiten*'s warhead did its work well: USS *Underhill* sank almost immediately with a heavy loss of life. The *Kaiten*, of course, went with her.

It was thought that *Kaiten* may have damaged five or six other US ships, but the most reliable reference makes no claims for these,[5] although passes were made at several vessels. Why, overall, did the Japanese midgets, of all kinds, achieve so little at such a vast cost in terms of both industrial effort and personnel? The obvious answer is that in the closing stages of the war the Americans enjoyed overwhelming superiority with their anti-submarine forces. Yet it *was* possible to succeed: the attack at Diego-Suarez proved that. Looking carefully at the all too scarce Japanese official records and personal accounts, it seems that poor organisation and planning by the staff (who did not understand the practical limitations), ill-defined and changing objectives, the virtual certainty of death and, above all, inadequate *operational* training were to blame for repeated failures by a band of suicidally gallant but literally misguided men.

The German Midgets

The German navy, like the Japanese, had several changes of heart about how miniature U-boats should be used—for harbour attack, coastal defence or aggressive operations in the open sea.

By the autumn of 1943 the German navy was at low ebb. The Atlantic tide had turned against the U-boats and, with Italy's surrender in September, an invasion of Europe was clearly imminent. The *Kriegsmarine* surface fleet was in no shape to meet an assault and there were insufficient regular U-boats. In desperation, Admiral Dönitz turned for defence to midget measures already demonstrated with success (albeit on offensive operations) by the Italian and British navies. A new special attack arm was created, with a sense of urgency amounting almost to panic, comprising explosive motor-boats, frogmen, human torpedoes and pocket submarines. Vice Admiral Hellmuth Heye was appointed head of this hastily conceived Kleinkampfmittel-Verband (small battle-weapon unit, Kdk or K-force) in December.

Heye, a great admirer of Lord Nelson, knew that high morale was the key factor and his stated aim was to establish a Nelsoniam 'band of brothers'. Many of the operations would inevitably be near-suicidal and all would be fraught with danger. He therefore decided that his men should not be subject to overmuch formal discipline: he expected and encouraged them to play hard in order to work and fight hard, following the Italian and British tradition that had demonstrably led to success. In fact, he went further towards non-conformity by discarding all badges of rank, but in doing this he was probably influenced by the thought that his teams would have to be drawn from the army and *Luftwaffe* as well as from the navy.

Human torpedoes were cheap and easy to produce by adapting existing G7e electric torpedoes, but the weapon that emerged, called *Neger* (Nigger)—after its designer Richard Mohr whose name in German meant 'negro'—could not dive. It was propelled awash at about 4 knots to the firing position (although the motor itself was capable of 10 knots); at this speed, it had a range of 48 miles.

Basically, the *Neger* consisted of two modified G7e's slung one below the other. The operator was encased in a Perspex dome forward on the upper carrier 'fish'. He was provided with rudimentary controls, a wrist-compass, a self-contained Draeger breathing set and a crude aiming device consisting of a graduated scale marked on the canopy and a spike on the body forward like the foresight on a rifle. A handle in the cockpit released the action torpedo which then started automatically and ran at a pre-set depth.

In theory, especially to shore-based tacticians, the *Neger* seemed attractive: the pilots thought otherwise. They were too low down in the water to see properly and wartime oil-slicks often smeared the canopy, rendering the operator blind: opening the canopy, either to see where he was going or to gulp fresh air, usually resulted in the craft being swamped. Several pilots succumbed to carbon dioxide poisoning. About 200 machines were built but the loss rate of those employed—60 to 80 per cent—was appalling.[6]

When *Neger* came to be used off the Normandy beaches in the summer of 1944, a number of canopies were painted to simulate the head and shoulders of a pilot: these dummies without torpedoes were floated off on the tide but they did little towards confusing or decoying the heavy enemy opposition.

The achievements of *Neger* (so far as they can positively be confirmed) were not numerous, but they were undoubtedly a nuisance. The British minesweepers *Cato* and *Magic* were sunk on 6 July 1944 while anchored off 'Sword' and 'Juno' beaches, and the Polish destroyer *Dragon* was damaged beyond repair on the following night, while another minesweeper, *Pylades*, was destroyed, probably by two *Neger* firing almost simultaneously. It is also possible that the destroyer *Isis* went down to a *Neger* on 20 July.[7] The destroyer *Blencathra* was hoisting in a human torpedo, which she had discovered, when the scuttling charge detonated and caused minor damage.

Marder (pine-martens) were a marginal improvement on the *Neger* because they could submerge to 30 metres to avoid counter-attack: about 300 were constructed and about half this number were flung into the fray at Normandy and, in September, off Monaco to attack a joint French and American force. These human torpedoes also suffered very heavy casualties, in exchange for sinking the destroyer HMS *Quorn* on 3 August, an LCF (Landing Craft, Flak) and a barrage balloon ship. Some other damage was inflicted on relatively unimportant invasion vessels. Further operations in the Mediterranean were wholly unsuccessful and resulted in the loss of practically all the *Marder* employed.

The first type of one-man midget submarine proper—the *Biber* (Beaver)—and its successor the rather larger *Molche* (Salamander), both armed with two G7e torpedoes or, alternatively, mines, were built in huge numbers. Some 330 *Biber* and 390 *Molche* were delivered[8] although by no means all became operational. The *Biber*

One of four *Seehund* adopted by the French navy after the war. They were discarded in 1955.

had standard Opel-Blitz motor-car gasoline engines for surface propulsion (with all the attendant hazards experienced with petrol in early submarines at the beginning of the century), but the *Molche* relied entirely on an electric motor. Neither of these types made any significant impact on the war but they did contribute to Allied anxieties: expensive and unwelcome defensive precautions had to be taken against K-force attacks of all kinds.[9]

The 14.7-ton type XXVIIB U-boat *Seehund* (Seal) was a very different kettle of fish. A total of 285 units was built before Germany surrendered. The first batch came into action in December 1944 and the two-man crews were delighted to find that their Seals were, in many respects, scaled-down models of a full-size U-boat with certain features discernibly derived from sections of the British X-craft salvaged in Kaa Fjord. The glass observation dome on the hatch cover safely withstood pressures down to 45 metres (150 feet). Her diesels drove her at nearly eight knots on the surface and she handled admirably submerged at three to six knots. The engineer of the boat handled the controls and fired the torpedo at command. During the approach, the boat was kept at periscope depth while being 'talked' onto the target by the Captain.

Underwater, a Seal's small size made it almost impossible for anti-submarine craft to locate her. Listening gear was incapable of detecting her propeller noise at slow speeds; and it was extremely difficult for Asdic to 'ping' on her small hull and detect an echo. Moreover, an excellent periscope enabled the Captain to sweep the skies for aircraft before surfacing to recharge the battery and refresh the air. The morale-breaking loneliness of the one-man submarine was gone in the two-man *Seehund*. A boat could cruise for 500 miles, staying at sea a week on patrol.

As many as 70 per cent of the Seals made approaches on Allied shipping before the war ended. In many cases the crews missed their targets due to inexperience and lack of training, for which there was very little opportunity, but it could well be (lacking adequate records) that something in the order of 100,000 tons of shipping was sunk or damaged between January and May 1945. *Seehund* losses, estimated at 35, were comparatively low and a score of these were probably due to bad weather rather than anti-submarine action.

Fortunately for the Allies, the type XXVIIB (like the very advanced type XXI U-boat) came too late. A little earlier, and Allied ships and landing craft might have suffered disastrously from the attentions of the *Seehund*: anti-submarine defences would have been swamped if large groups had been able to make co-ordinated attacks. It has to be asked whether the situation would be markedly different today.

The Future~Great and Small

The story of the monsters is an almost unrelieved catalogue of disasters, yet over recent years submarines in the major navies of the world have, in the main, tended to become bigger—much bigger than the old monstrosities. The Soviet *Typhoon*, for example, displaces more than a light aircraft-carrier and the American 'Tridents' displace more than many World War Two heavy cruisers. The bigger the submarine the bigger the expense (the tonnage/cost relationship is remarkably linear), so smaller countries with more limited resources have either kept to moderate-sized boats or are exploring more modest possibilities.

The new monsters do not, of course, bear meaningful comparison with the old. Nuclear propulsion has changed the situation radically: it would not make sense to try to learn too many lessons from the past. Nevertheless, increased size does imply increased detectability by one means or another, and a submarine's success continues to depend upon it remaining undetected: there are restricted and inshore areas where it is hard to think that a large submarine would survive for long in war. Here, at least, the navies which cannot afford nuclear power may find small, quiet, demagnetised boats at a fortuitous advantage—so long as they are prepared to invest in the right weapons.

The point arising in Chapter Two about submarine hulls being designed before weapon systems is, by and large, still true. There are good reasons nowadays for this and there is little use in moralising about it. A sophisticated weapon system takes between ten and fifteen years to develop, as a rule, from the initial bright idea to service at sea, and then continual and costly exercises are needed to ensure proficiency with it—something, in fact, that has seldom been achieved in peace but often been learned the hard way in war.[1] But a submarine itself takes three or four years to build and is then expected to last for twenty years, so the ideal order of things—with the weapon system being decided before the weapon-carrier—is hard to achieve in practice, unless outdated weapons are acceptable throughout a submarine's life. In fact, a compromise usually results, involving expensive major modifications during refits and overhauls. With a long multi-ship construction programme like the 'Los Angeles'-class nuclear attack submarines (62 complete or planned), it is, of course, possible to make radical changes when building the later vessels to accommodate a new kind of weapon system in the best possible way: the last 30 or more submarines in this class, from SSN 718 onwards, are to be equipped with twelve vertical-launch tactical-missile tubes outside the pressure hull but inside the outer skin.

Although research continues into miniaturised nuclear power plants there is not much hope of a breakthrough in the foreseeable future. However, a long-arm weapon system

The most monstrous monster: an artist's impression of the Soviet *Typhoon* with a submerged displacement of about 30,000 tons and a speed probably approaching 30 knots.

The Soviet navy's first answer to the American SSBNs—
a *Yankee*, first appearing in 1967. Carrying sixteen
1,300-nautical mile range missiles and displacing 9,500
tons, the *Yankees* bear a strong resemblance to the UN
Navy's 'Ethan Allens'.

lessens the need for a weapon-carrier to have sustained high speed (and hence for it to be large) for purely *tactical* purposes: the possibilities of new kinds of relatively small electric power plants and batteries—fuel cells amongst them—as an alternative to nuclear energy for short fast bursts have by no means been exhausted, and they might well meet most of the requirements for navies that do not envisage distant, rapid, strategic deployments for their submarines.

There are notable exceptions to the general rule about weapons having tended to come a rather poor second after hulls: ballistic-missile submarines (SSBNs) are one and Soviet cruise-missile attack submarines (SSGNs) are another. The 14,000-ton Soviet *Oscar* (SSGN) is a justifiable giant. It was conceived as a coherent weapon-package from the start, with 24 external missile tubes housing 270-mile range SS-N-19 cruise missiles, and it carries a formidable quantity of

torpedoes (probably all with nuclear warheads) as well. It represents, perhaps, the ultimate concept of the old British 'Mutton-boats'. And high-speed nuclear propulsion (35 knots for the *Oscar*) is a necessary part of the system conceived by the Soviet navy for specific targets.

The *Typhoon* (SSBN), 30,000 tons and nearly 560 feet long, is a logical means of providing a hidden, moveable bank of missiles, much less vulnerable than silos on shore. Vulnerability is something that the Russians have considered very carefully. Practically any normal submerged submarine will be destroyed by a single rupture, however small, of its pressure hull. To give some of the old monsters a degree of protection (in those days, primarily against gunfire on the surface), they were given double hulls, albeit mainly because the fairly narrow space between the outer skin and the pressure hull thus formed was convenient for fuel, water ballast and stability; but the *Typhoon* takes the idea a significant stage further with some fifteen feet between the thin outer hull and the tough (probably titanium) pressure hull. This makes it very difficult to

sink with ordinary non-nuclear torpedoes or other standard anti-submarine weapons because the force of an underwater explosion (which would occur against the outer hull) is inversely proportional to the cube of the distance.

The *Typhoon* has been widely reported as a submarine which the West has to fear because of its vast dimensions. It is indeed a fearful strategic weapon system with twenty SS-N-20 5000-mile range ballistic missiles, each with nine or possibly twelve MIRV nuclear warheads, but it is really no more than a well protected submersible bank of silos. It is hardly likely to be encountered in the usual submarine operating areas and its most probable habitat is below the protection of the northern ice-cap, within guarded zones such as the Barents Sea or in the remote South Atlantic Ocean. So far as submarining goes, it is not the super-submarine that size by itself has been assumed to suggest.

Submersible aircraft carriers are redundant by reason of long-range sonar, the whole gamut of electronic warfare, and satellites. Mine-laying is, however, another reason for building or adapting a big type of

Soviet *Alfa* attack-type 3,800-ton SSN with six torpedo tubes, a top speed of at least 42 knots and, with a titanium hull, an operational diving depth of about 3,000 feet.

Below
Soviet *Victor III* attack-type 6,000 ton SSN armed with six torpedo tubes for SS-N-15 Subroc type (partial air-flight) A/S weapons with a maximum range of 35 miles. Two reactors power a single propeller at speeds up to 30 knots but there are also two auxiliary propellers, presumably in case of damage under ice and for man-oeuvring in harbour. The large pod on the stabiliser fin is probably for a towed sonar array.

Top
An artist's impression of the gigantic Soviet *Oscar*, displacing about 14,000 tons, equipped with 24 missile tubes for 270-mile SS-N-19 cruise missiles and capable of about 35 knots.

Above
An *Oscar* breaking surface.

USS *Albuquerque* (SSN 708) at launch 13 March 1982.
This 6000/6900-ton *Los Angeles* class general purpose
attack-type SSN has a top speed in excess of 30 knots
and is heavily armed with Subroc A/S missiles and Mark
48 torpedoes: it is planned to fit Tomahawk cruise-
missiles shortly. The class has the particular capability
of co-ordinated operations with surface ships and other
units.

Above
The 16,600/18,700-ton *Ohio* class USS *Florida* (SSBN
728) at launch 14 November 1981 equipped for 24 Trident I submarine-launched ballistic missiles (SLBM).

Left
USS *Boston* (SSN 703) 'Los Angeles' class submarine,
commissioned on 30 January 1982, photographed at
moderate speed on the surface.

Below
USS *San Francisco* (SSN 711) in the James River,
Virginia. Great efforts have been made to improve
sound quieting in the 'Los Angeles' submarines and
considerable success has apparently been achieved
in this direction.

HMS *Minnow*, one of the Royal Navy's four postwar X-Craft built by Vickers in 1954–55. The Commander-in-Chief Home Fleet, Admiral Sir John Eccles, is inspecting her here at Portland in 1956 with (then) Lieutenant Compton-Hall (commanding officer) standing behind him.

Centre Left
HMS *Minnow* coming alongside at Portland in 1956, with the author on right at the induction mast.

submarine if mines have to be laid in quantity in fields far from the home base; it might have external mine chutes as well as, or instead of, internal tubes. However, a quite small submarine could serve adequately as a minelayer if only limited fields are required and distances are not great. Some of the larger Soviet boats could have a more substantial mine-laying capability than is immediately apparent and it is know that an *Oscar* can carry 32 mines internally instead of torpedoes. Mine-fields laid by submarines belonging to a power not directly engaged in the conflict could be used in scenarios far short of total war.

Meanwhile, the old title of Fleet Submarines, first used for the calamitous K-

Stickleback (X-51) looking aft through the control room. The first Lieutenant's pump control column enabled him to move large or very small quantities of water into and out of the trimming tanks to adjust bodily weight and to trim the boat fore and aft. The large handwheel in front of his seat worked the hydroplanes manually and, if the helmsman forward was otherwise occupied (assisting the diver to dress, for example), Number One could also steer by means of the smaller wheel. There were five men in the operational crew of this class, one more than in the wartime X-Craft. Three men, with a Passage CO of First Lieutenant's status, were enough for the passage crew.

Control room of HMS *Minnow* looking aft to the engine-room door. The evidence of a recent potmess is on the right!

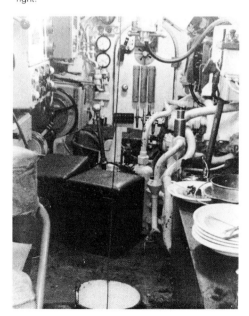

Diver climbing out of *Stickleback*'s Wet and Dry on the surface between exercises.

boats, has been revived for nuclear attack-type submarines which support a surface fleet. This role, too, demands size for speed and endurance.

Whether military or merchant submersible cargo-carriers will be purpose-built in the future is problematical. American designs for 300,000 and 400,000-ton submarine tankers were put forward in the 1970s but if oil is to be transported underwater it would be more economical to use a small nuclear tug towing a string of sausage-like containers.

Troop-carriers, on the other hand, are a more practical proposition: considerable numbers of troops could be ferried in a large submarine with only marginal modifications, although the carrier would be at risk off the beach-head. Soviet submarines are more likely to train saboteurs or shock-troops—combat swimmers from *Spetsnaz* special forces[2]—and use exit and re-entry techniques submerged (which are well practised in most navies) or launch them by means of mini-submersibles: the 4,800-ton 'India'-class has two of these on the after casing for rescue work and they would need but little conversion.

Even in peacetime submarining will always be attended by risks; but the bigger the boat, the bigger the disaster if it happens. The modern monsters are not immune from fatal or serious accidents[3] and they carry an awful lot of eggs in one basket. But that has to be accepted if it is clear that for some purposes, and particularly for strategic mobility, giants are the only answer.

So the pattern of the monsters today seems to be firmly established: but while attention is focussed on nuclear leviathans roaming the deeps, there is growing evidence that the Soviet navy is very quietly breeding midget submarines at the very bottom of the size-scale. Nor, while Western defences against midgets are generally neglected, is there any reason for much new technology to be applied for them to be successful. If any updating seems desirable for control and propulsion, there is all the experience of commercial mini-subs to draw upon.

Simplicity, ruggedness and reliability would be the watchwords from a submariner's point of view. The four, hopefully improved, postwar British X-craft (*X-51—X-54*) were not in fact as handy as their war-time predecessors and the USS *X-1* midget

launched on 7 September 1955 was too complex to be a weapon of war: after one year in service an explosion in the advanced hydrogen-peroxide propellant system tore the craft apart and put paid to the project. The British X-craft unit, with its two remaining craft, was finally disbanded in 1958. It was rumoured that Flag Officer Submarines was invited to reduce his flotilla by four hulls in the interests of economy and this was the least painful way of achieving the reduction, but the truth is that midget submarines simply did not fit the peacetime navy; the crews took risks which were not acceptable outside

Stickleback on the crane in 1956 with side-cargoes fitted. The small ball housed the rather primitive passive Asdic (sonar) set which was sometimes useful for gauging whether it was safe to come up from deep but was otherwise of little value.

The main periscope on the postwar X-Craft was both telescopic and periscopic, allowing, with its housing, a slightly deeper and more manageable periscope depth to be kept than was possible with wartime craft. A useful addition was the fixed net-cutting periscope right forward through which the electrician, lying on his stomach above the battery, guided the Captain while the diver used his hydraulic gun to cut through an obstruction.

USS *X-1*, launched at Jakobson's Shipyard, Oyster Bay, Long Island on 7 September 1955. An advanced but hazardous open cycle oxygen-diesel reciprocating engine powered the 35.1/36.3-ton craft submerged (with battery back-up), but this descendant of Bushnell's *Turtle* was not a success: it was concluded by Richard Boyle, the Engineer Officer and Officer-in-Charge, that 'high concentration unstabilized hydrogen peroxide has no place in a fighting ship'.

of war, and they worried the Staff ashore—which is always the most dangerous thing a submariner can do. Significantly, one of the postwar craft, HMS *Stickleback* (*X-51*), was transferred in July 1958 to Sweden, where Soviet midget activity has recently been suspected with good reason.[4]

What might the Soviet midgets be like today? A few clues from the scanty information made public about the alleged midget operations in Swedish waters suggest that one type could be amphibious. The German *Seeteufel* (Sea Devil) amphibian midget did not progress beyond an experimental model in 1944, and Vice-Admiral Hellmuth Heye (ex-Commander of the German K-force[5]) believed that the plans were unknown to the Soviets. Almost certainly, Heye was wrong about that; but this respected specialist with wide experience in the field was well qualified to voice his personal opinion about the value of further developments for Small Battle Units underwater when he summarised his views after the last war.[6] His notes (translated and abridged), dated 1949, need little comment beyond saying that if the Soviet navy did manage to get hold of them, despite their high security classification, they must have been read with great interest. They are, in any case, well worth recalling because they cover practically the whole range of possibilities:

1. SEETEUFEL (*Sea-Devil*)

a. *An amphibious midget. The pressure hull was placed on a tank caterpillar undercarriage. Engine could be coupled alternately to boat propeller or caterpillar gear.[7] Had a crew of two (with oxygen for 100 hours dived), two torpedoes or mines, one machine-gun, and one rocket or flamethrower. This was an experimental model that was completed and tested at Eckernfoerde. Tests showed that an efficient amphibious submarine can be developed along these lines. Caterpillar chains were too narrow in the experimental type, resulting in too heavy ground pressure. Engine was inadequate. Tests were suspended as industrial pre-conditions for speedy development no longer existed in 1944.*

b. *I consider the Sea Devil a promising weapon for use in commando raids. It is independent of mother craft and base personnel, can land on foreign shores, commit acts of sabotage and evade pursuit ashore or afloat. Can be taken to site by mother ship equipped with a powerful crane. With an engine of higher output than that of the experimental boat, a speed*

of 8 to 10 knots can be obtained submerged and 6 or 7 kms/hr overland. Speed and radius of action could be further increased by installation of a closed-cycle engine. Intended for use in coastal waters if weather is not too rough, and on rivers, lakes and artificial lakes.

2. THE SEEHUND (*Seal*)

a. *Complement, two; armament, two torpedoes or mines. Maximum endurance with a picked crew 6 to 7 days.*

b. *The Russians (German engineers) are also busy with development work on the improved type which was in the experimental stage at the end of the war i.e. the Seal with closed-cycle engine. This improved type would be about 18½ tons.*

3. TARPON

a. *One-man midget, very agile, carrying two torpedoes in the bow (one above the other). Launching of the torpedoes reduces the length of the boat by about 4 metres. Fully electric-drive. Radius of action—100/150 miles, depending on speed. Advantages: simplicity of manufacture, control and maintenance. Can be easily transported by mother ships or on undercarriage.*

b. *Very suitable for occasional use in commando operations (penetrating into harbours which are not too closely guarded). Design sketch was ready; construction of type became impossible due to industrial bottleneck.*

4. SCHWERTWAL (*Narwhal*)

a. *One man. 500 hp Walter turbine. Speed 28/30 knots. Carries two torpedoes. Experimental boat was scuttled in Ploen Lake at time of capitulation and not retrieved.*

b. *May open a possibility of replacing the standard type or remote-controlled torpedo by a one-man torpedo launched from ships. The man could be rescued either by a catapult which hurtles him out of the boat just before firing the torpedo, or by an arrangement (as in the German model) which permits launching the torpedo at close range whereupon the man would return with the boat.*

5. KLEINER DELPHIN (*Small Dolphin*)

a. *One man midget. Length 5 metres; weight 2.5 tons; speed 15 knots with Otto closed-cycle engine. Boat acted as 'crash-boat' with 1200 kg explosive charge. Operator is catapulted out of the boat, together with his seat, just before firing. Dynamic diving. Two experimental boats were ready and showed very satisfactory sea-going properties.*

b. *A promising weapon for close-range naval combat. Marks a further stage in the development of the one-man torpedo. Its future outlook depends on quality of engine.*

6. GROSSER DELPHIN (*Large Dolphin*).

a. *Two-man midget. The first boats were to have a diesel engine and electric power plant, to be replaced by Otto closed-cycle engine in subsequent units. Speed—about 15 knots; radius—about 500 miles. Carried two torpedoes or one trailing torpedo travelling nearer the surface than the boat and towed by the latter which dived under the target. Tests made with trailing torpedoes gave satisfactory initial results. Dynamic diving.*

b. *It is doubted that this type would have been worthwhile in competition with a good midget submarine of the Seal type, as it would probably have entailed too much outlay—beginning with construction —to be a paying proposition if used for occasional assignments only. Nonetheless, it shows a road along which future development of small combat craft may proceed with a fair chance of success.*

7. BIBER 3 (*Beaver 3*).

a. *A further development of the Beaver 1 and 2 designed by Professor Cornelius, with a closed-cycle engine of 65 hp. Radius of action—910 miles; weight—8 tons; crew —two men; speed—8–10 knots. Two torpedoes or mines.*

b. *Earlier Beavers were lost in Norway and in rivers on the Eastern front and subsequently salvaged by the Russians but Beaver 3 was unknown to the Soviets* [SIC].

8. GENERAL.

In my opinion further development of the Seal type appears particularly worthwhile. An improved type—such as the one we had in the experimental stage—would not only replace the standard submarine in some areas but might even be used to greater advantage than the latter. I consider it quite possible that some problems in areas such as the Baltic, Danish and any coastal waters can be solved with midget submarines more efficiently and with fewer losses than with large submarines. These types are also suitable as 'parasite' craft to be dropped from parent ships off an enemy coast. Pre-requisites for success are, first, availability of large numbers obtained through mass-production methods (as replacement would be preferable to repair) and, secondly, well-trained crews. I am inclined to believe that lack of trained personnel will prevent the Russians from getting large

Nets were laid to trap large as well as midget submarines. This is an old British *L-Class* entangled during boom-defence trials during World War Two.

numbers of midgets ready for combat assignment. German Navy experience showed that proper selection and training of crews is just as important as are the constructional features.

In the development of new types, attention must be given to greater simplicity of handling—a point which had already been considered in German naval planning. (One man should be able to rest while the other runs the boat, either surfaced or submerged.) Another item for consideration is whether the crews should consist of two or three men; I think that a crew of two picked men should be adequate and preferable from the designer's point of view, provided the controls are simplified.

There is no need to elaborate upon Admiral Heye's account beyond adding that midget submarine weapon loads could now include chemical or biological disseminators. In times of tension they are ideally suited to clandestine intelligence gathering or the landing and recovery of *Spetsnaz* units. But, if the Russians are using midgets, their invariable insistence on rigid political and military control implies the background presence of a mother ship or submarine; and that could explain the 'Whisky on the Rocks' incident when *W-137* went aground at Landskrona in 1981. Frogmen (with some kind of chariot) could equally well be based on a merchant vessel lying, innocently to all appearances, in a harbour of interest to Soviet military intelligence: Italian *Maiali* men used this ploy from 1942–43 when they berthed themselves

in the semi-sunken tanker *Olterra* at Algeçiras for attacks on Gibraltar across the Bay, leaving and returning through a hole cut in the ship's side below the water.

Outside the Baltic the obvious area for future midget operations is the Mediterranean and there are indications that human torpedoes may reappear along the North African coast. Israel would seem to be a prime candidate for adopting midgets proper, although there is no sign of them and the idea was said to have been rejected some years ago: she would certainly have no difficulty in recruiting first-class crews.

At the end of the day it is the men who count—much more than machinery and

Net-laying is an art that has largely been forgotten—a matter of no regret, perhaps, to those engaged in a difficult and unpleasant job but a defence system that may, nevertheless, have to be revived.

Naval Clearance divers: underwater skills are widely practised in most navies, particularly in the Soviet Union. (RN Commando Association)

Controls of Italian SSB human torpedo developed towards the end of World War Two but not employed operationally. With a top speed of 5 knots (but usually kept to 3½ knots), it is this kind of weapon that may appear again in the Mediterranean, but probably not in the Italian navy itself. The compass, depth-gauge and electric meters on the dashboard were luminous and waterproof. The upper wheel controlled.the four speed settings and the lower wheel worked the elevators and rudder. The handles operated the ballast and trimming pumps. The second crewman sat behind the pilot in the same cockpit.

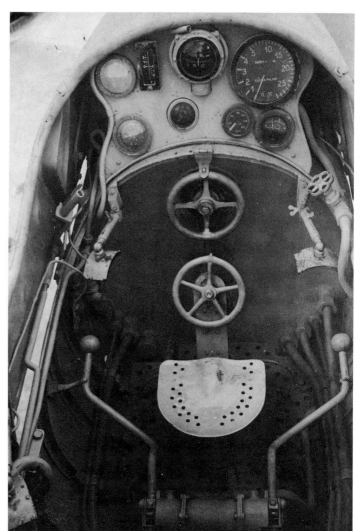

Wooden mock-up found in Germany in 1945, possibly of the amphibious *Seeteufel* described in the text.

materiel—in midget and, indeed, in large submarine operations; and it is this fact, amply demonstrated in war, that may make the Soviet underwater threat appear to submariners a little less worrying than it looks on the surface. When it comes to midgets, they require a very special kind of man and he may well not be outstanding in a normal naval career: among the Allies, Australians, New Zealanders and South Africans, none of them known to abide overmuch by custom or conformity, were excellent.

Men like Cameron, Place and—giving full credit to a past enemy now that the story is known—Saburo Akeida[8] were not only supremely brave: they possessed the rare quality of persistence: and it is upon persistence, against all odds, that successful midget operations will always depend.

All in all, it is arguable that big is not necessarily beautiful: the balance in submarine and anti-submarine warfare may shift in favour of smaller craft, particularly if there is a breakthrough or a significant advance in anti-submarine detection measures; and, meanwhile, midgets may already be fighting their way back to compete with the monsters.

German midget of a novel type: labelled 'tricky louse' by some humourist in the factory, this type has not positively been related to Admiral Heye's report. Nobody, in this case, could criticise the design for weapons not taking priority over the hull!

End Notes

Chapter 1

1 *Voyage of the Deutschland* by Captain Koenig; Hearst, 1916.
2 *Ibid.*
3 *Ibid.*
4 British reports and papers are held in the Public Records Office under references ADM 137/1262, ADM 137/503 and ADM 137/323.

Chapter 2

1 *The British Submarine* by Cdr F W Lipscomb (Conway Maritime Press Ltd, 1975).
2 *Maidstone Magazine*, 1914–15, in Submarine Museum Archives.
3 Submarine Museum Archives.
4 *Maidstone Magazine Vol. II 1916*, in Submarine Museum Archives.
5 *Ibid.*
6 Reminiscences of the late Lt Cdr R L Burridge, in Submarine Museum Archives.
7 The comprehensive diary of Leading Signalman H W Smith, in Submarine Museum Archives, reinforces this belief. Smith was glad to return to *K-6* after a short spell in *K-7* where things were easy going.
8 MS Confidential reports held in Submarine Museum Archives.
9 *Ibid.*
10 Unpublished reminiscences of George W Kimbell.
11 Quoted in *The K-Boats*, the excellent, readable and thoroughly researched book by Don Everett, first published by George C Harrap, 1963.
12 *Ibid.*

Chapter 3

1 Letter of 20 April 1904 from Admiral Fisher to 'My Dear Friend', probably the King's Private Secretary.
2 Letter to *The Daily Mail* of 2 June 1914.
3 Captain (S) in HMS *Conquest* to C-in-C Atlantic Fleet No. 21/7A, 3 January 1923.

Chapter 4

1 See the excellent summary of proceedings in *The Submarine and Sea Power* by Vice Admiral Sir Arthur Hezlet (Peter Davies, 1967).
2 Submarine Museum Archives.
3 Letter of 11 August 1928 from Commanding Officer HM Submarine *X-1* at Malta to Captain (S) 1st Submarine Flotilla.
4 Letter from Captain G H Roberts CBE, RD, RN (Rtd), the first Gunnery Officer of *X-1*. It is Captain Robert's letters (written in 1976), held in the Submarine Museum Archives, which have led to research into the true capabilities of *X-1*.
5 Suggestions for *X-2* written by Lt Cdr P Ruck-Keene in 1928.
6 'Pleasing' or 'Prepossessing'
7 Personal Letter from Winston Churchill to Mrs Sprague, dated 26 October 1949.
8 AKDM 119/1120.
9 D/NHB/14/2/61.
10 Quoted in *L'Épopée du Surcouf* by Maurice Guierre, (Editions Bellenand, 1952).
11 *Ibid.*

Chapter 5

1 C-in-C Atlantic Fleet to Secretary of the Admiralty, letter 1516/AF/1125, 8 October 1930.
2 *The Submarine and Sea Power* by Vice Admiral Sir Arthur Hezlet.
3 The Appendix to BPFLO—'Report on Japanese Submarines,' dated 1 November 1945.
4 The full story is given in the thoroughly researched, scholarly and non-sensational book *The Sacred Warriors* by D and P Warren with Cdr Sadao Seko (Avon, USA).
5 Dr Tom Paine (Chairman of Thomas Paine Associates, Los Angeles and formerly Administrator of NASA) was, as a lieutenant USNR, Executive Officer of the *I-400* prize crew which took the submarine to Pearl Harbor in company with *I-14* and *I-401*, arriving on 6 January 1946. He has written an objective private account about the *Sensuikan Toku* (Special Submarine) aircraft carrier and provided much information, including an invaluable account by Admiral Joe Vasey USN (retd), which assisted greatly in providing inside detail, from a submariner's point of view, for this chapter, supplementing the excellent essay which David Hill has generously allowed to be used.

Chapter 6

1 *Naval Warfare Today and Tomorrow* by Rear Admiral Hubert Moineville, translated by Richard Compton-Hall (Basil Blackwell, 1983).
2 But how valuable a 'Triton' might have proved during the Anglo-Argentinian conflict over the Falklands in 1982!
3 *The Fleet Submarine in the US Navy* by John D Alden (Naval Institute Press, 1979).
4 RA(S) to Secretary of the Admiralty, 14 May 1930.
5 Conference between RA(S) and DNC, 26 June 1930.
6 RA(S) to Secretary of the Admiralty, 14 May 1930.

Chapter 7

1 *Naval Chronicle*, Naval History of the Present Year, report from Deal 6 October 1805.
2 A basis for research is *Beginning of Modern Submarine Warfare* by Henry L Abbot (facsimile reproduction by Frank Anderson: Archon Books, 1966).
3 Amongst references which might be assumed most trustworthy are:
 (a) *General Principles and Construction of a Submarine Vessel* communicated by D Bushnell, of Conn., the inventor, in a letter of October 1787, to Thomas Jefferson, then Minister Plenipotentiary of the United States at Paris. (Transactions of the American Philosophical Society for Promoting Useful Knowledge, Vol. IV, p. 303, 1799. The paper was read on 8 June 1798, but very probably originated in 1778: *viz Thacher's Journal* 10 February 1778).
 (b) *Thacher's Military Journal* during the Revolutionary War, various entries 1776–1778.
 (c) Memoirs of Major General Heath.
 (d) I W Stuart's *Life of Jonathan Trumbull*, p. 294 (Boston, 1859)

(e) Dr Benjamin Gale, letters to Silas Deane Esq, dated 9 November 1775, 7 December 1775 and 1 February 1776 (Connecticut Historical Society).

4 HMS *Eagle* (Captain Henry Duncan); log kept by Lieutenant P Browne 9 February 1776 to 8 February 1777 and *Journal of the Proceedings of His Majesty's Ship* Eagle by Captain Henry Duncan, commander between 10 February 1776 and 28 February 1777 (Public Records Office).

5 *Thacher's Military Journal* October 1776.

6 *Cassier Magazine* Annual Marine issue 1897.

Chapter 8

1 MAS originally stood for *Motobarca armata SVAN* (*Societa Veneziana Automobili Nautiche*—the first building firm), but the same initials were later used for anti-submarine launches and subchasers.

2 Cricket, a jumping insect.

3 Jumping boats.

Chapter 9

1 *Deep Diving & Submarine Operations* by Robert H Davis (The Saint Catherine Press Ltd, 1935, with several succeeding editions), an invaluable reference book, which gave the first clue to the existence of this midget.

2 Letter 21/74 dated 3 January 1923 from Captain (S) in HMS *Conquest* to C-in-C Atlantic Fleet.

3 Engineer Captain C V Hardcastle RN was originally consulted by Herbert about the feasibility of this propulsion and saw no difficulties.

4 Confidential reports on officers held in Submarine Museum archives securely.

Chapter 10

1 Notably *Above us the Waves* by Warren & Benson (Harrap, 1953); *The Frogmen* by Waldron & Gleeson (Evans Brothers, 1950); *The War beneath the Sea* by W Brou, translated from the French (Frederick Muller, 1958); *Sea Devils* by V Borghese, translated from the Italian (Andrew Melrose, 1952); *The Kaiten Weapon* by Yutaka Yokota, translated from the Japanese (Ballantine Books, 1962); *Suicide Squads* by Richard O'Neill (Salamander Books, 1981).

2 As implied earlier, this point was widely expressed in the Admiralty and Parliament at the turn of the century when submarines were first seriously considered for the Royal Navy.

3 *Escape over the Himalayas* by Elios Tos-chi (Ed. Eur Milau).

4 Toschi *Op. cit.*

5 The Italian initials for 'Slow Speed Torpedoes'.

6 The pre-war associate of Commander Varley's mentioned earlier.

7 *The Second World War* Vol. IV by Sir Winston Churchill (Cassell & Co Ltd)

8 *The Sea our Shield* by Captain W R Fell (Cassell & Co Ltd, 1966).

9 Quoted by Captain Fell *op.cit.*

10 *Ibid.*

11 According to the report on Operation 'Principal' by Admiral (Submarines): SM 04349/600, dated 17 December 1943.

12 Preliminary narrative of *The War at Sea* Vol. V, 1946 (BR 1738(5)).

13 Now General Secretary of the Royal Naval Commando Association.

14 Statements and records held in RN Submarine Museum.

15 Lieutenant Commander (later Captain) W O Shelford, DSEA Instructional Officer.

16 Dr Balfour ended his active medical career as principal medical officer to the John Lewis Partnership (department stores and Waitrose supermarkets), where a more gentle approach to patients was encouraged.

Chapter 11

1 Lieutenant, later Captain, W G Meeke, MBE, DSC* RN. He transferred back to big submarines before X-craft became fully operational.

2 Lieutenant, later Commander, RN, D Cameron VC, RNR (awarded the Victoria Cross for his success in *X-6* during Operation Source).

3 Chief ERA K Richardson, BEM.

4 HMS *X-1* was the cruiser submarine (see Chapter 4) and *X-2* was the name assigned to the Italian submarine *Galilei* captured in the Red Sea by the armed trawler HMS *Moonstone* on 19 October 1940.

5 Lieutenant H E W Washington, RNVR.

6 Commander T I S Bell, DSC, RN.

7 Extracts from Donald Cameron's personal diaries and accounts are published by kind permission of his widow, Eve, now Mrs Richard Compton-Hall.

8 Lieutenant, DSC, RN, later Rear Admiral B C G Place, VC, CB, DSC (awarded the Victoria Cross for his success in X-7 during Operation source).

9 Captain W E Banks, CBE, DSC, RN.

10 Captain P Q Roberts, DSO, RN.

11 Lieutenant A Wilson, MBE, RNVR.

12 Lieutenant R L Alexander, RN, later Rear Admiral, CB, DSO, DSC.

13 Lieutenant P H Philip, SANF(V), MBE, widely known in South Africa as 'Uncle Peter' on the radio programme for children.

14 Sub Lieutenant J Lorimer, DSO, RNVR; Sub Lieutenant R H Kendall, DSO, RNVR; ERA E Goddard, CGM.

15 Sub Lieutenant L B Whittam, RNVR.

16 Sub Lieutenant R Aitken, DSO, RNVR.

17 Lieutenant M H Shean, DSO,* RANVR.

18 *Barenfels* and the floating dock were practically the same length and would have looked much alike in murky water from below.

19 Lieutenant, DSC, later Commander, H P Westmacott, DSO, DSC,* RN.

20 Lieutenant K R Hudspeth, DSC, and two Bars RANVR; Lieutenant, later Lieutenant Commander, G B Honour, DSC, VRD, RNVR.

Chapter 12

1 Imperial Rescript to Soldiers and Sailors, 1882.

2 The terrible damage and chaos caused by the air attack could conceivably have masked one or more torpedo hits from No. 5. Japanese propaganda made much of the midgets' operation, posthumously promoting the nine crewmen who had died by two ranks; but American sources did not believe that any of the Type A's scored.

3 Although the successful midget's crew were shot on shore after their attack it does not appear that the two men were positively identified as individuals. However, it is reasonable to surmise that is was Saburo Akeida with Petty Officer Masami Takemoto who carried out these devastating attacks on *Ramillies* and *British Loyalty*.

4 The full extent of the damage, remarkable for a 17.7-inch torpedo, is listed in BR 1886 (2) issued in 1952. (Submarine Museum library.)

5 *Die U-Boot-Erfolge Der Achsenmächte 1939–1943* by Jürgen Rohwer (JF Lehmanns Verlag, München 1968).

6 Figures given by the German naval historian Cajus Bekker.

7 BR 1886 (2) *HM Ships damaged or sunk by enemy action* states that there was one explosion on the starboard side abreast the boiler room followed almost immediately by two other explosions causing a large hole on the port side. *Isis* was on A/S patrol off the Normandy beaches and was specifically concerned with the midget menace. She must have been

attacked by two or perhaps three *Neger* simultaneously or run on to a group of mines: experts at the time were inclined to favour the latter theory.

8 Richard O'Neill in his excellent book *Suicide Squads* (Salamander Books Ltd, 1981) quotes figures of 324 and 363 respectively.

9 The lengthy preliminary narrative of *The War at Sea* (BR 1738) makes clear the effort expended. One authority estimates that 500 escorts and 1000 aircraft were diverted from more important tasks to deal with midgets of one kind and another.

The Future—Great and Small

1 See the analysis in *The Underwater War 1939–1945* by Richard Compton-Hall (Blandford Press, 1982).

2 According to a defector, *Spetsnaz* special forces (men and women) are an integral part of GRU, the Soviet military intelligence service and appear to operate in keen competition with the KGB. Sometimes referred to as *reydoviki* (raiders), their tasks are to create havoc behind the enemy lines, sabotage key facilities, mount terrorist operations and assassinate political and military leaders. They are said to include in their number some of the best athletes in the Soviet Union. Midget submarines are a logical part of the Spetsnaz armoury.

3 The tragic loss of the 4300-ton USS *Thresher* (*SSN-593*), in 1963, the 3500-ton USS *Scorpion* (*SSN-589*) in 1968, a Soviet 4000-ton November-class in 1970 and an unrevealed number of other Soviet submarines are examples of large

submarine disasters; but it has to be said that, since the war, there have also been a dozen fatalities (from various causes) involving small or medium-sized submarines.

4 HMS *Stickleback* (*Spiggen* in the Swedish navy) was eventually returned to Britain and is now on display at the Imperial War Museum annex, Duxford together with the remnants of *X-7*, recovered from Kaa Fjord.

5 See Chapter Twelve.

6 Admiral Heye's notes and comments drawn largely from the formerly SECRET document 'Small Battle Units' compiled by the US Office of Naval Intelligence in March 1949.

7 The tracks photographed in 1982 on the bottom of a Swedish inlet fit the pattern.

8 See Chapter Twelve: HMS *Ramillies*.

Index

References to photographs and drawings are in italic and bold respectively